16.76

Railway

In the same series

Railway

George Revill

REAKTION BOOKS

Published by Reaktion Books Ltd
33 Great Sutton Street
London EC1V 0DX, UK

www.reaktionbooks.co.uk

First published 2012

Printed and bound in China by C&C Offset Printing Co., Ltd

British Library Cataloguing in Publication Data

Revill, George, 1961-
    Railway. — (Objekt)
    1. Railroads. 2. Railroads—History.
    3. Railroads—Social. 4. Railroad travel—History.
    5. Railroad travel—Social aspects. 6. Railroads in literature.
    7. Railroads in motion pictures. 8. Railroads in art.
    I. Title II. Series
    385-dc22

ISBN 978 1 86189 874 6

Contents

Preface

The whistle of the locomotive penetrates my woods summer and winter, sounding like the scream of a hawk sailing over some farmer's yard, informing me that many restless city merchants are arriving within the circle of the town, or adventurous country traders from the other side. As they come under one horizon, they shout their warning to get off the track to the other, heard sometimes through the circles of two towns. Here come your groceries, countryman; your rations, countryman! Nor is there any man so independent on his farm that he can say them nay. And here's your pay for them! Screams the countryman's whistle; timber like long battering-rams going twenty miles an hour against the city walls, and chair enough to seat all the weary and heavy-laden that dwell within them. With such huge and lumbering civility the country hands a chair to the city. All the Indian huckleberry hills are stripped, all the cranberry meadows are raked into the city. Up comes the cotton, down goes the woven cloth; up comes the silk, down goes the woollen; up come the books, but down goes the wit that writes them.[1]

In this way the American nature writer Henry David Thoreau (1817–1862) describes the impact of the train from his rural retreat near the small town of Concord, Massachusetts. This description of the railway

Dale Creek Bridge, Wyoming on the Union Pacific Railroad, photograph by W. H. Jackson, 1885. The low angle emphasizes the height of this slender structure, suggesting the technological mastery of nature.

forms part of his rumination on the sounds of nature in his book *Walden*. In what has become one of the defining texts of modern environmentalist thought, Thoreau gives an account of his experimental attempt at living close to nature in a shack in the woods by Walden Pond (1845–7). The passage quoted above has become well known for its ambiguous portrayal of the railway as an influence that is both constructive and disruptive. For Thoreau, the railway links town and country, farm and factory, physical labour and philosophical contemplation in a landscape of busyness and progress. Yet at the same time, it brings the blight of industrialization, social alienation, loss of local distinctiveness and environmental destruction. For Thoreau the railway negotiates complex relationships between technology, nature and society. Thoreau is far from alone in recognizing the railway as a multi-edged force in the making of the modern world. In this guise it is an iconic marker of modernity, invading and transforming the world around it.

Substantially a product of the nineteenth century, the railway is a defining technology of the modern world and an archetypal symbol of progress and confidence in technological modernity. The most prominent elements of its technological novelty, its locomotives and rolling stock, buildings and engineering structures, have long captured the imagination. However the pioneering qualities of its technological apparatus extends well beyond such isolated and heroically represented artefacts. As an icon of the modern world the railway's importance also rests on its collectivity: machines, workers, structures, finance, route ways and various means of recording and decision-making assembled into functional networks of communication. The railway's innovative organizational cultures have had deep ramifications in wider society. Joint stock capitalization, complex bureaucracies and a variety of surveillance, accounting and control mechanisms indicate a social role for railways as a technological ensemble that is central to the production of modernity itself. Urbanization and suburbanization, nation building, colonial exploitation and global capitalism have all been facilitated by their networking properties. Evidence for the social and political as well as economic importance of railways in an industrializing world is manifest in the huge range of cultural materials, from painting to music and ceramics to film, that mediate its role in both popular and elite imaginations. It is certainly true that railways have left a firm imprint in the canons of high art; paintings by J.M.W. Turner, Claude Monet and Albert Bierstadt, novels by Dickens, Tolstoy and Emile Zola, poetry by W. H. Auden, Walt Whitman and William Wordsworth, all indicate the extent to which railways became subjects for 'serious' art. As such the railway signifies, amongst other things, death, loss, estrangement, reconciliation and fulfilment, alchemical power, mechanical energy and natural harmony. Yet the railway is an equally powerful symbol in popular culture, present in fireside songs, boys' stories, B-movies, tinplate toys and cartoon characters. From Casey Jones to Thomas the Tank Engine railways have marked out an everyday heroism which continues to fuel the imagination.

To a great extent the cultural proliferation and circulation of images and representations of the railway is closely related to the distinctively modern and technologically mediated society that railways helped to produce. Most directly, of course, railway companies were responsible for producing guidebooks, prospectuses and posters. They sponsored painters and photographers to advertise new companies and new routes, while the act of rail travel itself produced a demand for cultural products, including new forms of fiction written with the long hours of train travel in mind. Such materials created a public image for railways at the same time that they refigured the imaginative geographies of the places through which railways ran. More broadly, the speed and power of its locomotives and the impact

and extent of its networks generated a series of responses to its modernity which both reworked and extended a familiar cultural repertoire for coping with technological and organizational change. Railway locomotives were noble 'iron horses', destructive dragons or heroic figures from classical mythology; locomotive drivers, 'medieval knights'; railway directors, kings, tyrants and despots. Railway travel was often likened to flying, whilst stations were represented as the churches and cathedrals of the age, 'volcanoes of life', chaotic Towers of Babel or theatres for the conspicuous display of consumption and capital accumulation. Railway systems were frequently described using organic metaphors, such as the cardiovascular system of a huge body

This poster by Swain & Lewis, 1882, shows the Illinois Central Railroad at the centre of the nation. Set within are cameos redolent of an American ideology linking westwards expansion with settlement, resource exploitation and global trade.

or the giant tentacles of an enormous octopus. Both directly and indirectly, the systems created by railways played a significant part in engineering those changes in our experience of time and space by which the cultural dynamics of modernity were encountered on a day to day basis. The mail, the national daily press, the telegraph and the telephone are all technologies of communication that in one way or another developed in symbiosis with the railway. For many in the nineteenth century, the idea of 'railway time' constituted more than just the necessity to conduct business and communications over large distances by means of a regular and reliable schedule. Rather, it signified a disposition towards the modern world in which punctuality and specific rule-governed behaviour formed a cultural ideal for the respectable citizen. By these means railways enmeshed their rhythms and routines into the daily lives of rural and urban communities at the same time that they helped to rework those communities into larger

The old brings in the new, as elephants pull the first locomotive into Indore under the watchful gaze of British officials. Railways were central to British rule in India after the Great Rebellion of 1857.

networks of news, knowledge and social exchange extending across regions, nations and continents.

It is clear that the cultural imprint of the railway on popular and elite cultures has far transcended the realms of art, however this is defined, and etched itself on the ways we think and behave. Railways continue to play a role in the popular imagination. Evidence for this is not difficult to find, from the global fame of the magical Hogwarts Express carrying Harry Potter into a world of supernatural adventure to the London Bloggers website where individuals add their personal entries in a structure based on a local or favourite Tube station. The railway continues to be a cultural medium freighted with both utopian flights of fancy and everyday local attachments. Just as the idea of 'railway time' was a culturally meaningful construct with considerable social ramifications in the nineteenth century, so today in an age of air travel and the Internet, the deeper cultural associations of the railway change and live on. Thus we refer to bureaucratic or organizational failings by claiming that these represent 'no way to

This 1885 picture of the Bhor Ghat Gradient of the Great Indian Peninsula Railway near Khandala shows mastery of this extremely difficult terrain by a combination of European engineering and Indian labour.

run a railway'. That which is politically expedient is 'fast-tracked' while that which is administratively uncomfortable is 'sidetracked' or 'shunted into a siding'. Drawing on a rather different register of social values and behaviours associated with the railway, any compulsive or 'geekish' behaviour is referred to as 'trainspotting', while anyone who strays outside accepted social norms is said to have 'gone off the rails'.

As we move towards a future in which the mass individualized automobility characteristic of the second half of the twentieth century seems to be increasingly under threat, railways once again appear to hold a lifeline to sustainable mobility. Represented as such, the railway becomes essential to the continued existence of some form of modern Western lifestyle and its extrapolation into the future. In this context, ambitious cities promote investment in rail-based forms of mass rapid transit as boosterist symbols of their technological cutting-edge status, while vigilant consumer groups chart every failing in public transport as a marker of government short-sightedness, incompetence and betrayal. Thus the cultural meanings of the railway continue to play a role in organizing the ways we respond to modern environments, social problems, institutions and technologies.

Though the story of railway development has conventionally been told as one of technological progress and heroic personal endeavour on the part of engineers, labourers and entrepreneurs, it is clear there is a more complex tale to tell. In this respect the pioneering work of the cultural historian Wolfgang Schivelbusch has to be acknowledged.[2] Writing in the late 1970s, Schivelbusch raised a series of issues which transformed our understanding of the railway's place within cultural histories of modernity. Important aspects of his work show, for example, the extent to which train travel transformed the way we view landscape; how the railway itself was reimagined as a machine rather than a collection of parts, consisting of locomotives, tracks and station; and the ways in which the mechanized travel experienced through a multiplicity of physical and psychological shocks became an object for the new medical sciences. Schivelbusch's insight is still extremely influential and though scholarship has moved on since the 1970s this book remains in constructive dialogue with key concepts from his work. To understand the cultural impact of railways and their distinctive place in modern life is therefore to come to terms with a technology which is deeply engrained in the cultural imagination. In turn this suggests that we need to adopt an approach to culture which is able to recognize the wider cultural importance of the railway as it is embedded in everyday activities and objects, in addition to those things more conventionally thought of as cultural. The cultural meanings of the railway therefore are evident as much in toys, timetables and Temperance societies as they are in novels, poems, paintings and architecture. It suggests also that rather than portraying the railway as either unproblematically beneficial, bringing progress and civilization, or conversely unredeemably malign, a carrier for all the ills of industrial society, we can get closer to the cultural meanings of the railway by recognizing that it is the ambivalent and ambiguous marker of the modern condition described by Thoreau.

This book contends that understanding our love-hate relationship with the railway is central to understanding modern everyday life. Further, it argues that railways articulate a set of dilemmas and contradictions central to its construction. These can best be understood by considering the railway as a set of cultural symbols, meanings, images, artefacts and activities, some of which are finely crafted and consciously articulated, while others are tacit and taken for granted. There are five thematic chapters; in turn these examine a series of fault lines which help animate the ways in which railways have been co-constitutive of cultural modernity. Chapter One examines how the railway,

as a novel, risky and disruptive technology, came to be accommodated as part of our everyday lives as a safe, dependable and apparently natural part of the landscape. It explores the means by which railways became accommodated into the landscape and how its structures are often now interpreted as an intrinsic part of the natural surroundings. The chapter concludes by exploring the rhythms and sounds of the train in the landscape, as these formed a means for encapsulating and understanding its simultaneously creative and destructive energy. Chapter Two traces the ways in which railways became an instrument

British Royal Engineers on a narrow-gauge railway at Arras, France, on the Western Front during the First World War. Sometimes characterized as a symbol of mechanized warfare, the railway's most important role was substantially logistical.

of government and a means for enforcing political and administrative control through nation-states and across continents. Here railways participate in a powerful group of cultural practices by which political power is justified and enforced in both symbolic and material form. This chapter argues that counter to their familiar characterization as rigid and impersonal, it is the adaptability and versatility of railways as a simultaneously practical and symbolic resource which make them such a lively political force. Chapter Three looks at the ways in which the individual experience of mobility enabled by railway travel has shaped our senses of self and our experiences of everyday life in the modern world. Railways facilitated a variety of mobile lifestyles – the inveterate traveller, the self-made entrepreneur and the career professional – and together these are characteristic of modern society and fundamental to the cultural trajectories of modern everyday life. The chapter concludes by reflecting on the role of railways in marking out the distinctive experience of urban life. Chapter Four examines the railway as a cultural commodity. It explores the intersections of art, engineering, and commerce in railway design and marketing. It argues that railway design occupies a unique place straddling nineteenth-century and modernist aesthetics and that this is important for understanding the particularly valued place railways occupy as both historical heritage and hope for the future. Finally, chapter Five concerns the location of railways within currently developing cultures of sustainability. It returns to the theme of nature and technology raised in chapter One, this time in the context of ecology rather than landscape. The chapter examines how railways are being rehabilitated as a cultural symbol of the sort of sustainable future theorists call 'ecological modernization'. Drawing on a variety of current ecological metaphors, it shows how railways both hide and reveal the connections between natural and social worlds and consequently produce a very distinctive cultural ecology.

Though each chapter is thematic, there is some implicit chronology to the extent that earlier chapters deal with nineteenth century themes such as the coming of the railways and their role in the making of nation states, while later chapters engage with more recent issues such as the railway as heritage and its place within present-day debates concerning sustainability. The notion of culture is also expanded during the course of the book. Chapter One is mainly concerned with 'the arts', conventionally defined as painting, literature, poetry and music; however, later chapters begin to embrace all manner of socially meaningful materials and actions, including for instance operational systems and infrastructures, the actions of environmental protesters and indeed goods and products carried by railways, such as coal. In this book modernity is defined as an ongoing historical epoch roughly commencing with the rise of science and industrial society. It is also a range of aesthetic responses to the social forms generated by such changes; these are typified by the development of new subject-matters, aesthetic codes and media of representation. By implication it is also the experience we all have of living through, responding to and finding meaning in this world, which is characterized on the one hand by constant social, economic and technological change, and on the other by our apparent separation and estrangement from pre-existing 'traditional' social forms and the authorities represented by these. Together the five chapters in this book attempt to chart the role of railways in defining the contours of this cultural terrain. Central to this territory are notions of connection, isolation, proximity, distance, speed, flow, stasis, presence, absence, loss and excess that are intrinsic to the experience of modernity's cultural geography. By working with these terms in specific historical and cultural contexts, the book sketches out some dimensions for what is called in chapter Five a 'cultural ecology' of railways. Thus the book explores the railway's place as a means of communication in its broadest sense, carrying messages and meanings, creating connections and separations, senses of loss, belonging, estrangement, detachment and involvement, the banal routine of the commuter and the eager fascinations of the enthusiast.

Eurotunnel infrastructure, Kent, England. As high-speed rail plays an increasingly important role in plans for an integrated transport network in Europe, both positive and negative effects of increased railway infrastructure are brought into focus.

Drawn from Mr. Allen's Road

PRIOR PARK the Seat of Ralph Allen Esq.r near Bath.   PRIOR PARC la Residence de Raoul Allen Ecuyer pres de Bath.

Printed for R. Wilkinson, No. 58. Cornhill, London.

1 Nature, Culture and the Train Landscape

Recalling his time spent documenting the end of steam traction along the West Coast Mainline through the northern English Pennines, the photographer Colin Garrett waxes lyrical as he remembers a night-time train working its way through the fells:

> At night I deliberately lay awake and one morning at 01.00 the cry of a 'Britannia's' whistle rang out across the lonely fells as the engine prepared to start the long climb up from Tebay. The barking exhaust, interposed with that of the banker, cut through the stillness as it resounded over the hills as the heavy Pacific fought its way up the gradient with a northbound freight. As I watched its approach from my bedroom window, blazing coals were flung out of the chimney and the cab was bathed in a flickering orange glow that was reflected in the smoke trail. Spellbound, I watched the drama and listened to the rhythms – for surely a living presence was passing through the fells that night.[1]

Comparing the place of road and railway in this rugged moorland setting, Garrett laments the construction of a motorway through the fells at Shap with 'sheer disbelief that so wonderful a place could be defiled'. 'Today,' he says, 'the hideousness of the M6 has dissipated

Prior Park, Somerset, c. 1750. Ralph Allen revolutionized the English postal system and his quarries supplied the stone for the grand terraces of Georgian Bath. The tramroad brought Bath stone from his estate quarries down to the river Avon.

much of the magic almost as much as the disappearance of steam.' For Garrett the steam train is part of the natural landscape. Its exhaust beat a visible and auditory expression of power conveying a raw energy complementing the wildness of this bleak landscape. Such sentiments are a familiar part of the nostalgia generated by the passing of the steam railway. The new motorway represents the brash, impersonal and environmentally destructive against the shared experience, sense of community and obligations of public service and duty encapsulated in the idea of railway travel. In articulating the contrast between older and newer modes of transport, Garrett's words echo those expressed at previous moments of technological change. William Wordsworth's oft-quoted attack on the proposed Kendal & Windermere Railway (1844), a little further west from the scene of Garrett's reverie, parallels his sentiments by railing against the 'unnaturalness' of the new technology whilst at the same time mourning the loss of a more 'authentic' way of experiencing the landscape.

Is then no nook of English ground secure
From rash assault? . . . [2]

In writing about the Kendal & Windermere proposals, Wordsworth was not simply railing against the railway as a physical presence in the landscape. In this verse the railway stands symbolically for the encroachment of mass tourism in the Lake District, something which – ironically – Wordsworth had done much to popularize. In turn he felt this to be a symptom of larger changes taking place in English society resulting from increased physical and social mobility.[3] For Wordsworth, as for Garrett 160 years later, the place of the railway in the landscape was a marker for deeper and equally regrettable social changes. Because our conception of landscape is partly informed by pictures and images and partly by the material form and quality of land and territory, landscape is often perceived ambiguously as part nature and part culture; and that which becomes taken for granted as part of the landscape may itself come to be viewed as somehow natural. Landscape is represented in the arts through a long history of cultural conventions. Thus to trace the story of railways in the landscape as they are portrayed through such established cultural conventions is to follow a history of mutual transformation. Culture helps us to interpret our experience of the new at the same time that the new shapes our engagement with and experience of the world in which we live. Landscape therefore forms a useful medium enabling us to examine the ways in which we became familiar with and habituated to the railway as an unquestioned part of modern everyday life.

Railway structures form a distinctive component of the landscape; railways have transformed lands and landscapes, bringing agricultural development, urbanization and industrialization. At the same time they have enabled hitherto undreamt-of numbers of people to travel and experience new places, encounters which are themselves shaped by the speed, smoothness, rhythms and routines of railway operation. Thus landscape weaves together the intimate relationship between railways and the territories through which they run. The earliest evidence we have for railed ways is itself engrained in the archaeology of landscape. At Pompeii grooved stone tracks that would have provided a smooth road for wheeled carts are gouged into the rocky surface of the earth. In Britain similar Roman stoneways have been found, lending weight to the assertion that many of these were designed constructions rather than simply the product of many years of routine traffic.[4] The early horse-drawn railways or tramroads, for which there is evidence from the sixteenth century onwards, were short practical adjuncts to rurally based agricultural and landed estate economies, linking mine to river and

quarry to town.[5] Like lime kilns, horse gins, river wharves or flash locks they were substantially taken-for-granted features of the rural-industrial landscape. The earliest images of horse-drawn railways – often known as wagonways or tramroads – situate them unproblematically within a cultural domain of bucolic productivity little different from that used to illustrate agricultural innovations and the well-ordered landscapes of landed estates. While steam power in the form of its low-pressure antecedent, the atmospheric engine, had been used as a stationary power source in mining since the early eighteenth century, the application of steam power to railed locomotion subsequent to Richard Trevithick's (1771–1833) experiments in 1803 remained either a fairground novelty or a millwright's

Richard Trevithick, pioneer of high-pressure steam engines in mining, built several experimental railway locomotives. In 1808 'Catch Me Who Can' ran on a circular track in Bloomsbury, London, and admission to the 'steam circus' was one shilling.

experiment until the 1820s. In each of these cases railways did little to threaten established cultural conventions. Yet the development of the public steam-powered railway, from the opening of the Liverpool & Manchester Railway on 15 September 1830, heralded a much more turbulent and complex set of cultural engagements between railways and the landscape through which they ran.

Energy and alchemy

When Colin Garrett identifies the locomotive as 'a living presence' passing through the fells he invokes one of the earliest and most enduring characterizations of the railway locomotive as an 'iron horse'. The formal calculative description of mechanical energy in terms of horse power dates back to 1784 when James Watt, seeking a means of representing the power of a steam engine, standardized one horse power as the capacity to raise 33,000 pounds ten feet in

Middleton Colliery, Leeds (1814) by George Walker. In the middle distance is the locomotive *Salamanca* designed by colliery manager John Blenkinsop. It used cog wheels acting on metal lugs in the rails to give traction; four such locomotives were built.

one minute.[6] George Walker's colliery scene near Leeds (1814) is an early example of an image which makes this connection as both metaphor and engineering fact. The locomotive prominent in the middle ground is visually counter-posed with a diminutive horse at the pit head. Contrasting old and new technology by comparing horse power and locomotive traction, an accompanying text explains how the new machine saved the power of seven horses. It is a small step from Watt's cool, calculative, scientific use of the term 'horse power' to a much more animate and embodied version of the same metaphor. When, in a letter of 1830, Fanny Kemble welcomed the first locomotive out of Liverpool as 'the steam horse . . . this snorting little animal which I felt rather inclined to pat',[7] she drew on an increasingly conventionalized means of representing mechanical power as natural energy. Representations of the locomotive as an iron horse were balanced by those likening railway travel to flight. It is easy to imagine how travellers arrived at this analogy given the level line of the track, the smoothness of steel wheels on steel rails and the apparently detached view of the landscape as the train ran across viaducts and bridges and through cuttings and tunnels with little regard for the actual lie of the land.[8] Yet flying of itself suggests a sense of effortlessness not completely in tune with the experience of railway travel. The rhythmic sound of hooves and breath suggested by the metaphor of the iron horse compliment and contrast with representations of railway travel as flying because they suggested the mechanical power expended in locomotion. As a result, the two sets of images were often concatenated, fused together by a sense of the supernatural, as suggested by *A Poet's View of a Railroad* (1847):

> We feel ourselves as powerful as the sorcerers of old! We put our magic-horse to the carriage and space disappears; we fly like the clouds in a storm, as the bird of passage flies . . . [9]

Sometimes juxtapositions of horse and landscape were designed to engender a sense of melancholy for the passing age. Henry Alken's (1785–1851) chromolithograph of 1840–45 sets a derelict and decaying mail coach against the modernity of the railway. In an image heavy with symbols of decay, the grounded mail coach, accompanied by a superannuated and melancholy horse, is overshadowed by a dead tree. Given that Alken made his name by portraying horses and hunting scenes it is likely that there is a genuine nostalgia in this image.[10] In contrast, progressive voices celebrated the hard efficiency of railway locomotives in terms of their relation to horse power. In *Our Iron Roads* (1852) F. S. Williams celebrated the move from organic to mechanical means of transport while hanging on the homology between horse and locomotive; 'no foaming mouths, nor turgid veins . . . but that giant power (with) bones of brass and iron and nerves and muscles that cannot tire.'[11] The metaphor of the iron horse both enabled painters and cartoonists to contrast the old and the new, the slow and the outmoded with the new and technologically sophisticated and provided a means of connecting the new technology with a set of historically well-established moral equivalences; thus the locomotive driver was a chivalrous knight and the locomotive his trusty steed. J. M. Ballantyne's boys' adventure story *The Iron Horse, or Life on the Line* (1871) provides a good illustration from the mid-Victorian period. Introducing the hero of the story, the engine-driver John Marriot, Ballantyne describes him as a combination of chivalrous medieval knight and respectable Victorian citizen, 'a steady, sober, trustworthy man. None but men of the best character are nowadays put in so responsible a position.'[12]

Alternately in the United States, for example, the metaphor of the iron horse cast the engineer as a brave member of the cavalry, or a lone 'cowboy' figure fighting the retrogressive forces of chaos and disorder at the frontiers of civilization. In the painting *Opening of*

the Wilderness (1858) by Thomas Prichard Rossiter, railroad locomotives gather round a turntable at a depot in a clearing as if they
are themselves frontiersmen gathered round the campfire, while
Theodore Kaufmann's painting *Railway Train Attacked by Indians*
(1867) suggests the unequal struggle between the power of the railroad as a force for modernity and indigenous ways of life. John Ford's
epic silent western *The Iron Horse* (1924) draws on longstanding
representations of the American railroad evident in pictures, novels
and popular song. The film tells the story of the building of the
transcontinental railroad, simultaneously wrapping this story in the
landscapes and mythology of the western frontier and helping to
define the genre of the western movie itself.[13] Thus in North America
the metaphor of the iron horse played a central part in the myth-
making bound into the story of nation building, an image most
famously encapsulated in Francis Palmer's lithograph *Across the
Continent – Westward the Course of Empire Takes its Way* (1868).
Thus the iron horse became more than mechanical energy natural-
ized in the familiarized form of equine power: rather, it was co-opted
to a theological vision as part of a divinely ordained means given
to humans and enabling them to build civilization out of wilderness. This forms an essential part of what David Nye has called a
teleology of second creation in the United States. Here the railway
is an essential vitality driving human progress and animating the
conquest of land and landscape as physical resources. From this
perspective railways are more than simply a human fabrication:
rather, they became a God-given extension of the natural resources
given to humans in order to construct the world in God's image.[14]
Railways were therefore intrinsic to the very processes by which a
civilized and humanized landscape was wrought from the natural
environment. Thus many saw railroads and other engineering works
as elements of a larger divine plan. Writing at the completion of the

Baltimore & Ohio Railroad in 1857, William Prescott Smith imagined the topography of the USA as a set of divinely inspired challenges to be overcome,

> thus provoking the concentration of effort and active exercise of reasoning and inventive faculties, necessary to advancement and indispensable to a people's preparation for its new duties . . . [15]

A scout looks down on railway construction as a strange threatening cloud looms above. Cinema audiences would recognize this symbolism: popular images often used obscuring locomotive smoke to represent the eclipse of Native American civilization.

Many preferred to see technological achievements not as violations of nature but as extensions and imitations of it. Images which juxtaposed the sublime grandeur of mountains, deserts and great rivers with engineering structures such as bridges and tunnels both demonstrated human ability to conquer natural obstacles and rendered to such sublime structures the qualities of a new human-made nature as a rival and equal to divine creation. Such images are evident in early representations of the railway in Britain. Many express the supreme sense of Victorian confidence expected from the world's major industrial and imperial power. The Chancellor and reforming politician Lord Henry Brougham (1778–1868) talked of 'the gigantic power of man penetrating through miles of solid mass, and gaining a great, lasting, and almost perennial conquest over the power of nature', while the essayist and commentator Thomas Carlyle (1795–1881) viewed railway development as part of a war with 'rude nature'.[16] Not surprisingly, therefore, images of the railway in a situation of colonial expansion and conquest figure prominently, for example in photographs and lithographs showing the development of railways in British India. However, some of the most eloquent examples are provided by the photographs and paintings of the American transcontinental railroad (opened in 1869) by Thomas Moran and Albert Bierstadt, who were commissioned by the Union Pacific Railroad to document the line. The natural sublime intertwined with technological conquest, creating tensions within the imagery.[17] Thus Nye describes

the vastness of the American West literally put into perspective by the railroad track; the geometry of new cities juxtaposed with the panoramic vista of mountains; man [sic] dwarfed by the monuments of nature, while technology stands triumphant in the wilderness.[18]

In the USA such dramatic contrasts were complementary forms of the sublime and expressed an energy that dramatized an unfolding national destiny. In 'The Young American' the poet and essayist Ralph Waldo Emerson portrayed the railway as a vital energy planted in humanity and nature alike. Breaking with a simple opposition between nature and culture to find a unifying force underlying both, for Emerson the railroad was 'a magician's rod, in its power to evoke sleeping energies of land and water'.[19] Nature was not being invaded or destroyed but awakened, and the metaphor of 'sleeping energies' suggests that the transformative energy of the railroad is as much a product of nature as of human design.

In the painting *Westwards the Star of Empire Takes its Way – Near Council Bluffs, Iowa* (1865) by Andrew Melrose (1836–1901), the train cuts a path through a prairie landscape, opposing a human-made world on one side of the tracks and nature on the other. On the left-hand side of the image a homestead sits within fields newly won from the virgin forest. On the right, as can be seen in the procession of wildlife crossing the line in front of the locomotive, the forest forms a dense wilderness teeming with vitality. Rather than simply demonstrating the triumph of civilization over nature, the image seems to suggest something rather more ambiguous. The farm appears small and fragile, its smoking chimney and lighted window symbolizing domesticity, yet there is arguably also a sense of sadness suggested by the ravaged remains of standing timber. Though the cleared land is made ready for agriculture, it is presented as barren and lifeless in comparison with the residual forest. At the same time the train cuts through the landscape, separating civilized homestead from virgin woodland. The locomotive both emerges from and illuminates the natural world, spotlighting the flora and fauna of a fast-disappearing wilderness.

From the earliest years of public railway operation representations of the railway as a creative and progressive strength were balanced

against conceptions of the railway as an energetic force for destruction. The death of William Huskisson MP at the opening of the Liverpool & Manchester Railway on 15 September 1830 is often cited as a key moment. The novelty of the technology, and the newness of many of its operational systems, resulted in a version of the railway in the popular imagination from the 1830s through to the 1870s characterized by accounts of accidents, boiler explosions and fatalities to railway workers.[20] In contrast to its characterization as a friendly draft animal, the physical features of the locomotive were just as easily animalized, as monstrous or demonic. For the cartoonist George Cruikshank, the locomotive boiler easily metamorphosed into a head and face, while the smoke, steam, exhaust beat and whistle became roaring, shrieking and fire breathing. Cruikshank's *Railway Dragon* (1845), for example, demonizes the financial speculation associated with the railways. The sulphurous smoke, snorting steam, clanking machinery, dark tunnels and awe-inspiring depth of cuttings and earthworks further contributed to representations of railways as

Andrew Melrose, *Westwards the Star of Empire Takes its Way, Near Council Bluffs, Iowa*, 1865. Tracing the boundary between wilderness and civilization, here the railway is an ambiguous presence, a technology both derived from and transcending nature.

something infernal. An American diary from 1839 mused on the experience of encountering a train on a dark night:

whizzing and rattling and panting, with its fiery furnace gleaming in front, its chimney vomiting fiery smoke above, and its long train of

The Railway Dragon by cartoonist and illustrator George Cruikshank, 1845. The railway invades a domestic dining room, eating up everything in its path. Drawn at the height of 'railway mania' in Britain, it suggests both physical danger and financial greed.

cars rushing along behind like the body and tail of a gigantic dragon
– or the d–l himself . . .[21]

Charles Dickens, who so often described industrial scenes in terms of
infernal imagery, characterized the railway in *Dombey and Son* as the
'triumphant Monster Death'.[22] For an author who narrowly escaped
death in a derailment, and for an audience who were familiar with
railway disasters dramatically reported in contemporary newspaper
accounts, this was not an extravagant metaphor.

Taken together, the simultaneously creative and destructive power
of railways were a defining characteristic of the new technology. Such
arguments most frequently appeared in politically charged debates
concerning the modernization of the nation-state, for instance in
Karl Marx's 'The Future Results of the British Rule in India' (1853).
Marx argued that railways played a central role in the process of
annihilating the old Asiatic society and 'laying the foundations of
western society'.[23] Such a conception of railways as a technology of
creative destruction was, of course, picked up by artists of the futur-
ist movement in the first and second decades of the twentieth century,
celebrating the aesthetic of the machine age for its potential to over-
turn the restrictions and vested interests of a socially repressive past.
However, rather earlier than this the railway had also formed a highly
cryptic vehicle for the elaboration of such potentially 'revolutionary'
thoughts. J.M.W. Turner's painting *Rain, Steam and Speed* (1844)
shows a Firefly class locomotive crossing the River Thames on the
Great Western Railway mainline from London to Bristol at Maiden-
head. Characteristically unconventional, the train, bridge, river and
landscape emerge from the canvas through dramatic swirls of paint.
Yet Turner sets up a series of familiar contrasts; new railway bridge
and old road bridge, speeding train and drifting boat, steam-driven
locomotive and horse-drawn plough, direct track and meandering

river. To this extent the painting is little different from many other contemporary railway images. Yet where many pictures happily strive to balance symbols of the old and the new, Turner's *Rain, Steam and Speed* appears to dissolve and fragment these symbols between a set of force lines which merge natural and mechanical energy. The train hurtles relentlessly through the storm and out of the picture towards the viewer. Its wheels seem to barely touch the ground, while the front of the train appears to glow, an incandescent cipher for the energy expended in locomotion. Thus the painting expresses the apparent effortlessness of express travel by steam train whilst simultaneously demonstrating the superhuman effort needed to make this possible.

This is but one dimension to the painting.[24] The location of this painting at the point where Brunel's London–Bristol mainline crosses

J.M.W. Turner, *Rain, Steam and Speed*, 1844. When exhibited at the Royal Academy some critics felt they could feel the speed of the locomotive as it rushed towards them in this blur of light and colour.

the river Thames is significant. The intersection here of two of the nation's most symbolic transport arteries on their way to the capital would have been recognized by Turner, who elsewhere expressed an interest in economic circulation as a marker of national strength. Here the historic Thames gateway to the sea, symbolic of naval supremacy and maritime history, and the railway part of Brunel's integrated transport system linking with the new transatlantic steam ship route at Bristol, provided a contrast between old and new which was rather more nuanced than the popular prints from which it drew a symbolic vocabulary for the railway. Little wonder that contemporaries saw something in the picture that paralleled Turner's *Fighting Temeraire* (1839), which depicts a small black steam tug towing the majestic hulk of a redundant sailing 'man of war' up the Thames to be scrapped.[25] In these works a quite modernist sense of patriotism is at work, at once nostalgic for the past and yet fully cognisant of the need for reconstruction and change. Here Daniels finds parallels with Turner's paintings which 'celebrate' the burning of the Houses of Parliament (1835) with their implications of democratic and constitutional change.[26] Perhaps Turner, like Thoreau, recognized the simultaneously creative and destructive energy of railways which Marx made central to the making of modernity. At the same time, there are perhaps clear parallels with the balanced sense of loss and gain which haunts the landscape of Andrew Melrose's *Westward the Star of Empire.*

Landscape and the naturalization of technology

Wordsworth was not alone in opposing railway development during the 1830s and '40s. Notable early examples of opposition to its physical intrusion in the landscape include the then young economist John Stuart Mill and, most vociferously, the art critic John Ruskin, who was appalled by the construction of cuttings and embankments creating an artificial regularity set against the natural lie of the land.[27] It is certainly true that critics had something to complain about. In the UK and elsewhere in Europe railway development not infrequently rode roughshod over ancient monuments and through historic town-scapes. Noise and especially smoke remained contentious issues for neighbouring communities on some parts of the British railway system into the 1880s.[28] Much, for example, has been made of the opposition to railways made by the English landowning aristocracy and it is certainly the case that lines were sometimes diverted around the landscaped parks and fox coverts of aristocratic estates, or placed in tunnels or cuttings, and that some stations were built to flatter the ancestral home of a local grandee.[29] It was feared that the railway would devastate field sports, a recurring theme in early rail-way caricatures. In *Out with the hounds – meeting something like a check* from *Punch's Almanack* for 1846, John Leech depicts a balked field of huntsmen watching a train bearing down upon the hounds in a culvert. In fact the railway energized sporting life. Railway companies put drop carriages, which were detached at intermediate stations, on to express trains, for the accommodation of the hunting fraternity. At the same time railways made such pleasures available to the masses. The arrival of the railway at Epsom boosted atten-dances at the Derby to huge proportions in the 1860s and '70s.[30]

In Britain, there were loud complaints that railways would or did desecrate the landscape, complaints that usually assumed an idea of landscape that embodied rural interests, especially those of the gentry. Perhaps one factor influencing the English gentry's attitude was that the major period of railway construction coincided with the moment at which parklands planted in the eighteenth century were reaching maturity. As one MP protested in the 1830s, '[m]ountains were to be cut through, valleys were to be lifted, the skies were to be scaled: the earth was to be tunnelled; parks, gardens and ornamental grounds were to be broken into'.[31] However, in Britain the relationship between landowners and railway development remained complex and pragmatic. Not only were many aristocrats railway shareholders and directors, but for much of the nineteenth century and into the twentieth industrial investment such as that provided by the railways proved to be both more reliable and a more significant source of income than agriculture. Ironically, the grand houses of the aristocracy and their landscaped parks were substantially dependent on the industry, trade and urbanization more or less directly facilitated by railways.[32] Indeed, Wordsworth's relationship with railway development echoes this complexity and perhaps also some of its nimbyist hypocrisy. In spite of his protestations against the Kendal & Windermere line, Wordsworth was himself a railway shareholder and in his sonnets 'Steamboats, Viaducts and Railways' (1833) and 'At Furness Abbey' (1845) he wrote positively about the new technologies of steam-powered travel and transport. The railway propagandist John Francis poured scorn on the double standards he observed in the behaviour of the English gentry. In his *History of the English Railway* (1851) he derided those gentry who protested at the prospect of the railway crossing their land, usually, he maintained, as a ploy to raise the price of land to the railway companies. 'Fancy prices of fancy prospects', he sneered; in contrast 'the imaginative vision of the (railway) shareholders beheld Titanic arches and vast tunnels, magnificent bridges and fine viaducts'.[33]

Books of railway prints, often published in conjunction with railway companies themselves, provided an antidote to the accounts of railway construction that emphasized conflict and chaos.[34] T. T. Bury's prints documenting the early years of the Liverpool & Manchester Railway show a landscape in which the railway dominates without disrupting. Their cool documentary style suggests a world which is

calm and well-ordered, and in which everything has its place. John Cooke Bourne's views of the London & Birmingham Railway are unusual because they address the process of railway construction, not seriously addressed elsewhere until the 1860s. Though Bourne made sketches of excavations on the line in 1836 without any intention to work them up for publication, he was persuaded to publish partly to counter anti-railway propaganda. In *Building a Retaining Wall near Park Street, Camden Town* (1839), Bourne sets out a visual record of the work necessary to construct a cutting through the urban environment. Everywhere gangs of men are busy engaged on specific well-defined tasks; there is little evidence of the chaos and cacophony with which Dickens describes the same scene:

> Houses were knocked down; streets broken through and stopped; deep
> pits and trenches dug in the ground; enormous heaps of earth and clay
> thrown up; buildings that were undermined and shaking, propped by

John Cooke Bourne, *Building a Retaining Wall near Park Street, Camden Town, London*, 1836. These documentary style views show railway construction as orderly and rational. Perhaps not surprisingly Bury was an associate of the Society of Civil Engineers.

great beams of wood. Here, a chaos of carts, overthrown and jumbled together, lay topsey-turvy at the bottom of a steep unnatural hill; there confused treasures of iron soaked and rusted in something that had accidentally become a pond. Everywhere were bridges that led nowhere; thoroughfares that were wholly impassable.[35]

Where Dickens describes to dramatic effect the collateral damage caused by development, Bourne focuses on the practical processes of railway construction. Thus he portrays the navvies to be hard-working, steady and reliable and railway construction to be orderly and efficient.

One means by which railways became acceptably embedded in the landscape was by being cloaked in familiar historically based styles. In this respect railways merely followed the lead of early factory and canal design where buildings were variously styled to look like country houses, lodges or small garden temple structures. Eighteenth-century writers and artists endeavouring to depict the new scientific and technological processes, like iron-making, and machinery, such as the stationary steam engine, had frequently couched science and technology in the language of classical mythology.[36] So it is perhaps not surprising to find that imagery derived from classical sources was prominent in early railway design. Early railway locomotives fre-quently had names inspired by classical mythology: Vulcan, Cyclops or Ariel. Their design, like that of many line-side structures such as station buildings and bridges, often used elements from the vocab-ulary of classical architecture. Tall early locomotive chimneys were reminiscent of Doric columns; their domes and safety-valve covers derived their shape from classical vases and urns. Some of the finest and most imposing early railway architecture in Britain adopted a classical style, including Philip Hardwick's work for the London and Birmingham Railway and James Thompson's for the North Midland

Railway.[37] On the whole, examples of such sensitive and generous design did not continue to be built subsequent to the economic crises of late 1840s. On the one hand, economic stringency severely curtailed any tendency towards decoration and elaboration in railway design. On the other, the increasing experience, confidence and professionalization in both civil and mechanical engineering resulted in design which was increasingly functional and utilitarian. Perhaps by the 1850s Britain's railways were sufficiently well established as an economic and political force to enable them to be designed and built with less explicit regard for their surroundings. This growing confidence resulted in both increasingly utilitarian design for functional structures and explicitly elaborate and monumental design for many important and city centre stations.[38]

Artists both in Britain and the USA adopted the conventions of Picturesque aesthetics to portray the railway as an integral, harmonious and historically understandable part of the landscape. The theory of the Picturesque had come to prominence in late eighteenth-century

Curzon Street Station, Birmingham, designed by Philip Hardwick, 1838. The terminus of the London & Birmingham Railway was one of the world's first mainline stations. Its classical proportions pay respect to polite taste, lending an air of permanence and solidity to the new technology.

Britain as a set of visual conventions enabling the spectator to judge the aesthetic qualities of natural landscapes and compose landscape designs in paintings, gardens and parks. It was based on the style of picture-making developed especially in seventeenth-century Italy and particularly by painters such as the French/Italian Claude Lorrain (1600–1682) to portray historical scenes of classical civilization. The rules of Picturesque composition organized the elements of landscape to produce works which were balanced and harmonious in terms of their visual construction and their symbolic and historical associations.[39] The whole aimed to evoke the sophisticated and nostalgic rustic melancholy of the classical pastoral, combining nature and culture, quietude and stimulation, heroism and domesticity. Thus it situated its subject-matter in a history of Western civilization that itself, like early railway architecture, referred back to ancient Greece and Rome. In the pre-railway era a Picturesque aesthetic was often adopted to portray working machinery as old and decayed in a manner which softened its impact and encouraged spectators to imagine it an old, established part of the landscape. So it is not surprising that Picturesque images of the railway are prominent amongst early portrayals of the trains in the landscape. In Britain such views came closest to incorporating the railway into a dominant aristocratic view of social and landscape order. In *Chirk Viaduct, Shrewsbury and Chester Railway* by G. Pickering (1848), the railway viaduct with a train crossing is seen in the distance on the left across the fields, framed in the trees that line a country lane. In the foreground a scene of rural life is shown unaffected by the railway. The framing trees, the rustic foreground scene and the portrayal of the viaduct itself, reminiscent of a Roman aqueduct 'marching' across the Campagna, characterize this image as Picturesque. Significantly, the landscape is crowned by a parish church and a country house to the left centre above the viaduct. The train itself

is displaced further to the left; even its smoke fails to obscure these twin foci of rural power.[40]

Landscape painting of the Hudson River School in the USA also adopted Picturesque principles to situate railways in an idealized pastoral landscape whose inspiration was drawn from classical antiquity.[41] In Thomas Doughty's *A View of Swampscott* (1847) a tiny train is hidden in a grove of trees, while in *Starrucca Viaduct* (1865) by Jasper Francis Cropsey the railway follows a sinuous course observing the contours of the landscape before emerging onto a viaduct reminiscent of classical Italy.[42] However it is a picture by George Inness which most subtly harmonizes train and landscape in an image which at first viewing might be interpreted as a striking image of landscape change and contrast. Inness's picture *The Lackawanna Valley* (1855)

George Pickering, *Chirk Viaduct, Shrewsbury and Chester Railway*, 1848, adopts the conventions of the classic Picturesque aesthetics.

43

was painted as a railroad company commission and portrays a locomotive roundhouse and other industrial plants associated with the
railroad. Placing the train between the idealized pastoral landscape
and the clear evidence of change, urbanization and agriculture in the
foreground, the railroad buildings themselves are partly lost in the
heat of the day. Subordinating these buildings in height to the church
steeple, and framing them with mountains and trees, suggests a visual
language shared by many Picturesque railroad views. Similarly familiar is the way in which Inness harmonizes the trackbed itself into
the topography by representing the rails almost as if they are country
lanes leading away from the town. Historian John R. Stilgoe comments
perceptively on the train which appears to run through the newly made
fields almost without tracks; 'By de-emphasizing railroad scenery,

George Inness, *The Lackawanna Valley*, 1855, provides a distinctively American resolution
between technology and nature. Technological disruption is only temporary: when the train
passes, natural order will be restored.

especially the roadbed and tracks beneath the train, Inness stressed the ephemeral nature of the train in the landscape. When the train passes out of sight, everything – in the foreground and the middle distance, at least – is again traditionally rural.'[43]

Here Inness moves beyond the accepted visual conventions of the Picturesque to portray a landscape whose temporality concerns renewal and the re-establishment of order rather than decline and decay. Like the train whistle in Thoreau's account of Walden Pond, or indeed the steam train in the fells described by Garrett, the passing of the train disturbs the landscape, whilst at the same time signalling the temporary state of this disruption and the impending return to a state of rest and quiet. David Nye characterizes this sense of temporal disruption as a key component of what he calls the technological sublime.[44] Rather than emphasizing the disjunction between train and landscape and by implication the separation between nature and technology, the temporary character of such events work to effect a resolution between the two. The interruption of the landscape by the railway is resolved peacefully by the passing of the train. Nature appears as both precious and vulnerable while at the same time retaining its power to reclaim the socialized energy represented by the mechanical technology of the railway.

Railways, routine and the rhythm of landscape

In the final decade of the nineteenth century the proliferation of advertising and postcard material cast the train in the landscape as an increasingly commonplace image. A substantial proportion of this material was produced by railway companies themselves as they learned the commercial advantage to be gained from shaping public perceptions and expectations of the territories they served. In the UK from the early 1860s railway companies also began to employ professional photographers to document their lines, rolling stock and station structures. In the USA the photographs produced to document the building of the First Transcontinental Railroad, completed in 1869, illustrate the extent to which railway companies attempted to control the public image of themselves as a powerful force that was simultaneously making history and transforming landscapes.[45]

The development of railway-based tourism proved to be a major new source of images situating railways in the landscape. Though early railway guidebooks provided some information concerning towns and places of interest along the route, the guides produced from the 1880s were increasingly pitched at the tourist and frequently aimed at guiding the visitor towards an appreciation of the landscape's scenic value. The Boston & Maine Railroad's 1887 *Down East Latch Strings; Or Sea Shore, Lakes and Mountains,* a 256-page softcover book, states its purpose as 'presenting to the intending summer tourist a description of the scenery along the line'. Among the first such guides in the UK was that produced by the Highland Railway, which had reached its twenty-first edition by 1902. This boldly stated that 'the scenery traversed by the Highland Railway far surpasses in interest and variety that of any railway route in the United Kingdom'.[46] The Great Eastern Railway first placed photographic images in their railway carriages illustrating rural scenes in 1884. However, it was not until the 1890s that British railways began routinely to produce views illustrating and advertising the scenic qualities of the landscapes through which their lines ran.[47] These were displayed on posters in stations and above the backs of seats in railway compartments. Such views and the tourism they supported tapped into the nostalgic ruralism within British culture which ironically harked back to a pre-railway age. This is reflected, for example, in the popularity of novels by Thomas Hardy (1840–1928) set in a semi-fictionalized West Country just before the coming of the railways, the development

The Peak District for Picture Makers, a poster for the Midland Railway Company, 1930. Fashionably dressed women with cameras and sketch-pads in such posters gave a contemporary twist to the Picturesque tourism that had helped popularize this region of England in pre-railway days.

of preservation movements such as the National Trust (1895) and the widespread appeal of leisure pursuits such as rambling and cycling.[48] In both the UK and North America competition between railway companies was a major factor encouraging them to promote the distinctiveness of their routes and the attractions of the landscape through which they ran. Such competition was to gather pace in the 1920s and '30s, by which time the completion of competing rail networks, consolidation and amalgamation between companies and the growing threat of road competition resulted in a very real commercial need for distinctive high-profile company identities and aggressive marketing strategies on both sides of the Atlantic.

The experience of railway travel also shaped the way landscape was viewed. As Wolfgang Schivelbusch has shown, the conventional way of looking at landscape prior to the railway was to observe a receding vista from a static viewpoint,[49] a detailed and closely observed foreground giving way to a more generalized middle ground which guided the eye towards a specific distant object of interest. From the moving train perspectives were constantly shifting, eye-catching focal points in the middle distance were alternately visible and obscured, close and distant, while the foreground whizzed past in a perpetual blur. The speed of travel by rail made it impossible to form such well-ordered and closely observed landscapes in the mind's eye. The experience of landscape as a kaleidoscopic blur of sensory impressions is perhaps best represented in such works as Arthur Dove's semi-abstract expressionist painting *Fields of Grain as Seen from a Train* (1931), or indeed in the sort of rhyming verse which suggests early accounts of the experience of railway travel as akin to flying. Perhaps best known is Robert Louis Stevenson's poem 'From a Railway Carriage', published in *A Child's Garden of Verses* (1885):

Faster than fairies, faster than witches,
Bridges and houses, hedges and ditches;
And charging along like troops in a battle,
All through the meadows the horses and cattle:
All of the sights of the hill and the plain
Fly as thick as driving rain;
And ever again, in the wink of an eye,
Painted stations whistle by.[50]

Schivelbusch traces how the habit of reading came to restore order to the experience of landscape from the train as people learned to divide their time while travelling between reading and gazing out of the carriage window into the middle distance. The spread of railway bookstalls, such as those operated by W. H. Smith from the 1840s, and the development of novels specifically written to entertain while in transit are testimony to this. In this way, he argues, the book replaced the detail of the foreground in the experience of travellers and allowed them to observe the landscape as fragments of an ever-changing panorama dissolving one into another in counterpoint with the solid thread of narrative constituted by the words on the page.[51] Where once the traveller engaged directly with the landscape through which they journeyed, experiencing every undulation, skirting round puddles, fording rivers and accommodating their footfall to variations in surface texture and solidity, now they glided effortlessly through the landscape while glancing passively out the window at the passing scene. For many passengers, railway travel was thus transformed into a substantially routine and commonplace event.

By the 1870s depictions of the railway journey as variously disembodied flying or the visceral graft of horse-powered locomotion had been joined by perspectives which moved beyond immediate sensations of speed. Partly this is reflected in novels and paintings which looked inward towards the complexities of social mixing within the railway compartment; however, it is also evident in representations which turned outwards to take in the view from the carriage window. As the railway became an established feature of the social and economic fabric of everyday life, so the railway's presence increasingly came to act as a marker for the everyday and the unremarkable. In Monet's paintings of railway stations, for example *Train in the Snow at Argenteuil* (1875) and his pictures of Gare St Lazare in Paris (1877), the railway is little more than a medium for exploring atmospheric effects within commonplace urban environments.[52] In these images there is none of the sense of technological novelty apparent in Turner's *Rain, Steam and Speed*. Here the artist's focus on atmosphere sensitizes us to the mundane rather than the spectacular demonstration of mechanical energy. Yet railways also continued to serve as a marker for change as well as stability. As such, portrayals of the railway came to dramatize a very human engagement with landscape. Marcel Proust uses the juxtaposition of railway and landscape to describe the intersection of routine and extraordinary moments in everyday life. In the second part of *Remembrance of Things Past, Within a Budding Grove* (1919), he describes the moment at which the narrator's train stops at a wayside country station early one morning.

The scenery became broken, abrupt, the train stopped at a little station between two mountains. Far down the gorge, on the edge of a hurrying

Camille Pissarro, *Lordship Lane Station, Dulwich*, 1871. In this painting of an unremarkable south London suburban station, the train is taken for granted as part of the everyday landscape.

stream, one could see only a solitary watch-house, deep-planted in the water which ran past on a level with its windows. If a person can be the product of a soil the peculiar charm of which one distinguishes in that person . . . such a person must be the big girl whom I now saw emerge from the house and, climbing the path lighted by the first slanting rays of the sun, come towards the station carrying a jar of milk. In her valley from which its congregated summits hid the rest of the world, she could never see anyone save in these trains which stopped for a moment only.[53]

Proust contrasts the girl's rootedness in everyday routine, or 'habit' as he calls it, with the uncertainty of the narrator's position in the

Claude Monet's *Train in the Snow at Argenteuil*, 1875, is one of a number of works by this artist exploring the atmospheric effects of railways.

course of a long journey taking him to a new life. Taken together, the physical beauty of the 'milk girl' and that of the landscape are for Proust given stereotypically gendered human meaning by the peaceful, domestic habituation of a life lived close to the land and in harmony with the rhythms of nature. The train forms a convenient vehicle connecting the ordinary and the extraordinary, unquestioned everyday routine and the carefully considered life-changing journey. Perhaps significantly, by placing the girl's work serving milk and coffee to railway passengers as a central part of her daily routine, Proust marks out a place for the railway as a link between modernity, urbanity and culture on the one hand and nature, tradition and rurality on the other. Whilst the girl lives in an apparently natural and cyclical world, the narrator lives in a linear world of modern change and progress. Tomorrow she will return to the station but the narrator will be long gone; the railway connects these worlds and holds them separate.

Increasingly a conception of railways in the landscape developed during the first half of the twentieth century which emphasized the relationship between railway and landscape as an interpenetration of mutual dependencies rather than the juxtaposition of irreconcilable fragments. This is evident in the work of other artists who used railways as a means of documenting quotidian routine within everyday landscapes, including the painters of the Euston Road School, who portrayed everyday street scenes of suburban London, and American photographers such as Walker Evans.[54] Evans was employed during the years of the Great Depression by the Farm Security Administration to document the social upheaval it caused. This work is well represented in his portfolio *Along the Right of Way* (1950), which comprises a series of views taken from a moving train.[55]

Some of the most effective images representing the view from the train portray a fleeting and momentary landscape snapshot similar to those of Walker Evans and reminiscent of Proust's description of the encounter between the traveller and the milk seller. Edward Thomas's poem 'Adlestrop' portrays such a momentary encounter which, though it does not involve human-to-human contact, is equally freighted with social meaning. Written in 1915 after he had signed up for military service in the army, it was published posthumously in his collected works (1920).[56] Amongst the most widely known and loved of railway poems, it depicts an unscheduled stop at a rural station during a hot summer's day. In the pause after the train has come to rest and before the signal drops and the train moves off again, the author's attention is drawn beyond the railway in the stillness and heat of the afternoon. The sound of a single blackbird punctuating the silence catches his attention. As its sound resonates out across the landscape, so the author becomes sensitized to the natural sounds of the day and he becomes increasingly aware of a world beyond the tracks. Resounding at greater and greater distance, birdsong transforms the dull silence of the moment created by the train's unscheduled stop. The sense of detachment initially felt by the author is characteristic of Schivelbusch's description of the railway journey, yet this is soon transformed into an intimate and connected experience of a landscape full of life, vitality and hope.

And for that minute a blackbird sang
Close by, and round him, mistier,
Farther and farther, all the birds
Of Oxfordshire and Gloucestershire.[57]

Though a product of the Second rather than the First World War, the painting *Train Landscape* (1940) by the English artist Eric Ravilious occupies similar territory to that of Thomas's Adlestrop. It shows the chalk hill figure at Westbury, Wiltshire, as seen from a train window. Most famous for his engravings and book illustrations, Ravilious worked as an official war artist during the Second World War. Framed by the carriage window, the picture is redolent with a symbolism of possession and belonging in which patriotic pride is projected onto the landscape. The carriage door is improbably marked on the inside with a '3', indicating that this is a third-class carriage. The window frames the view for the spectator and we are encouraged to imagine that we occupy the empty seats of the railway compartment and look out on to the landscape beyond. As third-class passengers the moral of the picture is perhaps that this landscape belongs to us, the ordinary folk of Britain. The downland landscape itself with its white horse represents the highly valued southern English landscape encapsulated in ideas of 'deep England' and suggests a history of farming and settlement traceable in this landscape back into pre-history.[58] The painting persuades us to pause for a moment and feel a connection with this landscape and the countless generations who have shaped it through their routine actions. At the same time, the act of framing, like the passing momentary encounter enabled by the railway journey, creates a distance between us and the landscape that implores us to feel the preciousness and vulnerability of this moment and, by implication, to share in the wider perceived threat to this landscape, the history and way of life it represents during a time of war.

As one of the defining works of English pastoralism in the period between the wars, Thomas's 'Adlestrop', like Ravilious's *Train Landscape*, fed precisely the sort of ruralist myth represented in advertising posters and guidebooks produced by major British railway companies. They share with Proust, Walker Evans and others a conception of the train in the landscape as a means of connecting that which is routine with that which is exceptional in such a way as to transform our sense of the commonplace. Yet the experience described by Proust, Thomas and Ravilious seems to belong to more than its historically specific moment. The unscheduled stop, the stillness and the building sense

of irritation and disquiet, followed in the resigned idleness of the moment by a growing awareness of the world beyond the train is familiar to many travellers. The experience of landscape from a railway train is one simultaneously of isolation and connectivity. The straight, level line of the railway track and smooth progress along metal rails remove us from direct contact with the undulations of topography; carriage windows frame the view just as our guided progress through the landscape provides perspective, sequence and distance. At the same time, railway journeys heighten and dramatize the experience of travel. This experience is marked out upon boarding the train in a contrast between the frenzied tumult of the station and the quiet, reposed reflection of the railway carriage. The rhythmical counterpoint of stillness and motion, interruption and connectivity feeds senses of belonging and loss which are deeply seated in our experience of railways. Such a sense seems fundamental to the 'romance' of the railway and has become an increasingly important cultural

Eric Ravilious, *Train Landscape*, 1940. In this work Ravilious, an official war artist, encouraged the British to find patriotic pride in landscape symbols through the democratic vehicle of railway travel.

resource, part of the nostalgia generated after the Second World War by modernization and deindustrialization. Garrett's steam train in the Cumbrian fells, punctuating the dark cool solitude of the night, its exhaust beat reverberating around the hills and casting sparks into the blackness, is a poetic trope common from many cultural representations of the railway. As Garrett looks back longingly to a lost age, so poets such as Rupert Brooke and Lawrence Durrell and songwriters like Ewan McColl have equally contrasted communication with isolation, safety with danger and energy with stillness. The rhythms of railway travel built nostalgia into the experience of train journeys long before railways became heritage.

Connections, gatherings and the train in the landscape

The roaring, clanking, wheezing, drumming and screaming sounds which herald the proximity of the train give it a material impact which goes well beyond its visual appearance. Like many others before and since, Garrett's reminiscences of the steam train in the fells demonstrate the overwhelming physicality of this auditory encounter. Such a complex rhythmic material presence is expressed in a range of modernist and progressivist artistic responses to the railway locomotive from Walt Whitman's (1819–1892) 'To a Locomotive in Winter' (1881) to Arthur Honegger's (1892–1955) orchestral work *Pacific 231* (1923). In this context the sound of the train acts as a signal marker, a symbolic focus for expressing mechanical energy, a kind of cultural safety valve marking out moments of excess and loss, presence and absence, meaning and chaos. At the same time the rhythms of motion also act as a unifying force gathering together and refracting the separate rhythms of mechanical motion into one single reverberating propulsive energy. Thus in Honegger's *Pacific 231*, originally entitled simply *Mouvement Symphonique No. 1*, a sequence of initial block chords fragment into a series of cross rhythms, and syncopations emanating from different parts of the orchestra overlaying a steady marching beat. These are slowly resolved into a series of ensemble orchestral chords as the work gathers force towards its climax. Working with such rhythms in the abstract, it may not be surprising that Honegger insisted that he wrote the work as an exercise in writing music that built momentum against a slowing tempo. Reputedly, he only gave the work its descriptive name after its completion. However, the sense in which the music collects and directs the energy of motion is palpable and its analogy to the steam locomotive transparently evident. This was made most explicit in French director Jean Mitry's award-winning *Pacific 231* (1949), a film which used Honegger's orchestral work as its soundtrack. In a more popular and accessible genre, there are parallels with Richard Rodney Bennett's (1936–) iconic railway melody *Waltzer* from the film version of *Murder on the Orient Express* (1974). Here the music adopts a triple-time rhythm whose lopsided underlying pulse continually reclaims the joyful exuberance of its broad expansive melody. By this means the rhythmic complexity representing the moving parts of the locomotive are contained within a centrifugal vortex of sound, a kind of *perpetuum mobile* that propels the train forwards.[59]

Close up of locomotive valve gear from the film *Pacific 231* (dir. Jean Mitry, 1949). The abstract images match the modernist aesthetic of Arthur Honegger's music.

Yet it would be a mistake to see the rhythms of railway travel as simply about sound. The three sections of this chapter share a common concern for the multiple rhythms generated by the railway as a means for both experiencing and understanding the energy and power of the railway as a source of mechanical force and as a vehicle for social, economic and cultural change. In turn, these sections have been concerned with the rhythms of motion, the momentary shock of the technological sublime and the routines and connectivities of everyday belonging. Thus Whitman's 'To a Locomotive in Winter' draws the forces of landscape and nature together with the components of the train in order to stress a theme developed elsewhere in his poetry, that of parts working together 'merged in verse', to create a sense of movement, power and beauty:

> Thy knitted frame, thy springs and valves, the tremulous twinkle of
>   thy wheels,
> Thy train of cars behind, obedient, merrily following,
> Through gale or calm, now swift, now slack, yet steadily careering;
>   Type of the modern – emblem of motion and power – pulse of the
>   continent,
> For once come serve the Muse and merge in verse, even as here
>   I see thee.[60]

From a broader perspective our sense of railways in the landscape is built from experience of the overlapping of these rhythmic regimes. Moving through landscape, interpenetrating rhythms of hill, valley and plain intersect with the routine of everyday lives coordinated with railway time, while the tempos of locomotion, the beat of exhaust, the thrumming of the rails and the shriek of a whistle energize, dramatize and punctuate this experience. Turner's *Rain, Steam and Speed* exemplifies this eloquently, set at the intersection of symbolically important transport routes and bound together by the elemental cross-currents of driving storm and speeding train. So, too, does the harmonic resonance of stillness and vitality which opens out from Thomas's poem 'Adlestrop'. Music has of course provided a suitable means for exploring these forms of rhythmic encounter between train and landscape, most famously in the Toccata from *Bachianas Brasileiras No 2* (1933), known as 'The Little Train of the Caipira', by the Brazilian composer Heitor Villa-Lobos (1887–1959). In this work the composer binds together the rhythms of the moving train, its acceleration, progress and deceleration, with melodies inflected by the folk music of the rural hinterland through which the train runs. Together these cross-currents weave together the physical progress of the train through the landscape and the social and cultural world it inhabits. After the revolution in 1930, Villa-Lobos was central to the awakening of a national cultural consciousness in Brazil and therefore this music and his work can be interpreted more broadly as an attempt to bind the nation together culturally and politically.

As we have seen from the discussion of work by Turner, Ravilious and Thomas, portrayals of the train in the landscape speak eloquently of the physical and metaphorical power of the railway to connect

This poster advertising the GPO film *Night Mail*, 1936 (dir. Harry Watt and Basil Wright), draws on the abstract modernist qualities of the film to convey a sense of speed, power and dynamism.

people and places in the service of national identity and nation build-ing. In this respect, perhaps the best example is the GPO film *Night Mail* (1936), which follows the journey of a mail train from London to Edinburgh. With words by W. H. Auden and music by Benjamin Britten, *Night Mail* was made with an all-star cast drawn from the now highly celebrated British documentary movement of the 1930s. Certain aspects of *Night Mail* are echoed in Mitry's film *Pacific 231*: both films portray the locomotive through a sharply intercut and abstracted celebration of mechanical motion. Inflected by modernist avant-garde aesthetics, the film has a complex rhythmical structure juxtaposing real-time footage of mail-sorting with an overall sense of gathering momentum as the train accelerates through the night on its journey to Scotland. Images showing snapshot views from the train are balanced with those showing it streaking across the landscape. Sedentary farmers and sleeping children are contrasted with frenetic activity, frightened horses with speeding locomotives, factories and bridges with mountains and fields, the slow cadences of conversa-tion with the repetitive urgency of Auden's verse. Thus the film draws widely across the rich history of representational strategies for imagin-ing the train in the landscape. As the train slows towards its Edinburgh destination, so the tempo of Auden's verse slows and gathers the fragments of the film together.

Thousands are still asleep
Dreaming of terrifying monsters,
Or of friendly tea beside the band at Cranston's or Crawford's:
Asleep in working Glasgow, asleep in well-set Edinburgh,
Asleep in granite Aberdeen,
They continue their dreams,
And shall wake soon and long for letters,
And none will hear the postman's knock

Without a quickening of the heart,
For who can bear to feel himself forgotten?

As the train brings communications from London to Scotland, symbolically tying the nations of England and Scotland together, the aesthetic of the railway in the landscape as a polyrhythmic interplay of distance and connection reaches a fitting destination. In this respect the powerful imagery of *Night Mail* points towards the railway's very practical role in nation building. This assertion is strongly echoed in many of the examples discussed in this chapter. However, culture is much more than an apparently passive reflection of events, and the place of railways in government and military strategy, administrative and bureaucratic procedure is equally given purchase on the world through culture. The ways in which this is given form and meaning are the subject of the next chapter.

2 | The Machine Ensemble and the Nation-state

Democracy and the totalitarian machine

There can be few more powerful images of the railway as a tool of military power and political control than that showing the gates to the concentration camp at Auschwitz. The tracks converge on a single rail entrance watched over by a guard tower. In the foreground, belongings lie strewn across the rails in the snow. In this stark black-and-white photo the railway tracks foreground evidence of suffering and make a visual connection with the guard post's oppressive presence. It has been estimated that about 3 million Jewish people were transported to their deaths by the Reichsbahn during the Second World War. The mass murder of Jews in death camps involving industrial methods began in 1942 when the SS developed a system of mass murder using poison gas. This triggered the movement by rail of large numbers of Jews from Western Europe to the death camps of Auschwitz and Treblinka.[1] Adolf Eichmann, head of Gestapo Section IV B4 of the Reich Main Security Office and responsible for implementation of Nazi policy toward the Jews in Germany and all occupied territories, created an organization designed to funnel Jews to the death factories in Poland and Silesia. The railway played a central and highly planned role in this genocide as the death camps themselves were located at convenient places on the railway network. Railways clearly

Driver Jacques Lantier (Jean Gabin) studies the track ahead from the cab of his locomotive in an opening sequence from Jean Renoir's 1938 film of Emile Zola's novel *La Bête humaine*.

played a crucial role in the Holocaust, even to the extent that, at his trial, Adolf Eichmann claimed he was merely a transport officer.[2]

It is not surprising, therefore, that the idea of the railway as an impersonal, monolithic, unstoppable war machine has been an enduring one. The novel *La Bête humaine* (1890) by Emile Zola (1840–1902), concludes with the main protagonist, Lantier, a driver on the Paris–Le Havre line, driving a train carrying troops towards the front at the outbreak of the Franco-Prussian War. Fuelled by a complex web of desire, envy and murder, a fight breaks out between driver Lantier and his fireman as the train is travelling at full steam. Both fall to their deaths as their train of blissfully drunken, patriotic soldiers heads relentlessly for destruction. It is as if the train, and the capricious passions aroused by the network of people and events connected by it, is a motif for the pointless carnage of war itself. Perhaps the most clearly articulated example of this sort of thinking is represented by the historian A.J.P. Taylor's elaboration of a railroad theory to explain the start of hostilities at the beginning of the First World War.[3] Taylor argued that none of the great powers were consciously intent on war prior to 1914. Rather, he suggests, they held in common the belief that an ability to mobilize their armed forces faster than any of the others would actually serve as a deterrent sufficient to avoid war. In this context the decision to mobilize was in itself not necessarily an aggressive act. Yet Taylor claimed that in the case of Germany, once the railway mobilization timetable had been activated hostilities were in fact inevitable. German plans took the troops not to their mobilization centres but straight into Belgium and France. An aggressive military situation was consequently an inevitable outcome of railroad timetable logic. Taylor's account is hotly disputed by other historians, so perhaps it is not unreasonable to look to Taylor's own politics in search of reasons why he might portray the start of the First World War in this way.[4] A.J.P. Taylor was a popular media figure, a committed pacifist and a staunch member of the Campaign for Nuclear Disarmament. Writing about these matters during the 1960s at the height of the Cold War, it is not difficult to see how for Taylor the railway becomes an allegory for the systems and technologies of highly mechanized warfare epitomized in the nuclear doomsday machine that haunted many during the post-Second World War period. [5]

In the nineteenth century, liberals, reformers and progressives often championed the railway as a force for democracy, able to eradicate privilege and vested interest in its wake. The reforming headmaster of Rugby School, Dr Thomas Arnold (1795–1842), celebrated the coming of the London & Birmingham Railway at the end of the 1830s: 'I rejoice to see it . . . and think that feudality is gone for ever. It is so great a blessing to think that any one evil is extinct.'[6]

Such examples can be multiplied many times over as commentators came to terms with the fact that railways moved rich and poor people together in the same trains and at the same speed, simultaneously rendering outlying and remote places and regions more accessible. Thus in 1839 the French progressive thinker Constantin Pecqueur (1801–1887) claimed that

> the railways quite prodigiously advance the reign of truly fraternal social relations and do more for the sentiments of equality than the most exhalted sermons of the tribunes of democracy.[7]

The network properties of railways fuelled such opinions and stirred the modernizing imagination. Railways linked hitherto semi-autonomous and disconnected locations, moving everyone closer to the 'national hearth', as an article in the English *Critical Quarterly* termed it in 1839. By implication, railways connected formerly static and relatively isolated populations into greater regional and national systems of travel and communication.[8] Railways, as the *Critical Quarterly* suggested, built the nation both physically and psychologically.

The history of the railway is closely tied to the history of modern politics. Railways developed during a period of political change and revolutionary violence in Europe and advanced across the globe along with both European-derived models of the nation-state and the structures of formal empire. At the same time, movement and mobility became watchwords for that basic tenet of democracy, public participation in the nation itself. During the early 1830s, the relationship between mobility and citizenship was elaborated in this context within French enlightenment thought by the Saint-Simonian and future French senator Michel Chevalier, who encapsulated this in the concept of 'circulating civilization'.[9] All this took place during a period in which much of the world's political map took the shape we would recognize today, culminating in two world wars in which railways played significant if very different roles.

However, the growth of railway systems in the UK, Europe and USA, their use as a tool of military control and their emergence as corporate capitalist enterprises on a hitherto undreamt-of scale also

Edward Keller, *Impending Retribution*, a cartoon which appeared in California's satirical magazine *The Wasp* (7 October 1882). It related to a dispute over land titles between the Southern Pacific Railroad and homesteaders in Mussel Slough County, California, in which eight people died.

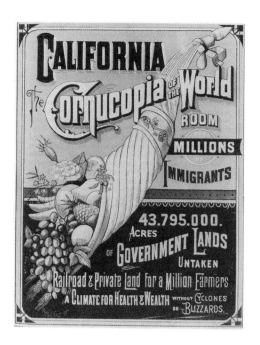

produced a conception of the railway as an impersonal, monolithic and callous machine. Frank Norris's novel *The Octopus* (1900) fictionalizes the conflict between wheat farmers in the San Joaquin Valley and the Pacific & Southwestern Railroad. In this conflict the Railroad attempted to take possession of land that farmers had been improving for many years, forcing them into conflict. Through the eyes of the character Presley, a poet and a thinly disguised cipher for the author himself, the railway is on the one hand the kind of deadly monster familiar from earlier representations, 'the galloping monster, the terror of steel and steam, with its single eye, cyclopean, red, shooting from horizon to horizon'.[10] On the other it is something on a vastly different scale to the familiar image of the demonized locomotive, thus Presley

California, The Cornucopia of the World, one of the major 19th-century Western promotional books, written and published in several editions by the Southern Pacific's immigration commissioner in Chicago between 1883 and 1886.

saw it now as the symbol of a vast power, huge, terrible, flinging the echo of its thunder over all the reaches of the valley, leaving blood and destruction in its path; the leviathan, with tentacles of steel clutching into the soil, the soulless Force, the iron-hearted Power, the monster, the Colossus, the Octopus.[11]

Here the railway system as an entity in itself holds the country in a vice-like grip. Its branch lines act like a 'veritable system of blood circulation, complicated, dividing, and reuniting, branching, splitting, extending, throwing out feelers, offshoots, taproots, feeders – diminutive little bloodsuckers that shot out from the main jugular'.[12] The very confusion of Presley's metaphors indicate his difficulty in finding adequate means for representing the railway as a geographical dictatorship, where the corporate drive for profit constituted a form of feudalism every bit as exploitative and coercive as that of a medieval monarch. The activities, for example, of the Grange Movement in the USA (National Grange of the Order of Patrons of Husbandry, founded 1867) demonstrates the scale and importance of the conflict between farmers and the railroads, which were operating as territorial monopolies, such as that symbolized by the 'Mussel Slough Tragedy' of 11 May 1880. The Grange's early success was based on mobilizing farmers politically against railroad and grain-elevator monopolies that controlled the process of marketing agricultural goods. The so-called Granger states, which included Minnesota, Iowa, Illinois and Wisconsin, were located in the upper Mississippi Valley, the region where conflict between farmers and railroads over transportation costs was particularly sharp in the 1870s.[13] In the Midwest as on the Pacific coast, railroads facilitated settlement and held out an economic lifeline while also holding those dependent on them as captive markets. As technological systems of hitherto unknown scale, railways bound the transactions of the nation into their particular medium. In the process they forged a conception of the modern nation based on connection and circulation. Both a conduit for the transactions of the nation and a means of shaping the patterning and direction of such flows, railways created unprecedented dependence on this particular and frequently privately owned means of communication.

The railway machine and the corporate–state metaphor

The idea that railways formed a system involving track, trains and locomotives, co-ordinated and regulated by signalling and telegraph systems and operating as a single machine whose totality was greater than the sum of its parts had been firmly established by the 1850s. By this time some railway companies in the UK, for example, had established regional networks employing in excess of 10,000 employees and constituted corporate commercial organizations of previously unimaginable size. Accounts of the railway prior to the 1830s recognized no distinction between railways and other modes of transport such as canals and turnpike roads. When in 1802 Richard Lovell Edgeworth published the first proposal for a public railway he imagined a type of routeway where individual private carriages would be conveyed independently of one another.[14] The world's first public

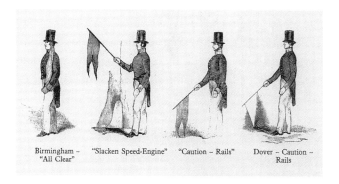

Birmingham –   "Slacken Speed-Engine"   "Caution – Rails"   Dover – Caution –
"All Clear"   Rails

This demonstration in *The Illustrated London News* in 1844 shows the system of hand signalling derived from military practice used to control trains by railway policemen before the establishment of mechanical signals controlled from strategically located cabins.

railway, the horse-drawn Surrey Iron Railway (1805–38), for instance, allowed private owners to pull their own wagons over the tramway in much the same way as a turnpike allowed anyone to use the road subsequent to paying the requisite toll. As the implications of railway operation became better understood, commentators recognized that this was an inadequate model, but were equally unable to think beyond it. In his *Observations on a General Iron Railway* (1820) Thomas Gray concluded that 'In order to establish a general iron railway, it will be necessary to lay down two or three rail-ways for the ascending, and an equal number for the descending vehicles. In the immediate neighbourhood of London the traffic might demand six rail-ways.'[15] Gray's singular vision of London's citizens travelling at their own discretion down any one of a substantial number of parallel tracks was, of course, never to be realized. Privately owned vehicles were conveyed by the new steam-powered railways which developed from the mid-1820s and indeed continue to this day to be carried on many of the world's railway systems. However, there are no instances of a system which could accommodate the sort of loosely coordinated individual free passage familiar from other forms of routeway.

From the earliest years of commercial railway operation there were both organizational and mechanical dimensions to the apparent fusion of technologies into a single unified whole. Ownership and control of both the means of locomotion and the routeway itself required them to function as a single entity. Partly this resulted from simple economics and logistics. Steam locomotives were expensive, requiring regularly spaced servicing points and the personnel to staff them. Investment in such technology and the necessary supporting facilities was only financially viable when this expenditure was built in to the railway's overall cost structure. It was simply not economically feasible to operate as one common carrier competing with others on a shared network and to support the infrastructure costs demanded by the new technology. Most recently in the early twenty-first century, neo-liberal policies designed to bring competition to the railways have wrestled with this same set of problems with varying degrees of effectiveness. In addition to this, safety considerations and the need to sequence trains efficiently on a system of tracks limited by both expense and space to perhaps one or two tracks in each direction necessitated that the individual train movement should be subordinated to the functioning of traffic on the system as a whole. In 1839 a British Parliamentary Committee urged the necessity of prohibiting free competition between carrier companies on the same line precisely on these grounds. Looking back in his book *Railway Economy* (1851) Dionysius Lardner, writer on science and mathematics and sometime professor of natural philosophy and astronomy at University College, London, concluded:

A railway, *like a vast machine*, the wheels of which are all connected with each other, and whose movement requires a certain harmony, can not be worked by a number of independent agents. Such a system would speedily be attended with self-destruction. The organization of a railway requires unity of direction and harmony of movement, which can only be attained by the combination of the entire carrying business with the general administration of the road.[16]

Lardner's characterization of the railway as a single 'vast machine' recognizes a system which is mechanically interlocked and organizationally co-ordinated. For Wolfgang Schivelbusch the resulting sense of unity and autonomy is complimented by the qualities of rail travel itself. The smoothness of the train's motion coupled with the synchronization of technologies and organizational structures rendered the railway a *machine ensemble*, a coherent spatially extended techno-bureaucratic entity, rather than simply the coming together of trains and track.[17] It is this sense of the railway as a single, logical and impersonal large-scale technological system that we recognize in Taylor's 'railroad theory' and Norris's 'octopus'.

Quite early on, the idea of a railway as an autonomous, organized and managed territory drew parallels with the organization of the nation-state itself. Superficially at least there was much in common between the management of a railway network and the government of a state, and these similarities were not lost on contemporary commentators. Both involve the organization and control of territory, the management of people and the supervision of productive capacity and service provision, frequently by an elected group (directors) in the name of and on behalf of many (shareholders). Parallels relate both to the sheer scale of railway undertakings and to the particular circumstances of railway operation, including the necessity for both physical and financial public safeguards: a degree of public accountability; a legally binding constitution; an independently policed system of legally enforceable rules; a measure of welfare provision and a necessity for personnel management on an unprecedented scale; the high degree of self-sufficiency necessary to maintain a regular and uniform service; and, perhaps most importantly, their role as an easily identifiable high-profile public service.[18] In one of the first treatises on railway management, Lieutenant Peter Lecount RN emphasizes the importance of centralizing control of a railway company in a single location, 'that terminus which is best situated to effectually overlook the whole of the various businesses, should be made the seat of government'. Lecount further relates his model to the experience of decision-making within Government Commissions and particularly to the Navy Board which formed part of the Board of Admiralty. In a letter to the *Railway Times* dated 1840, 'Examiner' suggested:

The management of a Railway requires the same kind of intellect as the management of a state . . . The Shareholders are the railway community and the Directors are their house of representatives.[19]

Not surprisingly what James Ward calls the corporate–state metaphor was equally prevalent in North America. In the US, he argues, beginning in the 1850s and continuing for almost three decades, railroad officials pictured themselves as sovereign rulers 'wielding vast authority over their economic domains while beset on all sides by the same vicissitudes and dangers that assailed their public [civic] counterparts'.[20]

As Lecount's treatise shows, railway companies drew significantly on experience from the military sphere. Borrowing from the military sphere involved technology, organization and rhetoric.[21] Early attempts to develop a semaphore signalling system to warn of approaching trains derived substantially from the methods of coastal defence devised during the Napoleonic Wars, while the language of railway promotion frequently adopted the metaphors of military conflict. In the UK for example, the *Railway Times* regularly described the 'Campaigns' to promote new lines fought out annually in Parliament. The verbal battles and diplomatic strategies by which schemes were amalgamated and modified and votes were traded sometimes initiated physical conflict: for example, between land owners and railway constructors. Commenting on Captain O'Brien's period as General Manager of the North-Eastern Railway, one contemporary writer commentated in language typical of the period 'with no ordinary satisfaction . . . Not a position of importance had been surrendered, not an inch of territory lost'.[22] Such language was equally evident in the USA, where Ward traces its most widespread adoption to the post-Civil War period, particularly in the north and east. Here, competition was already keen between well-established

networks, giving such recently familiar military rhetoric a new and civilian value.[23]

The problems set by everyday organization also shared much with those of the military. Describing the unsatisfactory organization of the Chicago, Burlington & Quincy Railroad, Charles Elliott Perkins claimed the difference between high-level strategy and day to day management in military terms: 'the Vice-President and the Auditor are generals not having anything to do with the regimental organisation. The working organisation of a Railroad, the *daily machine so to speak*, may I think be modelled on the Army, the Co. being the unit!'[24] Communicating orders and intelligence to headquarters and the logistics of maintaining maximum availability amongst men and machines were certainly common to both. In the early years of

As this example of a stewardess on a Japanese Shinkansen high-speed train shows, style and practice derived from air travel is only the latest manifestation of a working culture in which efficiency, comfort and safety are made visible in uniforms, rank and authority.

railway operation, management tended to be dominated by engineer-entrepreneurs and railway promoters. However, by the mid-1840s gross overexpenditure by many companies on expensive civil engineering projects or wasteful and idiosyncratic operating practices were beginning to emphasize the necessity for improved administration. Following the reduced influence of the engineer in executive management, men with military backgrounds became popular. Managers were often drawn from the ranks of captain and lieutenant; such middle-ranking military men with either army or navy backgrounds had experience of accounts and book-keeping, and were familiar with the direction of substantial groups of men, sometimes under difficult circumstances.[25] The impersonal authority structure developed by the railways in order to maintain constant spatial and temporal coverage, maximizing the interchangeability of both personnel and equipment, further promoted the association of railway work with that of military service. As personal qualities were subordinated to symbols of authority, uniform and rank, so railway workers were encouraged to think of themselves as subject to a military form of discipline and authority.

Corporate culture, loosely coupled systems and the limits of control

Military-bureaucratic methods of management were fundamental to providing railway organizations with their distinctive corporate culture. Most important was the functional division of responsibility into a hierarchical departmental structure. Early railway management was frequently undertaken directly by the Board of Directors. The Board of the Liverpool & Manchester Railway, for example, met five times in January 1831 to deliberate on all aspects of the railway's day to day operation. However, it was soon realized that the directors were overwhelmed with work and needed to delegate responsibility.[26] One principal problem was the relative importance of strategic planning, generating traffic and operating trains. If the director-managers were more sensitive to the propagation of traffic receipts than to complexities of running trains, conversely, the major complaint against the ex-military men was that while they were strong on discipline and organization, they often neglected the commercial aspects of railway operation. It was readily obvious that railway companies had to encompass a range of functions and services never before brought together under the auspices of one private corporation.

The growth in railway bureaucracy is evident in the employment structures of railway companies. By the 1870s many British railway companies employed in excess of 30,000 workers, of whom at least one-third were clerical and administrative grades.[27] Railway management theorists represented the hierarchical qualities of railway management as a form of tree-like structure divided by a combination of both functional and geographical separation of functions. Common to almost all versions of this model at what may be termed ground-floor level, the functions were frequently combined in one officer. A stationmaster, for example, was responsible for operations, including control of cartage, vehicles and also some commercial matters at the depot attached to the station.[28] The tension inherent in this structure was frequently manifest in disputes between departments over specific areas of responsibility. Describing development of the divisional structure of the Pennsylvania Railroad in the *Railroad Gazette* (1882) the anonymous author acknowledges this, saying: 'It seemed impossible to have both geographical divisions and departments in the same system of organization without involving a conflict of authority.'[29]

Such interdepartmental disputes were central to the workplace culture of the railway industry. The resultant confusion in the zoning of responsibility created unsupervised spaces. These enabled railway workers to have sufficient discretion in their duties to enable them to turn the formal rules of the company into working and workable practices. Reporting systems supported many areas of central control, from financial regularity to labour discipline. This created a spatially extended web of authority, based on a system of cross-accounting and affecting all spheres of railway operation, that made all workers party to the surveillance of their own conduct and that of immediate colleagues. In writing their daily reports, for example, each member of the traffic staff not only recorded the actions of his colleagues but also set down a record of his own labour.

The system of triple accounting for the supply of stores and sundries put into place by the Midland Railway in England during the 1850s is indicative of such corporate bureaucratic culture. This set of procedures was described by the company's chief accountant as 'placing a cordon around the men'. Such financial and physical safety checks were common across many systems in an industry notorious for generating paperwork. Built into the operation of the railway network, these 'cordons' regionalized the organization into operational cells. Such cells mapped out the territorial and functional extent of each railway worker's daily routine. At the same time, within such cells railway workers were able to exercise considerable discretion in their work.[30] The signal worker in the signal box, the driver on the footplate or the stationmaster on the platform all needed to reinterpret the structures and procedures of the company in order to undertake their work. Thus at each point in the system, irrespective of the mechanical rigidity of its structures, the rationality of its administrative procedures or the military discipline of its rules, the operation of the railway as a single machine was and undoubtedly still is dependent on the discretion of individual workers as they interpret and reinterpret the formal organization of the company in a way which might translate it into a practical operational reality. It is no accident that the strategy of 'working to rule' as a means of disrupting the system was invented by railway workers and has been used very successfully as a strategy in the pursuit of collective action.[31] If the railway does function as a 'machine ensemble', then this is arguably dependent as much on the points of discretion and play in the system as it is on its seamless mechanical interconnection.

In contrast to powerful images of the railway as a logical and impersonal doomsday machine, flexible, adaptable and robust technologies rather than tightly enmeshed and highly calibrated ones have formed the mainstay of railway design throughout much of its history. Considered alongside those ambiguities in its typical administrative structures described above, this would suggest that railways exhibit some characteristics of what organizational sociologists sometimes call 'loosely coupled systems'.[32] These might be described as systems in which discretion and flexibility result in the component parts having a high degree of autonomy. In comparison, closely coupled systems are characterized as those where a high degree of standardization and finely coordinated components result in a system where each part responds directly and precisely to the functioning of the whole. It is certainly true that adaptability and durability are central to the design of some of the railway's most basic components. Sometimes this has been at the expense of network integration and the functioning of the railway system as a single extensive machine and sometimes it has been at the cost of mechanical and economic efficiency. Few issues illustrate this better than the choice of track gauge, one of the most basic design choices to be made when planning a railway. A cursory glance at a map showing the variety of railway gauges in use around the world shows the diversity of standards which inhibit interconnection between railway lines, both between and within particular countries. 'Breaks

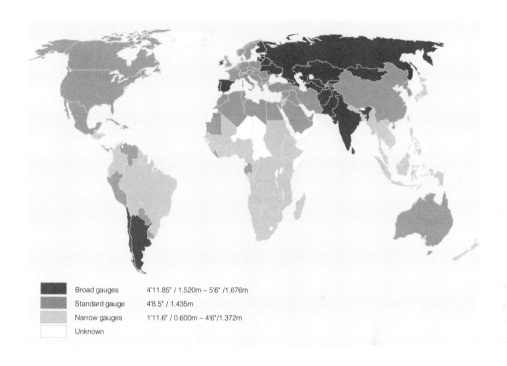

Broad gauges	4'11.85" / 1.520m – 5'6" /1.676m	
Standard gauge	4'8.5" / 1.435m	
Narrow gauges	1'11.6" / 0.600m – 4'6"/1.372m	
Unknown		

of gauge' hinder through-services across many international borders, including that of France with Spain and most external borders of the former Russian and Soviet empires.[33] The US and Canada had six gauges in widespread use until the 1880s. In recent decades, both Australia and India have made substantial progress in reducing their diversity of gauges.[34]

Widespread adoption of so called 'standard gauge' in which the lines are four feet eight and a half inches (1,435 mm) apart rests on a combination of historical precedent, unreflected working practice, common availability of resources and equipment and simple inertia. When George Stephenson used standard gauge on the Liverpool & Manchester Railway he merely adapted common practice used on

Even today there is a wide variety of track gauges throughout the world. As trade and travel increasingly involve transcontinental movements this becomes progressively more of an issue.

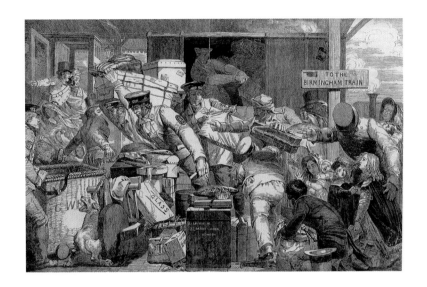

the Stockton & Darlington Railway and its predecessors, the horse-drawn tramroads of north-east England. Here the width of the track roughly approximated the distance between the wheels of a horse-drawn cart (about four feet eight inches); this in turn was informed by the distance between shafts comfortable for hitching a horse. To this Stephenson added an extra half-inch to allow for some play between rails and wheel flanges, enabling the wheels to run freely, especially where the track bends.[35] The immediate success of the Liverpool & Manchester Railway meant that it was sensible for the network of lines that developed through the highly industrialized counties east into Yorkshire and south into Staffordshire and towards Birmingham to adopt a common standard enabling the free interchange of traffic within neighbouring and already economically interconnected industrial regions.[36] Thus a model was established that was difficult to change, even in the face of apparently superior technology such as that of the Great Western Railway's broad gauge network (seven feet and

The chaos ensuing as passengers and luggage transfer from broad to standard gauge trains at Gloucester. *The Illustrated London News*, 6 June 1846.

one-quarter inches), designed by Isambard Kingdom Brunel (1806 –1859), the visionary chief engineer to the GWR between 1835 and 1859. At the time Brunel's system enabled greater speed and hauling capacity. Ultimately, the economic imperative to connect with the wider British railway network in combination with political expedient, entrepreneurial zeal and managerial brinksmanship played a much greater part in the downfall of the GWR broad gauge system than technical performance.[37] Elsewhere, in the US for example, where lines often originated as links between navigable rivers and between inland waterways and the coast, or operated as isolated systems serving a distinctive region or locality, common standards were less important. Only the changing priorities related to the expansion and amalgamation of systems after the Civil War resulted in the need to standardize.[38]

Douglas Puffert has persuasively argued that standard gauge might be thought of as a 'suboptimal compromise' lying on a design continuum between narrower gauge lines – where topographical difficulties and other environmental obstacles such as land availability and price are major design constraints – and broader gauge lines designed to maximize speed and mechanical efficiency.[39] Thus it is possible to recognise a dynamic and contextual technological history in which the compromise standard gauge was challenged during the period of initial mechanical innovation in railway design by a variety of broad gauge lines. Subsequent to the 1870s many of these either consolidated as independent systems, or were converted to standard gauge where network interchangeability was an issue. However, from this period the extension of the railway into continents, countries and regions in which the costs of construction and operation were paramount – for reasons of difficult terrain, scarcity or unreliability of traffic – resulted in the construction of many narrow gauge lines. These either supplemented and fed into or simply stood as cheaper alternatives to standard gauge lines. Thus many routes constructed to exploit agricultural and mineral reserves in Africa, South and North America or rural branches in Europe, particularly France, Spain and Portugal, adopted narrow gauge standards during the period 1870–1910. In this context the discretionary and compromise qualities of the railway as a 'machine ensemble', a flexible and contingent combination of close and loosely coupled parts within the overall system, provides a high degree of system resilience. Adaptability of the basic railway formula is evident both in its flexibility to cope with a wide variety of circumstances and conditions and a high degree of what historians and technologists call path dependency. Path dependency might be thought of as the ongoing dominance of a particular combination of technological and organizational components once initially established. As we have seen from the example of railway's 'standard' gauge, this particular compromise system has proved difficult to change irrespective of its pros and cons. More generally, very few railways have successfully departed from the combination of flanged steel wheels running on twin parallel steel tracks where a powered vehicle pulls a group of unpowered vehicles within a systemwide co-ordinated timetable of movements. System resilience and discretion as much as path dependency and seamless mechanical connection define the cultural characteristics of the railway as a machine.

Attempts to create technological systems with greater functional specificity have only been as successful as political determination and commercial interest has allowed. Though for example much of Europe today shares the same (standard) track gauge, the greater height and width of vehicles able to run on French railways precludes them from free access to the British system in spite of the fact that the systems have been physically connected by the Channel Tunnel link since 1994. From 1891 onwards successive attempts have been made to create pan-European standards. Those set by the Berne convention of 1914 and the International Union of Railways formed in 1922 in the aftermath of the First World War have resulted in greater inter-changeability of rolling stock but certainly not universal standards.[40] In developing the railway system across Europe the particular circum-stances in each country have created and continue to create barriers.[41] Even on the high-speed European TGV (Train à Grande Vitesse) system trains have had to negotiate a range of regional and local standards in order to move seamlessly across the network from country to country. Trains that pass through the Channel Tunnel between London and Paris or Brussels have to cope with three different electrical power systems, five different train-control and signalling systems and differ-ences in loading gauge (clearance dimensions) and other parameters.[42] As a result, duplicate technical systems have raised costs, and train performance could not be optimized for any part of the network.

Though the superficial appearance of railways as unified and smoothly operating 'machine ensembles' gives rise to their metaphor-ical association with the nation-state and their characterization as an impersonal doomsday machine, it is clear that there is much more to the railway as a political force than metaphor. If politics is basi-cally a matter of how we decide who gets what, when and where, then railways clearly play an important part in this process both within and between nation-states, enabling movement and providing access for citizens gathering and distributing the resources, goods and services which make modern life possible and represent our mater-ial stake in the national collectivity. In this context, the practical battles by which railways needed to define and redefine their organ-izational spaces and operational territories as variously closely and loosely coupled constitute a ground on which issues of real political importance are played out. Rather than encouraging us to focus solely on issues of technological and organizational rationality, such practical battles serve to highlight the broader location of railways within specific economic, social, cultural and national circumstances.

The importance of railway systems in nation building and national strategy has meant that, most frequently, the shape of its technologies, systems and networks intersect closely with wider political debates. In France, for example, the high-speed rail technology of the TGV won out against the revolutionary technology of the Aérotrain within the context of highly politicized decision-making. The Aérotrain project was funded between 1962 and 1974 by the government as part of France's high-profile science and technology programme. Running on a cushion of air along a concrete monorail track, the Aérotrain adopted aircraft technology to promise high-speed land travel, challenging air travel's growing dominance on intercity routes. Though the technology certainly fulfilled its promise in terms of speed, the project never moved beyond the experimental stage.[43]

Transport historian Vincent Guigueno shows how the fortunes of Aérotrain became associated with ease of mobility for a privileged

The TGV network, centred on France, is a potent symbol of European integration, yet trains still have to negotiate a range of regional and local standards in order to traverse national boundaries.

elite, an image at odds with its design conception as an inter-city prime mover for the masses. In this context Aérotrain's aerospace technology worked against the new system's political acceptability. In this regard its planned adoption for a dedicated link between Paris and the new Roissy (now Charles de Gaulle) airport worked to transform it into a symbol of costly and technologically oversophisticated luxury at a time when air travel was a relatively rare and expensive option. Directly threatened by the new technology, French national railways (SNCF) developed a high-speed rail solution in response to Aérotrain. In 1970 the Government awarded SNCF the contract to construct the first high-speed intercity line between Paris and Lyon (opened in 1981); this left few options to develop Aérotrain beyond the airport link and a few short, contentious and expensive Paris suburban routes.

A Eurotunnel train carrying heavy goods vehicles enters the Channel Tunnel. Such piggyback operations are becoming an increasingly important means for transporting goods across Europe while retaining the flexibility offered by road-based loading and delivery.

Thus Aérotrain became embroiled in debates peripheral to its original purpose concerning the costs of urban infrastructure within the Paris region. In a nation living with a political history polarised between right and left, Aérotrain became freighted with the symbolism of a modern but socially divided France. It was a technological success but a cultural failure.

Today, high-speed ground transport is no longer viewed as contributing to social and spatial inequality. One reason for this is the way it is embodied in technologies such as the TGV, readily understandable and identifiable as an adaptation and supplement, rather than a replacement, for traditional rail services with their associations of democracy and transport for the masses. Thus Guigueno says:

> It was not a passion for speed that made the TGV acceptable, but its unification of technology and shared political values that were implemented by a company that was the model of public service à la française.

Commemorated in 1970 on this French postage stamp, the Aerotrain endeavoured to bring jet-age speed and technology to rail travel.

Moreover, it may be no coincidence that the TGV was inaugurated in 1981, when France elected its first socialist president. Perceived as reinforcing national cohesion, high speed rail could become socially, as well as economically, profitable.[44]

Networks and nation building

In many respects, the contrasting fortunes of Aérotrain and TGV in recent French history recall the arguments concerning democracy and participation in the nation expressed by Michel Chevalier in the concept of 'circulating civilization' during the 1830s. The place of technology within the making of a modern and progressive national culture has been embedded in French culture since the eighteenth century, and the history of its railway system certainly reflects this broader history. In France, state-sponsored institutes for training

Built in 1912 to carry tourists to the Alpine views of Europe's highest station at Jungfraujoch (3,454 metres above sea level), the Jungfraubahn is one of many narrow gauge railways in Europe currently dedicated to leisure travel.

engineers such as the Ecole de Ponts et Chaussées (founded in 1747) and the Ecole Polytechnique (founded in 1794) played a central role in building the nation.[45] Their histories have been closely bound up with building the infrastructure for national defence and integration; fortifications, roads, harbours, bridges and canals. In terms of railway development, they provided the graduates who designed the civil and mechanical components for railways in France, the Austro-Hungarian empire and later Spain and Portugal. Their influence has been practical and theoretical, scientific and philosophical, helping to shape both the material infrastructure and the ideologies driving the idea of the French nation. Michel Chevalier studied at the Ecole Polytechnique, obtaining an engineering degree at the Paris Ecole des mines in 1829, and went on to become a major economic theorist advocating liberalism and free

The Darjeeling Himalayan Railway was built between 1879 and 1881. At 86 km in length it snakes up through the mountains following the pre-existing Hill Cart Road. It was declared a World Heritage Site by UNESCO in 1999.

trade built on international co-operation and relatively cheap, efficient means of transport and communications.[46]

Given both the strategic importance of railways and the predominance of liberal free-trade ideologies as expounded by Chevalier, it is not surprising that France adopted a system of control for its railways that encouraged private enterprise but subjected it to strict government supervision. The relationship between liberal free trade and state regulation was articulated most eloquently by Adolphe Thiers, French Minister of Commerce and Public Works in the 1830s. Quick to set out the limits of government intervention, Thiers also recognized the strategic role railways might play for the greater good of France. Envisaging a north–south rail axis from Le Havre to Algiers, he claimed it would bring untold commercial and military advantages to the nation. The main line would attract a dominant share of European trade thus 'preventing this transit from falling into the hands of Germany. At the same time, it would provide an avenue for French troop movements everywhere from the Belgian frontier to North Africa'.[47]

The result was a plan developed from 1837 onwards for what became known as the Legrand Star. This was named after Baptiste Alexis Victor Legrand (1791–1848), who was also a graduate of the Ecole Polytechnique and the Ecole de Ponts et Chaussées, and an engineer who held a variety of important government posts including Director General of Roads Bridges and Mines (1834–7) and Under-Secretary for Public Works (1837–47). His plan placed Paris as the communications capital of Europe. The main railway lines should radiate from this centre to major French cities and borders in every direction: to Lille and Belgium in the north, to Strasbourg and Germany in the east, to Marseilles and the Mediterranean in the south, to Bordeaux and Spain in the south-west and to Le Havre and England in the west.[48] Thus the French set up a unique combination of free enterprise and state planning for their national rail network with

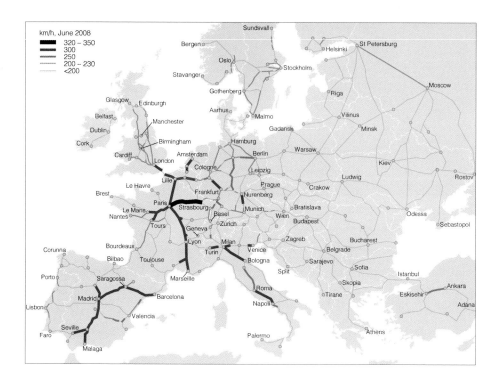

a law passed on 11 June 1842. The state assumed responsibility for infrastructure by determining routes, confiscating property when needed, surveying and laying roadbeds and designing bridges and tunnels. Private companies would then provide the rest by acquiring rolling stock, hiring personnel and operating and maintaining regular services. As Alan Mitchell concludes, many ambiguities remained which would form a constant source of friction well into the twentieth century. However, the Legrand Star would serve to make Paris 'the rendez-vous of all Europe' and as such it is easy to see how such later schemes as the TGV and debates concerning its merits vis-à-vis Aéro-train fit into 200 years of French cultural, political and technological history.[49] Within this history, railways act variously as both a particularist and localizing force facilitating the consolidation of rationalist enlightenment values in the centrally planned social geography of

This map of the developing high-speed rail network linking European cities shows the centrality of Paris to the existing system. It recognizes at least partial fulfilment of the promise held out by the dream of the Legrand Star.

France and as a universalizing force, providing a vehicle for a greater pan-European enlightenment project. As such they embody some of the central contradictions in the European enlightenment ideal of the nation state, the privileging of specific identities and localities in the name of a supranational humanist ideology.

The creation of the Legrand Star illustrates some of the key roles played by railways in nation building within Europe and on other continents. These include the forging of trade links and economic development; the enforcement of uniform internal regulation; social integration, internal security and policing; military strategy and the symbolism of national pride. Elsewhere in Europe railways also played an important part in nation building during a period in which many of Europe's nation-states took their modern form. The precedent was set by the state-owned railway network developed from 1834 by the Belgians, who had successfully revolted against Dutch control in 1830. Railways proved to be of practical, military strategic and symbolic importance, proving to the world that the country could

Celebrations as the first train emerges from the St Gotthard rail tunnel in 1880. Linking Switzerland with Italy, the tunnel was both a major technological achievement and an important step in the construction of a European rail network.

grow and prosper without Dutch supervision or finance.[50] Unlike France or Britain, the network was to be nationally controlled; private railways were granted only twenty-year licences before they reverted to state control. Nation-states such as Germany and Italy, formed in the third quarter of the nineteenth century from formerly separate or semi-autonomous kingdoms, states and principalities, used railways strategically to bring together disparate, competing and sometimes antagonistic regional economies and cultures. Thus railways took on both practical and symbolic roles in nation building, frequently acting as distinctive markers for modernity within specific geographical contexts. Japan, for instance, represents the outstanding example of a modernizing and expansionist state outside Europe. By the first decade of the twentieth century the country itself was one of the railway-building imperial powers, with a strong presence on the Asian mainland in China and Korea. By the time the greater part of the system was nationalized in 1906–7, the Japanese had built an alliance of indigenous political, military, state-bureaucratic and private business interests that proved capable of attracting foreign investment into a system built and operated according to the precepts of the Japanese military and domestic capitalists.[51]

Issues of defence, security and internal control were fundamental to the role that railways played in nation building. This was recognized even in Britain where railway development took an unashamedly demand-led, private capital, free enterprise model. Legislation existed in Britain from the earliest years of operation, allowing the railways to be taken into state control in times of national emergency. Indeed British railways, like those in France, were brought into full state control during both the First and the Second World Wars, leading to their eventual nationalization under the Labour government in 1947. In fact the developing railway system across Europe proved to be most useful during the series of conflicts and

uprisings in the period 1840–70, in which much happened to consolidate the nation state within Europe. In Britain during the early 1840s, rail was used to 'pour troops into the disturbed districts' in response to Chartist agitations in favour of universal suffrage.[52] In 1846 the Prussians moved 12,000 troops by rail in order to quell the 'Greater Poland uprising'. The largest imperial power within Europe, the Russians made increasing use of railways. In 1849 they sent 30,000 troops by rail to help the Austrians in Hungary and later to quell the Polish uprising of 1863.[53] Beyond Europe perhaps the best known example is that of British India (which included present-day Pakistan, Bangladesh and, until 1937, Burma), where railways were central to the exercise of colonial power. The Indian Revolt of 1857 resulted in the wholesale reorganization of the way in which India was controlled, including the transfer of power from the private East India Company to the government department of the India Office.[54] Under the auspices of Lord Dalhousie, Governor-General of India,

Axel Herman Haig, *Victoria Terminus, Mumbai, Great Indian Peninsula Railway*, 1878, watercolour. Inaugurated on Jubilee Day 1887, named after Queen Victoria and designed in an exuberant free Gothic style by F. W. Stevens, the terminus demonstrates the confidence and splendour of empire.

one consequence was a rapid escalation of railway building from 1858 onwards using a system of 5 per cent loan guarantees underwritten by the British government. By this means the system expanded from 838 miles in 1860 to 10,198 in 1883 and 25,619 in 1901.[55]

Though characterized as a 'war machine' in fiction and political rhetoric, the extent to which railways fulfilled any of this dystopian potential is hotly disputed. From the early use of an improvised line by the British to bring much-needed supplies to the front in the Crimean War (1853–6), railways at best constituted a useful link in the supply chain rather than an instrument of advanced military strategy. Railways played a prominent role in the American Civil War (1861–5), where they were a supreme symbol of the gap between the

India's railway system in 1909, from the *Imperial Gazetter of India* by Sir W. S. Meyer. It shows how by the early years of the 20th century the railway network had extended to most parts of the sub-continent.

industrial North and the largely agrarian South. The war demonstrated the extent to which military supremacy came to be based on a combination of technological supremacy, industrial and manufacturing capacity and organizational structure, which in the twentieth century, marked by industrial-scale warfare, came to be known as the 'military industrial complex'.[56] Yet the use of railways for military purposes was an imperfect art at the best of times. During the German civil war of 1866, the Prussians made relatively poor use of military transportation by train. Plans had provided for bringing troops to railheads but not for supplying them once they fanned out onto the battlefields. Backed-up freight cars and shortages of food and munitions were the inevitable result and neither problem was solved. Sometimes figured as a victory brought about by the use of rail, the decisive battle at Königgrätz arguably resulted from something of a fluke when one Prussian unit stumbled onto the enemy and was saved by the arrival of another – on foot. Yet ironically, the result

The Grand Crimean Central Railway, built 1855, supplied ammunition and provisions to Allied soldiers engaged in the siege of Sevastopol during the Crimean War. It also carried the world's first hospital train.

was growing recognition of the railway's strategic value and the strengthening of Prussian control of railways across the federal states of Germany under the chancellorship of Otto von Bismarck (1815–1898). Ultimately, this led to the unification of German railways and consolidation of the German state.[57] Whether in France, Germany, Japan or elsewhere, the place of railways as large technological systems in nation building demonstrate the same complex, messy and compromised but ultimately highly resilient outcomes characteristic of their internal organizational and mechanical structuring.

Railway, communication and nation building

Rather than rigid impersonal structure, it is the railway's adaptability as a simultaneously practical and symbolic resource which makes it such a lively political force. Variously characterized as democratic or totalitarian, railways are implicated in a wide variety of nation building strategies. These range from liberal-enlightenment European models and empire-building monarchies to despotic totalitarian regimes and post-colonial democracies. As Benedict Anderson has shown, nation building is about more than institutions and infrastructures: the building of a shared sense of belonging through collective senses of history, heritage, culture and most particularly language are fundamental.[58] As a means of communication, railways fulfil a crucial role in nation building which has some parallels with the roles played by other media of mass communication such as the postal system, telegraph and more recently radio and television. All these media facilitate the sharing of news, matters of common interest and concern, language and culture across the nation, helping to provide a shared focus for experience, history, myth-building, community and solidarity. In Britain as in many other countries railway communication helped popularize and make accessible a national daily press as

a forum for broader social engagement and political debate. Railways have also enabled citizens to become part of the body politic in ways hitherto unknown, if only for fleetingly brief moments. The 'whistle stop tour', for example, became characteristic of canvassing in US Presidential elections from the time of Andrew Johnson (1808–1875, President 1865–9).[59] Railways have also formed a vehicle for the delivery of official and government messages, as evidenced by the use of propaganda trains in, for example, the Soviet Union and Nazi Germany. In this context railways are agents of the sort of national homogenization symbolized by the standardization of time zones and their cross-calibration with railway time. However, as Lisa Mitchell

Loudspeakers at the ready, President Dwight D. Eisenhower prepares to address the crowd, 5 July 1952. In the 19th century politicians became accustomed to travelling the vast distances of the USA on chartered trains and addressing the voters from the rear platform. In this way railways became a direct part of the democratic process.

has shown in her study of language and regional politics in Southern India since the 1950s, railways continue to act as a powerful and informal conduit for political communication and as sites for protests, violence and graffiti feeding back local and regional complaints and objections to the centre of power.[60] Such extraordinary means of political communication are especially important for those who are poor, believe their voice is not being heard or feel otherwise disenfranchised.

The apparently impartial spaces of station platform or railway carriage provide sites which unfold events of great political significance. In 1893 while in South Africa, the young barrister Mahatma Gandhi strongly objected when asked to move from his first-class seat to the luggage compartment. He consequently spent a cold and uncomfortable night on Pretoria station. Gandhi recalled these events as a turning point in his life, awakening him to social injustice and influencing his subsequent critique of colonial oppression and the social and political activism leading to Indian independence.[61] Yet at the close of colonialism, when British India was in the process of partition, railway carriages provided little protection from physical violence and political turmoil. In October 1947, amid large-scale migration between Hindu and Muslim regions, 3,000 passengers were killed on a Muslim refugee train in Amritsar. Though conceived by both Gandhi and the former colonial authorities as rational and dispassionate national spaces, the murders, beatings and rapes in and around trains during this period challenged the ideal of India as a secular nation and undermined civil dreams of modernity.[62] The spaces of the railway – its stations, trackbeds, carriages and compartments – seem to focus, condense and amplify political concerns, social issues and cultural fears. From this perspective we can perhaps better understand a range of incidents from the Dutch train hostage crisis in 1975, involving a group claiming independence for the South-east Asian islands of South Molucca, to the Madrid train bombings of 2004,

October 1947: Margaret Bourke-White's photo of the fly-covered bodies of the victims of Sikh attacks at the station intended as the departure point for the Pakistan Special Train carrying Moslems to liberty in West Punjab. After the Partition of India in July 1947 the transfer of over 14.5 million people between the two new states often resulted in tragic violence.

often attributed to al-Qaeda-inspired terrorists. In May 2007 full-scale riots broke out when services were interrupted during the evening rush hour at Constitución station, Buenos Aires, one of the largest stations in South America. One hundred police attended the incident, firing rubber bullets and tear gas as rioters pelted them with rocks, smashed windows, set fire to the ticket sales area, looted shops and ripped pay-phones from the walls as the protest spilled out on to the street. The riot was the second outbreak of violence within a year. The previous September train cancellations had resulted in three railway carriages being set alight and police making seven arrests.[63] Such behaviour was indicative of a complex array of otherwise pent-up frustrations relating to Argentina's recent history, especially its serious economic problems and the subsequent widespread unemployment, welfare cuts, raging inflation and neoliberal reforms. Passengers had com-plained for years about poor commuter rail services on lines leading from Constitución station in downtown Buenos Aires to the capital's

The Madrid train bombings, 11 March 2004, were a coordinated series of attacks on commuter trains that killed 191 people. Perhaps the trust placed in the transport system by ordinary commuters acts as a magnet for sometimes violent and destructive acts of protest.

poor southern suburbs. Privatized in the 1990s, failure of the Buenos Aires commuter lines to provide punctual services on overcrowded routes was merely a symbolic marker for a range of long-standing social concerns.

The practical functions played by railways only serve to compound their role creating the nation as a community of shared communication. Railways provide symbols of the nation, such as flags, insignia, uniforms and architectural styles, with a material presence at stations and on moving trains which carry them into the daily routines in the most obscure regions and locations. At the same time they transform the material products of national circulation embodied in the form of railway networks and trains themselves into highly symbolic artefacts. This may take the form of symbolically meaningful railway lines, such as the transcontinental railways in the USA and Canada and Shinkansen network in Japan, or specific named trains such as the British *Flying Scotsman* or the South African *Blue Train*. Station architecture has frequently functioned as a material presence of both national identity and political domination. This is given form in statuary and armorial devices, as at Antwerp Central (1895) or Hamburg Hauptbahnhof (1903–6); grand statements of an imposed colonial culture, for instance Howrah Station Calcutta (1906); and expressions of new and progressive national cultures, for example in Helsinki (1910–14) or Rome (1947–50).[64] In countries such as Belgium, railway workers themselves were state employees and, like members of the police force and postal service, their uniform carried state authority into towns and villages around the country. Even individual railway vehicles have achieved considerable national symbolic significance. The coach in which the Armistice was signed to end the First World War on 11 November 1918, for instance, was used by Hitler as the location for signing France's surrender in June 1940. Stored by the Germans during the Second World War, it was blown up by the SS

The grand eclectic Neo-Renaissance extravagance of Antwerp Central Station, 1895–1905, by Louis Delacenserie, demonstrates civic and national pride in its use of armorial devices.

Designed by internationally acclaimed architect Eliel Saarinen in 1904 and finally opened in 1919, Helsinki Station's design is a triumph of modernism.

Termini station, Rome, a huge modernist structure of the late 1930s and 1948–50.

Venice's Santa Lucia Railway Station, one of only a few modernist buildings fronting the Grand Canal. Reconstruction started in 1936 and was completed by Paolo Perilli in 1952.

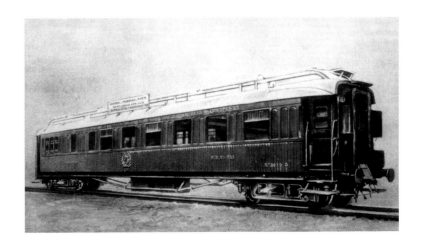

shortly before American forces arrived, thus foreclosing the possibility that the coach would be restored to its symbolic place as the site of German defeat.[65] Even today the railway can play a highly symbolic role in national and international relations and as a marker of good governance. The renewed movement of trains across the border between North and South Korea (May 2007) was undertaken with due ceremony and in the spotlight of global media as a gesture of reconciliation after 56 years of conflict.[66] Against a background of geopolitical struggle between European, American and Chinese influence in relation to development and reconstruction, failure of the railway system in central Africa is perceived internationally as a marker for political corruption within what are portrayed as chaotic and failing nation-states. A series of horrific fatal accidents between 1993 and 2000 attracted international attention, making Kenyan Railways notorious as the most dangerous in the world. In August 2000, for example, a passenger train rolled back due to failed brakes, killing 25, while just four days later another 25 people were burned to death after a train carrying gas ran into stationary wagons and exploded.

This coach, used by the German and Allied delegations during Armistice negotiations in 1918 and resonantly symbolic of German surrender, was destroyed by the SS shortly before the end of the Second World War.

Under the heading 'The Lunatic Express', the BBC News blamed the 'litany of disasters' on 'lack of investment', negligence and – quoting the Kenyan *Daily Nation* – 'sheer criminal incompetence'. In the neighbouring Democratic Republic of Congo, an accident in August 2007 involved an overturned freight train, brake failure and in excess of 100 fatalities. Decades of neglect were blamed on 'mismanagement under former ruler Mobutu Sese Seko and a 1998–2003 war [which] left the central African nation's transport infrastructure in ruins'.[67]

The transcontinental railway in the USA is perhaps the most eloquent statement of the European-American idea of manifest destiny. Yet there are many other historical examples in which railways have expressed expansionist and imperialist aspirations. A number of well known examples are intimately bound up with a global geopolitics centred on Europe. The Trans-Siberian railway (commenced 1889) at the behest of Czar Alexander II connected the Russian capital St Petersburg with the Pacific Ocean port of Vladivostok. It was the outcome of a long-standing urge of the European elite constituting the

In the late 19th century Siberia was hampered by poor transport links. In summer rivers were the main form of transport; in winter cargo and passengers travelled by horse-drawn sleds. The Trans-Siberian Railway boosted agriculture, carrying exports, especially grain, to central Russia and Europe and importing millions of peasant-migrants from further west.

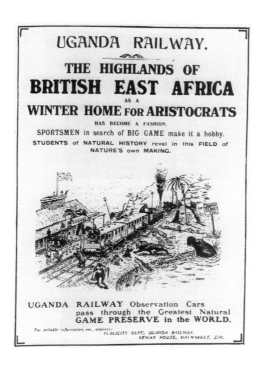

UGANDA RAILWAY.

THE HIGHLANDS OF
BRITISH EAST AFRICA
AS A
WINTER HOME FOR ARISTOCRATS
HAS BECOME A FASHION.
SPORTSMEN in search of BIG GAME make it a hobby.
STUDENTS of NATURAL HISTORY revel in this FIELD of
NATURE'S own MAKING.

UGANDA RAILWAY Observation Cars
pass through the Greatest Natural
GAME PRESERVE in the WORLD.

For reliable information, etc., address:
PUBLICITY DEPT., UGANDA RAILWAY,
DEWAR HOUSE, HAYMARKET, S.W.

Russian state to control its border territories through centralization of power, resulting in 'Russification' of the economy and of social and cultural affairs.[68] The plans for a railway throughout the north–south length of Africa from the Cape to Cairo was fundamental to the strategies for British colonialism on the continent. Cecil Rhodes (1853–1902) was instrumental in securing the southern states of the continent for the British Empire and envisioned a continuous 'red' link of British dominions from North to South. Never fully realized, the railway was to be a critical element in this scheme to unify and consolidate the regions of British control, facilitate governance, enable the military to move quickly to hot spots or conduct war, help settlement and foster trade.[69] In this sense the plan had something in common with British

This advertisement for the Uganda Railway, aimed at rich Western tourists, flatters prejudices and preconceptions by providing an almost comically stereotyped image of Africa.

practice in India. German plans for a line from Berlin to Baghdad, through the territories of the much enfeebled Ottoman Empire, would have connected Germany with its colonies in Africa and elsewhere via a port on the Persian Gulf. Though other major European powers including Britain, Russia and France initially reacted positively to Germany's proposals, the proposed railway soon came to be seen as a threat and Britain blocked a move to further develop the scheme in 1911. As a result Germany had to recognize southern Mesopotamia, as well as central and southern Persia, as the exclusive field of operations of the Anglo-Persian Company in 1914. Though the precise role of these events in the making of the First World War is a matter for debate, it cannot be denied that they form an important component in the geopolitical manoeuvrings leading up to conflict.[70] Thus A.J.P. Taylor's railway theory is not the only way to present the railway's culpability in the outbreak of hostilities.

As a vehicle for the transmission of national history, myth and mission, or indeed as a highly resilient system combining elements of both loose and close coupling, the networking and structuring properties of railway systems both connect and divide. On the one hand the neutrality of technology as a mere carrier of goods, people and meaning renders it readily available as a vehicle for realizing the aspirations of social and political groups from all persuasions. However, technologies themselves structure the nature of communication; thus, while railways bring places closer together by increasing trade and social interaction, they also shape the direction and intensity of encounters, sometimes in unexpected and unforeseen ways. At the same time, widespread acknowledgement of the shared symbolism of the railway as a means of bringing modernity, cohesion and progress does not necessarily imply that everyone means the same thing when they use these terms. Thus the dependence of national cohesion on the mechanized communications media that carry its

people, products and messages – what has been called technological nationalism – opens up both opportunities and pitfalls for nation building, and has resulted in a wide variety of historically contingent routes to statehood. Thus Andrew Marshall concludes, for instance, that Bismarck's attempt to bring the constituent states of the German Federation together through the unification of their railway systems resulted in retrenchment and the consolidation of particularist interests by member states rather than an open endorsement of federalism. This made German unification more rather than less difficult to achieve.[71] Ian Kerr likewise points to the highly uneven role of railways in the making of modern India. He quotes the British critic of the Raj, William Digby, who in 1901 compared what he called the relatively favoured and prosperous 'Anglostan' with the less-favoured 'Hindustan', which he defined as practically all of India beyond a fifty-mile limit each side of the railway lines.[72] Most recently, the opening of a railway line by the Chinese government into occupied Tibet from

A train runs on the foot of snow-covered mountains in north-west China's Qinghai Province, 24 October 2009. The railway is a major part of Chinese plans for development in the Qinghai and Tibet Autonomous Region.

Golmud to Lhasa (2005) has released a wave of protest by Tibetans worried about the cultural and political assimilation of Tibet's distinctive culture into that of a greater China.[73] The tensions between ideologies of universalism and particularism, cultural pluralism and social cohesion, closely controlled communal places and less supervised private spaces, are fundamental to making the modern nation state reflect eloquently through the cultural spaces of railways themselves, which connect and divide people and places in complex and sometimes unexpected ways.

One of the most well documented examples of such technologically centred nation building concerns the construction of transcontinental railways across Canada. The first of these, the Canadian Pacific Railway between Ontario and the Pacific coast, was completed in 1885. Its construction established Canadian claims to the remaining parts of British North America not yet constituted as provinces and territories

A Currier & Ives lithograph of the Niagara Suspension Bridge between the USA and Canada, 1856. This bridge symbolizes the technological triumph of nation building while also reminding us of increasing economic and cultural integration.

of Canada, acting as a bulwark against potential counter-claims by the US. Construction fed into a myth of nationhood encouraged by government rhetoric. As in the US, the powerful icons of railway technology, its mighty locomotives, soaring bridges and piercing tunnels, were gladly ascribed by Canadians to their capacity for nation building. Yet as Den Otter explains, in spite of this the scheme encapsulated a basic contradiction in Canada's sense of national identity.[74] While the country's leadership professed a basic conservative loyalty to ancestral British traditions, it enthusiastically embraced the basic tenets of American liberalism, particularly a belief in the liberating role of technology. Thus by adopting technological 'progress' as a national ideology in common with their southern neighbours, Canada left itself open to the effects of a stronger and more aggressive American economy and culture. While railway companies were building across Canada in the national interest, they were also connecting into the US rail system, drawing Canadian economy and society into a greater North American system. Simultaneously, this consolidated the economic and political control of Canada's central belt over both the peripheral Maritimes and the Pacific North West. Soon, these regions came to perceive the railway as an instrument of imperialistic domination, forcing their local economies to operate for the benefit of the central provinces. Thus technological nationalism in the form of railway development encouraged alienation and estrangement to become defining features of Canada's regional identities.

The railway then is perhaps best thought of as an open, flexible and connective conduit for a multiplicity of possible versions of the nation. The simultaneously unifying and alienating role of railways as a force in military domination, the construction of national myth and the forging of national identity is played out most poignantly in Jiří Menzel's film *Closely Observed Trains* (1966). Based on the novel by Bohumil Hrabal, the film was one of the most celebrated examples of the Czech New Wave.[75] Set in occupied Czechoslovakia during the Second World War, it centres on a small rural branch-line station. The title refers to the German trains that were given priority passage through occupied territories carrying munitions, troops and Jewish victims of the Holocaust. The story at its most literal is one of coming of age. It follows the trials and tribulations of a young trainee, Miloš, his romance with a young female train guard, his sexual frustrations and coming to sexual maturity with an older woman. In the closing sequences, he takes the place of the womanizing train dispatcher Hubicka and drops an explosive device from a signal gantry into a German munitions train, destroying the train and losing his life in the process.

In this film the train is indeed the totalitarian war machine suggested at the beginning of this chapter. German trains are run through the station under strict orders to the accompaniment of the electric telegraph and the ticking clock. Yet the station itself is an earthy, licentious and chaotic place where staff neglect their duties in order to breed chickens, skin rabbits and indulge in heated arguments, passionate day dreams and torrid sexual encounters. It is as if the station is a microcosm for an unselfconsciously visceral rural society. Such representations of anarchic sleepy branch-line stations sometimes appear in fiction as metaphors for the kind of employee discretion and opposition to formal authority associated with the concept of loose coupling discussed earlier. It is certainly true that in this, as in many such examples, it is the railway workers' intimate knowledge of the railway's technology and their ability to appropriate it creatively for their own personal benefit which is foundational to the story. Yet there is something more to this portrayal of a branch-line station than simply rustic opposition to the formal authority of the 'machine ensemble', or indeed the desperation suggested by the iron grip of Frank Norris's *Octopus*. In this film the railway represents

the intersection of two different ideas of nation. One is mechanical, impersonal, callous and associated with the German occupation; the other is relaxed, make-do, crude, emotional, artistic, humanly flawed and associated with the Czech people. Both are embodied in the railway and both connect universal ideals to particular localized ways of living: logical, dispassionate and regulated or passionate, communal, liberated and in tune with the rhythms of nature. The railway brings both of these complex conceptions of the nation into the lives of those living in the sleepiest backwater and demands that they decide between them. It is the railway that presents Miloš with the choice between these worlds and leads to his eventual selection of resistance and patriotism. At an important moment in the film he is commandeered to act as a human shield and forced to ride a train used by the SS as a defence against their fear of ambush. This moment of politicization serves as an important tipping point, ensuring his social acceptance by other station staff and leading to his eventual action on behalf of the resistance.

Made the on the eve of the flowering of Czech culture known as the Prague Spring, it is hard to resist the temptation to read this against the background of Czech–Soviet relations. The film also makes several appeals to contemporary Czech nationhood and identity. In one notable

example, the camera even picks out a poster defiantly proclaiming that the Soviets will never get Prague. By referring to Czech history, the film powerfully couples the fate of the individual and the fate of the nation. Thus Miloš' twin journeys towards manhood as he discovers sexual maturity on the eve of his act of patriotic sacrifice are both a call to individual action and a metaphor for the nation as whole. As both a cultural icon and physical means of forging the nation, the railway has a distinctive power to draw nation and people together through shared experience of the journey.

Still images from Jiří Menzel's film *Closely Observed Trains* (1966): title of film and picture of station; Miloš and Hubicka salute a passing train; kiss on the station office table; Miloš crouches on the gantry ready to sabotage the munitions train.

3 | Journeys, Stories and Everyday Lives

States of mind: the railway journey as personal biography

In one of the most iconic moments from the film *Closely Observed Trains* (1966), the hero Miloš stands beside a train which is about to depart as the attractive young female train guard Masa stands on the bottom step of the last coach. Their faces just millimetres apart, she puckers up to kiss him and as he moves towards her and closes his eyes in anticipation she waves her flag and the train moves off. Miloš is left alone, stationary, frustrated in his desire, as the flirtatious Masa disappears off into the distance. The moment is lost. The increasing distance between them symbolizes much more than the playfulness of a youthful tryst: ultimately it foretells of sacrifice, sadness and loss, the unfulfilled dream of life together. From *Brief Encounter* to Tolstoy's *Anna Karenina* meeting and parting, separation and union, desire, yearning and fulfilment are central to an experience of personal mobility which is distinctively modern and which is played out in the imaginative spaces of the railway carriage and the station platform.

From Dickens's *Dombey and Son* to *Murder on the Orient Express*, films, songs and novels portray lovers meeting and fugitives escaping by train. Wracked with guilt and despair, heroes and villains commit suicide under advancing locomotives, while chance meetings result

Their faces just millimetres apart, Miloš and Masa prepare to kiss as the train departs. In this moment from the film *Closely Observed Trains* (1966), meeting and parting, separation and desire are caught in a confusion of emotion.

in life-changing encounters in railway compartments and station waiting-rooms. Thomas Hardy (1840–1928) for instance, provides an early example of how the novelist might use the timetabling and scheduling of railways journeys to carry plots and animate storylines.[1] His semi-autobiographical novel *A Pair of Blue Eyes* (1873) describes a love triangle between a young woman, Elfride Swancourt, and her two suitors from very different backgrounds. Stephen Smith is a socially inferior but ambitious young man (perhaps Hardy himself) who adores her and with whom she shares a country background, and Henry Knight a respectable, established, older man who represents London society. The novel is propelled forward by the pace of the railway, relying on the distance between home and station, meetings at stations and in compartments and on the scheduling of the timetable

An iconic moment from David Lean's film *Brief Encounter* (1945), as Laura (Celia Jesson) and Alex (Trevor Howard) say goodbye, their unspoken, unsatisfied passion interrupted by the departing train.

to sequence events. As such it presages genres of railway-based fiction, including detective novels by Agatha Christie and others, of well into the twentieth century and beyond:

> In less than a quarter of an hour Elfride emerged from the door in her walking dress, and went to the railway. She had not told Mrs Buckle anything as to her intentions, and was supposed to have gone out shopping.
>
> An hour and forty minutes later, and she was in Stephen's arms at the Plymouth station. Not upon the platform – in the secret retreat of a deserted waiting-room.
>
> Stephen's face boded ill. He was pale and despondent.
>
> 'What is the matter?' she asked.
>
> 'We cannot be married here to-day, my Elfie! I ought to have known it and stayed here. In my ignorance I did not. I have the license, but it can only be used in my parish in London. I only came down last night, as you know.'
>
> 'What shall we do?' she said blankly.
>
> 'There's only one thing we can do, darling.'
>
> 'What's that?'
>
> 'Go on to London by a train just starting, and be married there to-morrow.'
>
> 'Passengers for the 11.05 up-train take their seats!' said a guard's voice on the platform.
>
> 'Will you go, Elfride?'
>
> 'I will.'
>
> In three minutes the train had moved off, bearing away with it Stephen and Elfride.[2]

In this and other novels railways formed a convenient vehicle for a technologically animated melodrama on to which was projected the cultural resonances of a romantic individualism which had been developing since the late eighteenth century. Railways not only produced new forms of personal mobility but, by defining the contours, parameters and possibilities of this experience, the railway has come to shape how we think about ourselves as distinctive individuals, able to build unique biographies from the circumstances and choices which present themselves.

In this context, railways provide highly articulate symbolic markers that dramatize the experience of life as a journey: its moments of decision, thresholds of transition and rights of passage. The continuing resonance of this set of cultural metaphors is exemplified by a recent set of television advertisements in the UK featuring a well-known bank. These show a cartoon version of a European high-speed train. The train weaves its way through a dreamlike landscape which collapses together many milestones of everyday life in the early twenty-first century: going to university, a first job, moving house, starting a family, a happy and active retirement. Stereotypical characters get on and off the train; they relax into their seats and look out of the windows at an uncertain and changing world. The strap line for this advertising campaign, 'For the Journey', seeks to draw parallels between the comfort, security and stability of the railway train and a range of financial products. Life is a like a journey, the adverts tell us: with prudence and careful planning, it can be as comfortable, structured and predictable as travelling by train. In Philip Larkin's (1922–1985) poem 'The Whitsun Weddings' (published 1964), for example, the train provides the author with a vehicle to reflect both on his own personal circumstances and those of everyday life in Britain after the Second World War. The poem takes us, with the author, on a journey from the provincial city of Hull, where Larkin was university librarian, to London. His journey down the industrialized reaches of the Humber estuary, along the broad flat agricultural landscape of the Trent valley and through the Midlands towards London and the Home Counties is one he had undertaken many times and that symbolized his feelings of alienation in provincial England.[3] Having collapsed into his seat in the stuffy carriage just as the train sets off one hot, sunny Saturday afternoon, Larkin becomes increasingly aware that at each subsequent station groups of excited and animated people are waving to departing passengers as the train heads south. The 'whoops and skirls' he hears 'down the long cool platforms',

I took for porters larking with the mails,
And went on reading. Once we started, though,
We passed them, grinning and pomaded, girls
In parodies of fashion, heels and veils,
All posed irresolutely, watching us go . . .

These are the Whitsun wedding parties of the poem's title and Larkin's scorn for their modish awkwardness and lack of sophistication is palpable. Yet Larkin's attitude is one of disdain mixed with pity. His empathy is built on a shared condition of loss and unfulfilment. Their goodbyes said, the married couples take their seats and the train gets under way again making for London:

– An Odeon went past, a cooling tower,
And someone running up to bowl . . .[4]

Larkin's poem is full of complex imagery but its central thread rests on the parallels drawn between the passage into wedlock and the journey of the train towards London. The station platform symbolizes the threshold of marriage and the train, both the journey into married life and into the future of modern Britain. Larkin sees the optimism generated by the marriage celebrations to which he is witness as a hollow charade. Modern life is merely an excursion into banal, commodified uniformity; the journey of life is something we undertake *en masse*, like a train trip. The moments at which we feel life is most distinctively ours are merely a common set of experiences shared by the bulk of humanity. Some critics see a hint of optimism and ultimately redemption at the end of the poem but, whether this is the case or not, this work transforms the railway into a vehicle for exploring deep and difficult ideas fundamental to thinking about the human condition in the modern world.[5]

It is not surprising therefore that over the years railways have figured in the work of a number of artists, writers and theorists as they have attempted to describe and explain the modern condition. Marcel Duchamp's painting *Sad Young Man on a Train* (1911–12) is both an abstract analytical study of the body in motion in the manner of his controversial painting *Nude Descending a Staircase, No. 2* (1912) and a psychological reflection on the state of melancholy.[6] Sigmund Freud entertained lifelong fears about missing trains, and about being caught up in railway accidents. His earliest thinking concerned with railways focused on the psychopathology of shock, what we might today call post-traumatic stress disorder.[7] Wolfgang Schivelbusch has most usefully explored this in his discussion of 'railway spine', the condition elaborated by doctors during the nineteenth century to explain human reactions to the experience of technologically mediated accidents and catastrophes.[8] However, Freud's more long-term interest is demonstrated in the case of 'Little Hans' and the study in infant sexuality. Here the train's psychological significance lies, not as one might first assume in the sexual symbolism of trains and tunnels, but in the rhythmical experience of motion. Freud claimed that

[t]he shaking produced by driving in carriages and later by railway-travel exercises such a fascinating effect upon older children that every boy, at any rate, has at one time or another wanted to be an engine driver or a coachman . . . A compulsive link of this kind between railway-travel and sexuality is clearly derived from the pleasurable character of the sensation of movement.[9]

Dread of railway travel here signifies repression, that blockage on the psychological journey to satisfactory adult sexuality in the modern human subject.[10]

Railways are a recurrent motive in the work of the Greco-Italian painter Giorgio de Chirico (1888–1978). Studying in Germany, De Chirico was influenced by the vitalist scepticism of the philosophers Nietzsche and Schopenhauer. His early work circa 1909–19 pioneered a style he called metaphysical painting, and which became an important inspiration for the Surrealist movement. These dreamlike works seem to echo Freud without owing him any direct influence. They are characterized by the juxtaposition of apparently random objects within a frequently Italian Renaissance city landscape inspired by the work of Giotto and others. Major themes in these works are nostalgia, melancholy and a sense of loss. The deserted streets, the harsh mid-afternoon sun, the indeterminate perspective and the menacing presence of objects without context present us with a series of images which suggest alienation and estrangement. De Chirico's father had been an Italian railway engineer who planned and built railways in Greece so, perhaps not surprisingly, the trains in these images invoke memories of his father, who died in 1905 and with whom De Chirico was never able to express his feelings of warmth and affection.[11] Pictures such as *The Anxious Journey* (1913) and *Gare Montparnasse (The Melancholy of Departure)* (1914) connect journeys and personal memories in such a way as to demonstrate the irredeemability of the present, the remoteness of the past and the irrepressible march towards the future. The railway train is an unsettling presence in these images, standing in a corner of the picture as if about to move off. Never the main focus but always just within consciousness, it is a disturbing reminder that, in the modern world, we will have to move on whether we like it or not.

For a number of notable thinkers in the late twentieth century the railway has come to signify connection rather than alienation. The French philosopher and cultural theorist Michel de Certeau (1925–1986) has given us one of the best articulated attempts to develop the biography/story/journey metaphor as a means of understanding

Giorgio de Chirico, *Gare Montparnasse (The Melancholy of Departure)*, 1914. In a dreamlike landscape inscribed with symbols of personal memory the train and the clock stand together marking time.

the complex interrelationships of modern social life. Drawing on a wide range of influences including Marx, Freud, anthropology and literary theory, his grandiloquent writing itself mirrors some of the self-confidence in narratives of Victorian railway enterprise. In modern Athens, he says,

> The vehicles of mass transportation are called metaphorai. To go to work or to come home, one takes a 'Metaphor' – a bus or a train. Stories could also take this noble name: every day, they traverse and organize places; they select and link them together; they make sentences and itineraries out of them. They are spatial trajectories.[12]

Certeau's transport-based social poetics suggests some of the ordering and networking qualities of the railway discussed in the last chapter. But more than this, he is trying to suggest an active role for travel

Giorgio de Chirico, *The Anxious Journey*, 1913. The waiting steam train and the labyrinth of arches seem to suggest an impending weight of choices for the viewer.

and movement in making the individual and collective fabric of modern everyday life. As we go about our daily business, commuting, going on holiday or visiting the shops, we write our journeys into our lives and on to the physical fabric of the landscape around us as if they were stories. Stories, like journeys, have a structure, a beginning, a middle and an end, context, central characters and outcomes. Such stories both describe activity in our everyday lives and give sense and meaning to quotidian experience as we reflect on our actions. By linking this idea to individual journeys and indeed to transport systems such as the railway, Certeau gives everyday life a sense of both adventure and structure. Yet it might still seem strange that such complex and abstract ideas derived from literary theory need to draw on metaphors of trains and transport systems in order to understand and explain a modernity which has been increasingly dominated by more contemporary means of transport and mobility. Perhaps the answer lies in how the modern world is enabled by and largely experienced through its means of communication. During the 1950s and '60s theorists explained this phenomenon mainly in terms of media such as radio, television and the press. However, recent developments in technology – for example, the development of the Internet as a globalized means of networking with economic, cultural and political ramifications – have encouraged theorists to think beyond the indiscriminate mass consumption of broadcasting and rehabilitate the structuring role of network technologies as a means for understanding the world in which we live today.[13] By invoking the railway in this context, theorists both acknowledge the historically central role played by railways in producing the physical and social fabric of modern life and draw on the widespread acceptance of the railway as a cultural signifier of technological progress.

Such writing has given the railway renewed power to explain back to us the world in which we live. These theoretical and philosophical formulations may, for instance, stress the importance of physical technological structures in the making of local, national and international relationships, as in the work of the philosopher and sociologist of science Bruno Latour. They may question and extend the idea of culture beyond that simply understood as 'the arts' in ways which are useful in studies such as this. Thus the French philosopher of science Michel Serres, echoing Certeau's metaphor-transport analogy, says: 'our universe is organized around message-bearing systems'.[14] For Serres and others, such messages are the stuff of culture and therefore by implication to study the conduits of communication, its transport systems, is to study the means by which social life is made and held together. In this respect, few have matched the subtlety of the historian and philosopher Michel Foucault (1926–1984) as he mused on the 'extraordinary' nature of the railway as a cultural product and producer of modern life. The train, he said,

> is something through which one goes, it is also something by means of which one can go from one point to another, and then it is also something that goes by.[15]

To a certain extent Foucault is merely reflecting ideas developed by media theorists during the 1960s encapsulated in Marshall McLuhan's slogan 'the medium is the message'.[16] It is certainly true that in works like Larkin's 'Whitsun Weddings' or De Chirico's *Gare Montparnasse (The Melancholy of Departure)*, which connect stories, journeys and biographies, the structures of travel, its stations, locomotives and coaches are intrinsic to the meaning of the work rather than just carriers for something else. For Larkin the journey from Hull to London is more than just a framing device or indeed simply a metaphor. It was a familiar experience central to the organization of his routine, linking his daily working life in Hull University library with his literary ambitions and intellectual circle in London and the south-east. For the newlyweds described in the poem the station platform is more than merely a symbolic marker for their life together: it is their actual point of departure as honeymooners into life as married couples. The journey to London is an experience in and of itself and the railway is both the poetic starting-point for reflection on that experience and the physical means by which the journey is made. Thus the cultural experience of railway travel challenges the model of passive consumption developed by early theorists concerned with radio, television and film. The railway constitutes a model for the sort of active and all-encompassing engagement with technology that characterizes this age of digital and computerized network communication. The philosopher Gilles Deleuze (1925–1995) calls this networked, technologized world 'virtual'. By this he does not mean unreal or immaterial: the 'virtual' world is full of potential, always emerging and constantly subject to change.[17] Stories, journeys and train travel take on a particular resonance in such a world: they speak simultaneously of familiarity, routine and an infinite world of possibility.

Mobile biographies and senses of place

As might be seen from the way individual lives are collected and juxtaposed in Larkin's 'Whitsun Weddings', railways link narratives of biography and mobility to senses of belonging, identity and purpose in ways which are both multiple and complex. In the poem Larkin works through a variety of local and national identifications. These senses of place enabled by mechanized mobility connect with moral geographies of tradition and progress, associating modernity with Americanization and superficial ugly commercialism and tradition with a sense of authenticity, beauty and loss. The final lines of the poem read:

And as the tightened brakes took hold, there swelled
A sense of falling, like an arrow-shower
Sent out of sight, somewhere becoming rain.

This imagery is sometimes thought to refer to the volley of arrows in the Battle of Agincourt scene in the 1944 film adaptation of Shakespeare's *Henry V*. This in itself suggests a complex linkage of belonging, place and identity. The original version of the film commences with a 'dedication to the commandos and airborne troops of Great Britain'. Its production and release coincided with the momentous events of the D-Day Allied invasion of France, and the film played an important role in boosting national morale at this most difficult time in British history.[18] Perhaps Larkin invokes a similar moment of collective biography signified by national crisis, or perhaps he simply expresses the dissipation of his own deeply rooted sense of self fragmented by multiple attachments to cosmopolitan London, a sense of national heritage, the promise of his own talent as a writer and the bland suburban banalities of working life in Hull. Either way, the railway journey epitomizes how mechanized mobility both calls into question and remakes those senses of local, regional and national identification important for senses of self and belonging. In this context and in addition to its role facilitating those aspects of mobile modern lifestyles such as commuting and tourism, trains themselves have become objects for the projection of biographical senses of self. Nicholas Whittaker's book *Platform Souls: The Trainspotter as Twentieth-Century Hero* (1995), for example, fits into a genre of autobiographical and semi-autobiographical writing that explores the obsessions and insecurities of contemporary everyday masculinities. The book draws on a world of substantially male enthusiasms in order to reflect on the experience of growing up as male in late twentieth-century Britain. Whittaker's schooldays, his parents' divorce, his time at college, his marital infidelities and his later efforts to bond with his young son are carried along, explored, understood and resolved through his all-consuming interest in trains and train travel. Rather than a means of escape, it is as if for Whittaker the enthusiast, railways become the medium through which life and the consequences of action become real and take on material form. On the one hand railways represent a mythologized and nostalgic past of steam locomotives, politeness, long summer days and packed lunches. On the other their workaday grubbiness, the crowded commuter trains and run-down suburban stations act as a reality check, demonstrating that the world carries on regardless even when life feels as if it is careering out of control. In this narrative, railways are a site of certainty cast against the doubt and insecurity of personal biography.

The railway station itself acts as a conduit and collecting point for biographical narratives. Stations clearly play an important role. Richards and MacKenzie call them 'an extraordinary agent of social mixing', simultaneously a centrifugal and centripetal force.[19] Most famously this is exemplified in W. P. Frith's painting of a crowded station platform at the Great Western Railway's terminus at London, Paddington. *The Railway Station* (1862) has all the qualities of a Victorian novel with its wealth of characters and incidents, plots and subplots.[20] The painting's carefully staged verisimilitude acts as a powerful platform for sentimental departures and phantasmagorical excursions that resonate with a range of Victorian fears relating to social mixing and the anonymity of the urban crowd. Frith provided a range of visual clues enabling his audience to identify characters and complete story lines. Some incidents are readily identified by a modern audience, but Victorians could also recognize the genteel family in reduced circumstances and the likely murderer because they habitually studied not only dress but also facial features and head shape for evidence of social standing and moral character. Contemporaries

were clearly captivated by the theatrical and melodramatic power of this painting. It was a sensational success – in seven weeks over 21,000 people paid to see it. John Schlesinger's documentary film *Terminus* (1961) echoes the cameos and conversations set up in Frith's painting by portraying a day in the life of London's Waterloo station in a series of vignettes. As earnest city gents, frightened lost children, irate holidaymakers and busy workers move in and through the station during the day, these tell the story of twenty-four hours in the life of the station as it intersects with a wide range of individual biographies. Produced by the British Transport Film Unit, a department of the nationalized British Railways at the point at which it was making record losses, the film makes an eloquent statement for the railway as common national property shared by all. Just one year later Dr Richard Beeching was appointed head of British Railways with a brief to cut the spiralling losses.

The idea of railways as common property can also serve biographical stories which are anti-authoritarian and countercultural. The New York graffiti artists who illegally spray-paint designs on the side

W. P. Frith, *The Railway Station*, 1862. A narrative approach to social mixing on stations and in trains. This monumental canvas used photography and an architectural draftsman to create a theatrical sense of illusion.

of subway trains inhabit a world where local personal status and citywide notoriety depend on anti-authoritarian individual heroism and artistic skill. Making such art requires intimate knowledge of the system, its points of access, the movements of security staff and stabling of trains. Works require patient creative planning, skill and stamina and are often executed in very difficult, dark and dangerous locations. Established graffiti artists often work with teams of helpers (crews) who thus learn the techniques and procedures necessary to become individual artists themselves.[21] Therefore the world of graffiti artists is a complex structured social network of neighbourhood allegiances, crew loyalty and personal admiration. Sometimes called the visual expression of rap music, graffiti art emerged in the South Bronx, New York, during the 1970s along with a do-it-yourself hip-hop culture which enabled young people and gang members in poor communities to find a positive and creative response to poverty and urban decay.[22] Thus for graffiti artists trains make mobile the visual expression of local pride, group identification, self-worth and personal esteem by carrying this message into a broader public domain in full public view on the sides of trains.

The individual freedoms enabled by personal mobility are, of course, central to ideas of both self and nation for many North Americans. Perhaps the archetypal mobile lifestyle associated with railway development in the USA is that of the hobo. The term hobo is often thought to be a corruption of 'hoe boy' a reference to the agricultural hoes itinerant migrant workers would take with them from job to job.[23] The end of the Civil War created an initial pool of landless, rootless men inured to life on the move. Completion of the first transcontinental railroad in 1869 and subsequent rapid agricultural and industrial development combined with a series of economic depressions, in 1873, 1893–4 and the 1930s for example, provided both means and reason to move. Railroad building, crop harvesting

Stills from John Schlesinger's documentary film *Terminus* (1961): Woman looking at watch underneath departure board; passengers waiting to board a train; policeman talks to a lost small boy sitting on a suitcase.

and lumberjacking all necessitated the movement of tens of thousands of workers. As a result, for the first time the US was home to a large pool of intermittently employed workers who were mobile on a continental scale.[24] Simultaneously tramp, outlaw, cowboy, vagabond, hero and villain, the hobo holds a mythological status in the North American imagination. Introducing his collection of hobo testimony, life stories and poetry, Cliff Williams (Oats) says 'they like to go their own way; they do not live within the rules and restrictions of everyday society; they cannot be tamed'.[25] For many in mainstream society, hobos are shadowy, dangerous, untrustworthy figures located on the margins who are glimpsed across the tracks and beyond in the makeshift encampments known as hobo jungles, situated close to freight yards. On the one hand their transience,

The practice of spray-painting designs on subway trains which began in New York during the 1970s is now regarded as an urban art form. Its origins in hip-hop culture speak as a creative response to poverty and urban decay.

lack of interest in personal property and drunken hedonism renders hobos a socially disruptive force. On the other their camaraderie, respect for 'natural' justice and most importantly their work ethic, with its concomitant message of personal responsibility, act as confirmation for some of the deepest beliefs of North American society. Thus riding the rails has become synonymous with the ideas of individual freedom and self-expression fundamental to North American culture. Both as part of a reserve army of casual labour vital to the economy and as the carrier for a shared ideal of individual freedom, the presence of hobos is a threat to settled society yet at the same time necessary to its continued functioning. Consequently their marginal

During the Depression of the 1930s unemployed workers often used freight trains to move round the USA in search of work. Such traumatic events are documented in the myths, songs, novels and popular culture of the period.

and transient position justifies in equal measure both society's worst fears of anarchic disruption and its greatest hopes of individual self-realization.

Perhaps it is no surprise that railways have been a fertile ground for the development of that most archetypal of American musics associated with itinerant workers – the blues. The composer and musician W. C. Handy (1873–1958), known as 'Father of the Blues', claims to have discovered the blues while waiting at a railway station in Tutwiler, Mississippi. He recalled, 'A lean, loose-jointed Negro had commenced plunking a guitar beside me while I slept . . . The effect was unforgettable.'[26] The development of the blues paralleled mass migration from rural to urban centres, as well as movement within the South itself. As African-Americans migrated, their music migrated with them. The period 1890–1939 saw the mass movement of African-Americans from the South to the industrial north as a consequence of both the end of slavery and the availability of employment in centres such as Chicago and Detroit. As Fleming puts it:

> because the blues are about the lives and surroundings of the people, the songs often reflect this movement, and offer up an image of migration and struggle for freedom and success, with the train being one of the principal players.[27]

During the time of slavery, attraction to the railroad was both real and symbolic. Southern railroads made extensive use of slaves during the Civil War and some railroads owned slaves themselves.[28] Many work songs were sung to the rhythm of the swinging hammer as spikes were driven into the rails. Trains passing by plantation fields represented to the slaves toiling in them a freedom for which they were longing. So strong was the symbolism of the train that white sympathizers who helped to organize escape routes north of the Ohio River and often into Canada were given the name 'underground railroad', where 'conductors' were met at 'stations'.[29]

For those suffering in southern prisons and for whom railroad travel was an impossibility, the free movement of the train took on a deeper symbolism. The blues musician Huddie Ledbetter, known as Leadbelly, wrote his version of 'Midnight Special' (recorded 1934) while in the Sugar Land Penitentiary, Texas. Leadbelly's own fabrication of the story surrounding this song was perpetuated by John and Alan Lomax in their book *Best Loved American Folk Songs*. According to this story, a train left Houston each night, heading for the West Coast. It went by the penitentiary around midnight, shining its lights over the prison buildings. As Leadbelly would have it, the inmates believed that any person illuminated by those lights in passing would be the next one released.[30] Hotly disputed by blues historians, the veracity of this story is of secondary importance compared with its eloquent expression of a widely accepted belief in the iconic, almost magical status of the train as the means of transporting individuals to a new and better life. With its focus on self-reflection, life, love, nostalgia for home and escape to freedom, the blues form a musical counterpoint to the hobo's life on the rails. Just as the hobo's travelling life embodies a fundamental characteristic of North American identity, so the blues themselves are a mobile music foundational to modern north American culture, fusing African-American slave songs and gospel music with European folk traditions from the Appalachians into a mix that helped produce jazz and rock and roll as soundmarks of American culture. Together they help forge a distinctly American sense of place grounded in personal mobility.

If the hobo and the blues illustrate important dimensions of the culture of modern mobile individualism forged through experience of rail travel, then the example of railway work forms both contrast and compliment. Railway work constitutes a defining example of modern individualized experience where narratives of mobility link personal biography to senses of purpose and possibility, belonging and identity. Beyond the obvious symbolic status enjoyed by locomotive crews and engineers as part of a technological avant-garde in the nineteenth and early twentieth centuries, one of the most important attributes of railway work, giving it high status, was the prospect of consistent and regular employment, 'a job for life', and the possibility of promotion, 'to be able to make something of yourself'. Railway companies, well aware of this attitude, exploited the long-term security of railway work to keep wages low. Typically, both in Britain and in many other parts of the world during the nineteenth century, railway companies drew a substantial number of their employees from rural backgrounds; railway work constituted a route out of poorly paid labouring work in the countryside.[31] Though wage rates for those entering the service were poor, the scale of railway operation and their service role within the economy greatly reduced the impact of cyclical economic fluctuations, which created great uncertainty for those engaged in manufacturing industry.[32] Continuity of employment gave railway work 'status' and its employees 'respectability'.[33]

Railway work created a new breed of corporate employees, economically sheltered, personally confident and upwardly mobile. As shown in the following extract from a letter to the *Derby Mercury*, dated 24 July 1872, this could be something of a culture shock in a society steeped in expectations of deference and tradition:

> I was a passenger on an excursion train to Melbourne last Saturday, and upon returning witnessed at that station a disgraceful proceeding on the part of several railway clerks . . . This young gentleman was drunk . . . on the platform he threatened if he did not actually molest a minister who had in no way interfered with him, he attacked and forced a man onto the railway and directly commenced a free fight . . .

He dared a porter to touch him, stating he was a clerk with a first class pass, which he frequently exhibited, and there is no doubt whatever that if it had not been for this – if he had been an ordinary passenger, unconnected with the company, who had thus acted, he would surely have been arrested . . .

This minor altercation between a drunken railway clerk and a platform full of day trippers must have been echoed in countless encounters and at many times and places. Yet in spite of its trivial nature, it seems so highly suggestive of the new social relationships forged by the experience of railway travel. The anonymity of the crowd on the platform, the mixing of ages, genders and classes, the vagaries and incivilities of the random encounters produced by such coincidence, all seem to suggest those anxieties and intensities by which late nineteenth-century sociologists distinguished modern mobile urban life from what they perceived as its sedentary rural predecessor. It is not without significance that the drunken railway clerk flaunts his first-class pass as a talisman protecting him from the sanction of those around him. A corporate perk for higher-status administrative staff allowing free first-class rail travel, the pass signifies both his social and physical mobility. Waving his pass in front of fellow travellers and railway workers alike, he tells the world: 'You cannot touch me, I am going places.'

As the many photos of station staff and locomotive crews standing to uniformed attention show, railway work produced a very particular form of militaristic masculine identity. This seems to have been the case not only in those countries like Germany and Belgium where railway work was closely aligned with uniformed government service, or imperial contexts where railways had a military and strategic significance, but in other places too. Like many tales of modernist mobile progressivism, this is one in which women are marginalized,

INTERIOR OF BOOKING HALL, NEW MAIN LINE STATION BUILDING, V.T.

fixed safely in place as homemakers and passengers. Nevertheless, women historically played important if largely hidden roles as railway workers, not only as caterers and cleaners but as station attendants, signal workers and crossing keepers, in carriage building, upholstery and uniform making, and in clerical work and engineering, the latter particularly during wartime.[34] Though sometimes characterized by historians as part of a 'labour aristocracy' comparable with skilled engineers, carpenters and other skilled trades, the fact remained that in the main, railway skills were designated by and assessed by the companies themselves and consequently had no direct parallel outside the industry. Through the close linkage between the individual career and the fortunes of specific companies, railway workers were provided with a job for life at the cost of economic and social dependence. Shift

This office interior of a main-line station booking hall in India shows members of the mixed-race Anglo-Indian class for whom railway employment became a special preserve. Typically they held middling ranking positions as engine-drivers and mechanics, or clerks and stationmasters at medium-size stations.

work for traffic crews and signal workers, for example, separated workers from normal social and family life, forcing workers to build a life story around their work.[35] The pursuit of a career required locational mobility: a willingness to move to other departments, or to other locations within the organization. Opportunism and a willingness to submit to the organizational requirements of the company were necessary conditions for success as good 'corporate men'.[36] It is not surprising that the railway workers caricatured in films portraying rural branch lines such as *Oh Mr Porter* or indeed *Closely Observed Trains* are represented as having been shunted into dead end jobs. Bypassed by progress, they are literally as well as metaphorically at the end of the line.

Compartments, platforms and the marketplace

As suggested in chapter Two, in the nineteenth century it was argued that railways democratized travel because they carried the poorest

Train crews lodging away from home at Stratford, East London, a century ago. Lodging allowances were a significant income supplement, with train crews having to trade domestic life for a peripatetic male camaraderie.

members of society at the same speed as the richest. If one could afford a ticket then one entered an egalitarian world in which everyone travelled together. Claims that railways democratized travel appear to have had good grounds. Simmons has estimated that in Britain between 1850 and 1910 the number of passenger journeys per head of the population per year rose from 3.2 to 31.3 and the number of passenger journeys by railway from 67,359 to 1,276,003.[37] Gladstone's 1844 Act introducing cheap workmen's trains resulted in the rapid growth in third-class travel, even though companies adopted this only with reluctance and their 'parliamentary trains' became a byword for

In the US before the Civil War, the South used slaves in preference to white employees in positions such as locomotive fireman. After the war, African Americans could be found in low-grade clerical jobs and as car attendants and porters or in unskilled work.

Women locomotive cleaners of the Chicago & North Western Railroad cleaning one of the giant 'H' class locomotives, Clinton, Iowa. War resulted in women engaging in a variety of skilled, heavy, dirty and dangerous work on the railways.

slowness, dirtiness and discomfort. The 5 per cent tax concession on passenger fares enabled by this Act constituted the first government subsidy for rail travel and a clear government endorsement of mobility as a common right of citizenship. By 1875 the percentage of third-class passengers had risen to 77.9 per cent from 17.15 per cent in 1845 and by 1913 to 96 per cent.[38] Yet as the contrasting examples of hobos and railway workers might suggest, fellow travellers do not necessarily share destinations. The common experience of travel does not everywhere uniformly result in a fairer and more equal society. Railways can accentuate and entrench inequalities, expectations and life chances just as easily as they can provide the means for them to be to overcome. This is at its most obvious with the inauguration of new high-speed lines and services. Limited-stop express trains and new dedicated lines improve access for those places fortunate enough to have stations but times and levels of service are inevitably reduced at those locations where new trains speed by without stopping. There is much to be gained and lost for those included and those left out.

Nineteenth-century railway travel was certainly not always democratic. In Russia early travellers on the line between Moscow and St Petersburg were strictly vetted and subject to police and passport control.[39] In a country where the peasantry were still tied to their home villages, it is understandable that mobility was perceived as socially destabilizing, if not openly revolutionary, by those in authority. As common carriers North American railroads had a duty to carry anyone who bought a ticket without fear or favour. However, in operation the open-plan saloon-type railway coach typical of American practice – and widely believed to be more democratic than its compartmentalized Euopean counterpart – reflected long-standing contradictions in American ideals of equality, opportunity and autonomy. In 1896 the *Railway Age and Northwestern Railroader* called attention to class stratification on the railroad 'under other names'.[40] Even with a first-class ticket, African-Americans were routinely relegated to part of the baggage car, a smoking car or a divided-off section in a sleeper.[41] Stations themselves consolidated in bricks and mortar the racial and class divisions experienced on the train. Throughout the Johannesburg commuter system during the apartheid regime all station platforms were divided in half for whites and non-whites, and the trains were similarly divided so that the appropriate part stopped at the relevant stretch of platform. At many stations in India, and particularly in Africa, the meagre third- and fourth-class waiting-rooms were often physically removed from the main range of station buildings,[42] while in Europe separate waiting rooms for different classes were familiar into the early twentieth century and indeed have been reinstated today for airline-style high-speed intercity and trans-European services.

Early in the history of railways it became clear that railway compartments and carriages formed a key site in which disparate and conflicting biographies might intersect. The compartment soon entered the popular imagination as a site of danger and social uncertainty in

Open-plan North American saloon cars were believed to be more egalitarian and democratic than European coaches, which were divided into compartments. The experience of African-Americans suggests otherwise.

everyday life. If the mobile lifestyles associated with railway work produced clear and positive senses of belonging, then to make a journey as a passenger was to place at risk both one's physical being and sense of self. The brutal murders of Chief Justice Poinsot on a train to Paris (1861) and chief bank clerk Thomas Briggs on a train in London (1864) and the consequent press coverage of them created a climate of near panic.[43] This even made its way into the typically dry and utilitarian prose of technical literature, as the following extract from the *Handbuch für spezielle Eisenbahntechnik* (Handbook for special railway technology) shows:

> The passenger is so pleased when he finds a vacant compartment; but he is not so fortunate when he acquires a fellow passenger who robs him in his sleep, or perhaps even murders him, and then ejects his body from the compartment piecemeal, without attracting the train personnel's attention.[44]

Paintings, novels and etiquette books illuminate the irritations and excitements, the social and cultural clashes and juxtapositions forged through the common experiences of railway travel. Though not the first of its kind, *The Railway Traveller's Handy Book* (1862) provides what is probably the single most illuminating guide to acceptable behaviour on the mid-Victorian railway. Cartoons, novels and journalism reveal considerable nervousness about the danger of contact with strangers during railway travel. In Benjamin Disraeli's novel *Sybil* (1845), the character Lord de Mowbray tells a cautionary anecdote about a countess chatting to 'two of the most gentlemanlike men sitting opposite her'. Beguiled by their intelligent conversation, the countess is shocked when the men stand up to leave the train and she discovers that they are notorious thieves chained together and on their way to appear in court; 'A countess and a felon!' says

De Mowbray. 'So much for public conveyances.'[45] Though one might assume such social anxieties were very much a product of the Victorian period, social situations created by the apparently random juxtaposition of people as passengers on trains certainly seems to have provided longstanding fascination for writers, artists and filmmakers.

Such situations have been the grounds for numerous volumes of crime and detective fiction. Alfred Hitchcock uses the railway carriage

Voicing bourgeois fears of social mixing on trains, this illustration from the cover of a popular song leaves the unwitting polite male 'holding the baby' but minus his wallet as a result of his ill-timed conversation with an attractive female traveller.

as a container for suspense and intrigue in his 1935 feature film adaptation of John Buchan's novel *The Thirty-Nine Steps* (1915). Hitchcock is of course known for his psychological approach to making thrillers, and both his work and his own personality have been subject to psychoanalytic investigation.[46] Perhaps it is not surprising that the railway compartment itself occupies a complex and troubled place in modern imaginations. As Schivelbusch says:

> That only two cases of murder, occurring four years apart and in two different countries, were able to trigger a collective psychosis tells us as much about the compartment's significance for the nineteenth-century European psyche as does the fact that it took so long to become conscious of the compartment's dysfunctionality. The surprising aspect of the history of the train compartment is, indeed, that it remained unchanged for so long . . . [47]

The rudimentary civility of third-class travel on a Parliamentary Train is represented in this engraving of a drawing by William McConnell of a train from Euston to Liverpool, 1859. Early third-class travel was in little more than open goods wagons.

A public space with some of the trappings of domestic comfort, the compartment encourages us to treat it like home while constantly reminding us that our state of repose is imminently vulnerable. Behaviour in the compartment is ambiguously both on public display and yet hidden from the censure of wider society. As such the compartment is a place of temptation, freighted with the wildest of fantasies, where the darkest recesses of our psyches might enable almost anything to be possible. The increasingly complex interpenetration of public and private worlds in the nineteenth century brought with it a modern public culture based on consuming the pleasures and luxuries of domesticity and recreation, for instance in department stores, cinemas and restaurants. Both in Europe and North America, many novels and newspaper reports emphasized the vulnerability of a woman's virtue whilst on railway trains and gave credence to the notion that women were incapable of navigating public life. Women thus appeared in accounts as the preferred victims of unscrupulous men. Popular depictions of travelling salesmen combined concerns about the spread of commercial interactions with anxieties about women's virtue. The travelling salesman was one of the new forms of mobile lifestyle, which was itself greatly facilitated, if not actually created, by railway travel. The skills that made successful salesmen – an outgoing personality, the ability to anticipate the needs or desires of others, a broad knowledge of the pleasures and discomforts of travel – were equally suited to taking advantage of inexperienced female travellers and compromising their reputations.[48] Etiquette books recommended that acquaintances made on board trains should terminate at the end of the journey. Ironically, this advice may have heightened the confidences shared by female passengers, adding to their potential vulnerability.[49] Today, trains are typically composed of open saloons and there are few compartments but we continue to experience some of the fragility and ambiguity associated with them on our overcrowded trains. This is reflected in typical coping behaviours as we endeavour to reclaim some portion of the railway coach as private space by listening to music through headphones, making phone calls and working on laptop computers.[50] Recent calls for the instigation of women-only carriages in India and Japan, where high-density commuting provides circumstances in which women are exposed to sexual harassment, constitute only the most recent example of long-standing social concerns relating to the incivilities of rail travel.[51] This example might remind us that barriers between public and private space, appropriate and inappropriate behaviour, accessible and inaccessible places are not so much removed but remade and frequently reinforced by the proximity and mobility enabled by railway travel.

In the 'new' integrated Europe high-speed railways play an important role in forging an apparently barrierless 'Schengen space' with a single currency and free movement of passengers and goods. Yet rather than witnessing a reduction in customs, checkpoints and border controls, an increasing variety of electronic information-gathering systems enable these to be folded into the system of surveillance at stations and transhipment points throughout the member states of the European Union. Where once migrants and refugees might gather at the periphery waiting to be let in, now they routinely assemble beside the tracks at the entrance to the Channel Tunnel and congregate at key city stations deep within sovereign territory. At Milan Central, for example, the city council fund a centre which provides refuge spaces for homeless and migrant people. These shelters are sometimes located in redundant railway property. Rather than simply trying to police vast stretches of highly permeable peripheral border, it has proved strategically more efficient to focus efforts on such popular and necessary points of passage.[52]

The dramatic differentials in life chances between rich and poor, developed and developing world which draw migrants from Africa and Asia towards Europe also pull flows of migrants elsewhere in the world. The US remains one of the most powerfully attractive destinations for migrants and its border with Mexico is one of the world's great fault lines between rich and poor. Cary Fukunanga's widely acclaimed film *Sin Nombre* (Without Name, 2009) is but one illustration of increasing disquiet concerning the unequal relationships between North and South America. The story concerns a Mexican ex-gang member (Willy) and a poor Honduran girl (Sayra), who find each other amongst the dozens of people trying to escape poverty and violence by hitching freight trains heading north in order reach the US border. Willy and Sayra team up to help each other make the dangerous journey to the border and an illegal crossing into what they hope will be a better life. Part violent gangland thriller, part drama documentary, the film pulls no punches in showing the cost, hardship, brutality and danger to which migrants submit themselves at the hands of traffickers, local traders and communities along the way as they jump trains and sleep rough.[53] The trains themselves, slowly rumbling through a Third World landscape of subsistence agriculture, heading to and from the US border with wagonloads of raw materials, shipping containers stacked with consumer goods and transporters loaded with cars, form part of a continent-wide traffic linked into a global free market economy. For migrants such trains embody their aspirations, parading before them physical evidence of a materially better life available in the USA and providing the means for gaining access to that life. At the same time such trains also represent the constantly shifting global patterns in manufacturing and services that draw on flows of migrants and cheap labour while also creating the circumstances of boom and bust, surplus and deficit which lead to the establishment and mobilization of pools of transient labour in the first instance. In this context and as a product of a modern mobile capitalist economy enabled by railway travel,

Cary Fukunanga's *Sin Nombre* (Without Name) (2009).

contemporary experience on the Mexican border resonates strongly with the structural circumstances which produced the original hobo phenomenon back in the 1870s.

Historically it would certainly seem that the market economics of railway development, the monopolies encouraged by high initial capitalization and networking costs in relation to geographical coverage and market share, seem to promote agglomeration, exclusion and inequality of opportunity. Perhaps it is not surprising that regulatory or other forms of government intervention have in one way or another been universally necessary in order to preserve the equitability of liberal freedoms provided by railways. Reflected in ongoing debates concerning the relative merits of railways as a public service, such tense relationships between liberal economics and public service obligation are exemplified by the White Trains of Buenos Aires. During the presidency of Carlos Menem (1989–99) neo-Liberal reforms were marked by the rapid privatization of state companies, including the railways, and the opening of finance to international

markets. These reforms resulted in significant job losses and capital outflow, leading to unemployment or irregular employment. From the mid-1990s increasing numbers of people previously in secure work were evident on the streets of Buenos Aires collecting recyclable materials, plastics, cardboard and cans.[54] As a result of the economic and political crisis of 2001–2, the presence of this underclass without formal employment, pensions, savings, security or welfare benefits was formally recognized when special trains were laid on to enable people to travel from the suburbs to the city centre in order to forage for cardboard and other recyclables from the streets. Called 'White Trains' because of their colour or 'ghost train' because of their stripped-out carriages and skeletal appearance, they are omitted from official timetables and run in the early evening and early morning. They bring trainloads of scavengers (called *carteneros*) into the city and take them, their carts and their rubbish out to the recycling points early in the morning. Thus they form a spectral counter-rhythm to the tidal flow of conventional commuters, reflecting their

White Train and *carteneros* today.

passengers' status as outcasts from society and the precarious informality of their economic status.[55] Provision of White Trains by the metropolitan railways of Buenos Aires is both a form of welfare and a mode of market-limiting regulation. However squalid, the trains establish a form of not for profit provision in the service of society's poorest. Coupled with new municipal legislation which seeks to incorporate *carteneros* into the official street-cleansing regime of the city, the trains constitute part of a mode of governance supplying some order to what was increasingly perceived as a disorderly and uncontrolled colonization of the city centre and its more prosperous residential districts by the vagrant poor.

Strangers on a train

In Theodore Dreiser's (1871–1945) first novel *Sister Carrie* (1900) a young woman flees country life for the city. Travelling by train from her home in rural Wisconsin to a new life with her sister and brother-in-law in Chicago, the eighteen-year-old Caroline, 'Sister Carrie', soon falls into conversation with Charles Drouet, a travelling salesman. There is an instant attraction between the brash, confident, opportunistic Drouet and the naive, diffident, but determined Carrie. They exchange addresses and thus set into motion a dramatic chain of events involving marriage, deceit, adultery, embezzlement, ambition, success, personal failure and ruin. After leaving Drouet and moving to New York with Drouet's associate Hurstwood, Carrie abandons Hurstwood and, poverty-stricken, he eventually commits suicide. At the end of the book, after discovering her true vocation on the stage, Carrie finds that success and the money that comes with it do not give her the fulfilment she craves. A chance meeting on a train, a travelling salesman, a vulnerable woman and a journey from provincial innocence to city worldliness lend this novel all the characteristics of the railway age.

In deeper ways too, the novel enacts the culture of its time. With only one semester of college, Dreiser, a newspaper reporter in Pittsburgh, discovered the work of the social philosopher Herbert Spencer (1820–1903), whose work was subsequently to become a seminal influence on Dreiser and *Sister Carrie* in particular.[56] Spencer's philosophy is a combination of nineteenth-century mechanistic and romantic beliefs. He believed that we live in a world composed of matter in motion describable in scientific and mechanical terms. As an advocate of evolution, Spencer thought that within the overall linear progress of time, each individual follows a cyclical pattern: birth and growth leading toward development and maturity, followed eventually by physical and mental decline leading toward death. At the same time, humanity could advance even while the individual was circumscribed within physical limits; as in nature, the fittest will survive (a Spencerian idea often attributed to Darwin). As Lehan argues, the novel can be read as an exercise in Spencerian principles of matter in motion overlapping cyclical and linear time: Carrie illustrates the move toward completion; Drouet, a form of stasis or equilibrium; and Hurstwood, a process of dissolution.[57]

In this story of society as mechanical motion, it is not without significance that the major characters enter the city by train and that the train articulates pivotal moments in the story: the initial journey to Chicago, the escape with Hurstwood to Montreal and their eventual relocation to New York. Spencer's dispassionate positivistic social philosophy overlays the hard scientific interpretation of the world as merely a collection of individual atoms grouped together in motion with the moral imperatives of a civilization built on circulation and enabled by modern technological means of communication such as the railway.[58] Indeed Spencer was himself the native of a railway town, Derby in the English East Midlands, headquarters of the Midland Railway Company and a centre for radical enlightenment and scientific thought.[59] Also significant is the city of Chicago itself as a focus for the novel. Dreiser describes the city in terms of physical force, as a magnet, possessing a compelling attraction that draws people to it with pulsating energy. Urban crowds are matter in motion, sweeping onward, like the sea through space and time.[60] Chicago is, of course, the epitome of a railway city. The development of the great Midwestern US cities from the 1870s onwards depended on their nodal status at the centre of extensive networks of lines bringing agricultural products, cattle and grain from across 1,000 miles of prairie farm and ranching country stretching as far as the Rocky Mountains. This transformed Chicago into the centre of a vast agricultural region and a centre for the processing and production of food products with global reach as meat products were exported both to the eastern seaboard by rail and across the Atlantic by ship via the Great Lakes.

Created on the flat prairie lands alongside Lake Michigan, a town of just 30,000 in 1848 when the first railway came, by the early years of the twentieth century Chicago came to be served by 22 separate railway companies. In the 1870s one-third of all the rail system in the US, amounting to the 21,000 miles of track, was controlled from Chicago.[61] Characteristic of Chicago were the vast rail-served stockyards south of the city and the factory settlement and carriage works of the Pullman Car Company. With both suburban and long distance lines radiating out from a central core, itself defined by an elevated commuter railway, the 'L' (the first part of which opened in 1892), the railway became a major influence on the shape and form of the city.[62] Thus Chicago became a model for the characteristically zoned patterns of urban development typical of the nineteenth-century railway city and familiar to us today in the urban fabric of many places throughout the world. In Chicago, from the late 1860s commuter settlements began to develop alongside railway tracks within the region surrounding the city. In all 35 such settlements came into

being, creating an extensive, prosperous, low-density residential landscape that came to be known as 'Chicagoland'. The first of these, the elite landscaped suburb of Riverside (1869), formed a model for suburban development in the US through the railway era and beyond.[63] Consequently, the railway became an agent of increasing social segregation as residential and industrial areas became more homogeneous and the wealthy began their well-documented flight from the city centre. Not without good reason did the idiom 'born on the wrong side of the tracks' take hold in North America as a means of signifying the prejudices, limited life chances and expectations of someone born in poor circumstances in a run-down part of town.

Lake Bluff station, in the northern suburbs of Chicago that became known as 'Chicagoland'. The Tudorbethan and ranch-style architecture of the stations in this area complement the domestic architecture of these comfortable residential settlements.

Dreiser's Carrie inhabits this increasingly differentiated urban landscape facilitated by the development of railways. Dreiser's narrative view of the city corresponds to the writings of a group of urban sociologists, themselves based in Chicago and interested in how physical laws applied to social phenomena. Robert E. Park maintained that the city was externally organized in terms of laws of its own. His colleague Ernest W. Burgess illustrated this point by insisting that the city grows in evolutionary concentric rings. These spread out from the central business area to an area of poor housing and low rents, a slum; to the working class area, which will become the next slum; to a residential area of high-class apartments; and finally to a commuter zone, a suburban area or satellite sites within thirty to sixty minutes of the central business area.[64] Chicago, uniquely situated and with a distinctive history, thus became the physical exemplar for the dominant theoretical model of the railway-age city. Represented as a series of concentric circles, Carrie clearly moves through these spaces. The business area in the centre is surrounded by factories, where Carrie works; this is encircled by cheap homes for the workers, where she lives with the Hansons. In turn this is bordered by more expensive apartments, where she lives with Drouet. Beyond these are the richest homes, at which Carrie marvels, and finally the suburbs, where Hurstwood lives with his ungrateful family. If, as Lehan argues, '[w]ithin the confines of the city, Carrie's role is purely mechanistic, she is matter controlled by principles of physical laws', then as both a migrant and a resident Carrie's experience of the structuring effects of urban life are embodied, given presence and effect through the railroad, its steel tracks, carriages and stations.[65]

In this way Dreiser articulates a series of contradictions central to the experience of modern mobility and evident from both the experience of train travel and our reflections upon that experience in literature and the arts. Increased social proximity and mixing seems to result not in familiarity and fellowship but in personal distance and detachment. Intense levels of social interaction result in greater degrees of social segregation. Greater sense of individual freedom seems to come only in the context of a range of externally defined choices. Self-fulfilment merely generates further frustration and disappointment. The railway carriage and indeed the station itself seem to dramatize these apparent inconsistencies in modern experience. As we have seen, the increasing interpenetration of public and private lives encouraged by the experience of railway travel forced people together in circumstances in which they felt both vulnerable and defensive. As Richter suggests, even as the social life of the railroad mirrored that of cities, train travel differed from urban life and created a distinctive milieu. Only rail travel demanded the constant and simultaneous negotiation of both urban social disorder and the systematic ordering associated with large technological systems and corporate business. In this way, 'the railroad stood squarely at the crossroad of the major social, business, cultural and technological changes remaking national life during the second half of the nineteenth century'.[66]

Important in this regard is the work of the German sociologist and philosopher Georg Simmel (1858–1918). Simmel was one of the most important intellectual influences on Chicago School sociology and his concept of 'the stranger' gives form, substance and voice to the half-conscious fears and anxieties experienced by people on trains.[67] For Simmel, the stranger represents a synthesis between 'freedom' (mobility) and 'fixation' (stability), between near and far, somebody who is connected yet disconnected.[68] Thus the stranger we meet on trains and station platforms disturbs our expectations of physical and emotional space. It is someone who brings into our intimate presence the kind of difference and otherness anticipated and tolerated only at a distance. Thus the stranger challenges our sense of self at the same time that our response to their presence both encourages us to assert our individuality and objectify the generalized presence of the crowd. In this way Simmel provides, for instance, textbook language to help us to begin to understand the behaviour of the 'clerk with a first class pass' we met on Melbourne station, the condescension of Philip Larkin and perhaps also the social positioning of the graffiti artists, hobos and *carteneros* encountered earlier in the chapter.

As discussed at the beginning of this chapter, the railway seems to have an extraordinary capacity to explain back to us the world in which we live. Little wonder then that the railway has become such an effective vehicle for travel writers and popular ethnography, typified by the work of Eric Newby (1919–2006), Paul Theroux (1941–) or indeed in the long running BBC television travelogue series *Great Railway Journeys* (1980, 1994, 1996, 1999). The complex metaphorical associations and indeed physical connections between journeys, stories and biographies have been central to this since at least the 1860s. In the work of social theorists no less than novelists the railway continues to enable us to reflect on the experience of modern life. It is a world in which electronic media of virtual and networked communications have failed to eclipse the social experience of proximate strangers, partial connections, and individualized conformity familiar from the experience of train travel. Characteristic of this is the 'London Bloggers' website, which classifies and organizes a multiplicity of ongoing personal biographical narratives according to the blogger's chosen home station. The website provides both location and distance, allowing authors a degree of intimacy and anonymity which echoes that of the railway carriage itself. Geoff Ryman's novel *253: The Print Remix* (1998) also gives expression to this world. Composed of 253 discrete short biographies, the novel is organized around the number of seats on a London underground train. Each 'chapter' is a free-standing description of a specific passenger's individual thoughts, telling of their immediate concerns, hopes, fears, expectations and impressions of other travellers as the train hurtles towards an uncertain and, for many, tragic fate. There is no continuous thread of narrative beyond the equal and individual experience of the train journey. Designed with the random access of a computer website in mind, the novel's chapters' can be read in any order, perfect for the commuter 'dipping in' while on the Tube.

Perhaps it is the connection between routine and purposive action which encourages this strange liaison between contrasting nineteenth- and twenty-first-century means of communication. Both railway and computerized information technology provide us with distinctive yet related experiences of singular and repetitive events. In the case of digital technology this strange liaison concerns the infinite repeatability of computer-generated actions and the individual choice associated with sequential and random access to its stores of information. In the case of the railway it rests on the contrast between individual journeys and the repetitive sequencing of the timetable. Both instances provide us with metaphors of linear and cyclical time which resonate powerfully with lived experience. The fusion of linear, secular time and cyclical, eternal time are foundational for the human capacity to tell stories about ourselves, and have been for at least several millennia. Historians and literary theorists recognize this combination as belonging to the structure of myth. The railway journey thus enables us to build stories about our origins and destinies that balance the frailties and tragedies of individual fallibility with the purposive and redemptive possibilities of human progress. It has the power to translate everyday life into narratives of mythical proportions. Little wonder that Proust believed the railway journey provided an opportunity to recapture lost time, to reunite distinct experiences in the essence of a common metaphor,[69] or indeed that the philosopher

Ludwig Wittgenstein (1889–1951) claimed that '[t]he only place where real philosophical problems could be tackled and resolved is the railway station'.[70]

4 Moving Objects: Stations, Locomotives and the Arts of Commerce

Stations, museums and malls

In the centre of Paris, on the left bank of the River Seine, stands the Musée d'Orsay. Opened in 1986, it holds mainly French art from the period 1848 to 1914, a period we might think of as defining the 'railway age'. Pictures such as Claude Monet's (1840–1926) *Train dans la campagne* (c. 1870), or Henri Ottmann's (1877–1927) *La gare du Luxembourg à Bruxelles* (1903) feature images of the railway as their primary subject-matter while others simply tell of a world which was increasingly urban, individualized, socially and physically mobile and animated by the fashions of mass leisure and consumption. How fitting then, that the Musée d'Orsay is itself a former railway station, the Gare d'Orsay. Its long, deep glass-canopied train shed forms a dramatic and imposing central hall from which open a series of more intimate gallery spaces situated in the station's former waiting rooms, booking halls, offices, railway hotel and its once luxurious assembly rooms.

Redundant railway buildings have certainly made imaginative and extremely versatile spaces for cultural activities. In London, the old locomotive roundhouse at Chalk Farm, Camden Town, built in 1847 for the London and Birmingham Railway, reopened as a theatre venue in 1964. In spite of several changes in ownership since then, it has

The main hall of the Musée d'Orsay, Paris, created from the space formerly occupied by the train tracks and platforms. The station clock remains as a reminder of its former use.

become a well-known venue for independent and contemporary arts. Its cavernous, utilitarian, warehouse-like interior suits the performance of art that is modern, urban and progressive.[1] Though many disused rural railway stations have been converted for cultural uses, restaurants, rural craft galleries and visitor centres, the Musée d' Orsay is relatively unusual as a major city centre station transformed for purely cultural use. More commonly, the economic value of city centre development sites and the consequent commercial pressures result in redundant railway stations forming the basis for mixed-use projects involving retail, commercial and residential in addition to cultural developments. The large open-circulation areas of main-line railway stations often convert easily into distinctive semi-public open spaces suitable for malls, gallerias and open air entertainment.[2] In this context it may not be surprising to discover that one of the earliest models for the mainline railway station was the English coaching inn. As architectural historian C.L.V. Meeks shows, the public commercial circulation spaces of the coaching inn shaped the pattern by which trains drew up alongside a range of buildings given over to servicing the needs of passengers. This is a model which still serves purpose in many locations.[3]

North America provides the best and most numerous examples for the reuse of city stations. The formerly extensive network of inter-city passenger services were severely curtailed during the 1960s and '70s, resulting in proportionately more redundant large city station sites than elsewhere. St Louis Union Station, St Louis, Missouri, built in a substantial Romanesque style and once the world's largest and busiest railway station, provides a good example. Once handling 100,000 passengers a day in 1940, it had three trains a day in 1971, subsequent to the takeover of national rail passenger services by Amtrak. The last train left St Louis Union Station in 1978 and Amtrak trains are now located one block to the east in the multi-modal St

The Roundhouse, London. This former locomotive shed, built in 1847, was first opened as a theatre venue in 1964.

Interior of The Roundhouse; its cavernous, circular industrial space converts well into a venue for contemporary performance.

Designed in a Romanesque style by Theodore Link and opened in 1894, St Louis Union station was among the world's largest and busiest railway stations.

Interior view of St Louis Union station showing the vast vaulted train shed converted into shops and restaurants.

Louis Gateway Transportation Centre. In August 1985, after a $150 million renovation, Union Station was reopened with a 539-room hotel, shopping mall, restaurants and food court. Devoid of trains, the Union Station complex is now marketed as one of the city's major tourist attractions.[4]

The change to predominantly cultural/civic usage has sometimes resulted from the failure to find other commercial uses for passenger stations.[5] Cincinnati Museum Centre, situated in the former Union Terminal, houses museums, theatres, and a library. Opened in 1978 as the 'Land of OZ', a family entertainment and shopping complex, the venture substantially failed to draw shoppers back to downtown Cincinnati. Reopened in 1990, the monumental art deco structure now provides a home to six museums and an 'omnimax' film theatre.[6]

The railway station has clearly entered the fabric of modern life as an object of culture and functions as such in a multiplicity of ways: as architectural icon, museum and gallery, locus of civic pride, site of public and private memory, space for leisure and consumption and as a resource for urban reconstruction and regeneration. As such railway stations exemplify also the different registers within which we experience something identifiable as culture in the modern world, including high art, popular entertainment, lifestyle and its associated commodities. The Gare d'Orsay certainly demonstrates this complex cultural positioning. Built on a historically sensitive site opposite the Tuileries Gardens, within sight of the Louvre and the Île de la Cité, the station was a highly politicized project from its inception. Extending the line formerly terminating at the Paris–Orlean Railway's Gare d'Austerlitz, it was constructed on the site of the former Orsay Palace. Showcasing French transportation technology for the Universal Exposition of 1900, the extension adopted advanced electric traction from American practice partly to soothe fears concerning noise and pollution.[7] This enabled the architects to create a highly ornate

and totally enclosed train shed, greatly facilitating its later change of use to a museum. In the station itself passengers and luggage were separated and luggage handling mechanized in a manner reminiscent of that of a modern airport. Yet in spite of this, the station's short platforms rendered it out of date within ten years of its opening.[8] In 1935, a scheme was put forward to transform the station into an entertainment and sports centre. The structure of the building would be retained and new, uncompromisingly modern facades would be erected in front of the existing buildings. The scheme remained unrealized.

Used as a headquarters by the German occupation in the Second World War, it was also the point of return for many detainees and prisoners in 1945. On 15 May 1958, General de Gaulle chose the still splendid assembly rooms as the venue for a press conference announcing

The monumental Art Deco exterior of Cincinnati Union station, which was designed by the firm Fellheimer & Wagner and opened in 1933, enjoyed only a brief period of prosperity before the postwar decline in rail travel. It was opened as the Cincinnati Museum Centre in 1990.

his return to politics. Though built using the modern steel-framed methods, the heavily decorated turn-of-the-century Beaux Arts style of the hotel and assembly rooms, designed by Victor Laloux, became increasingly unfashionable. In the post-Second World War period this style came to epitomize the sort of comfortable complacent bourgeois taste despised by many who embraced the modernizing spirit of post-war reconstruction. Plans to demolish the building and replace it with an uncompromisingly modern hotel complex in the international style were only halted by fears relating to visual sensitivity in this historic site. In its semi-derelict state, the station housed charity collections, a car park and a temporary home for an auction house, had

Too small and cramped for expansion, the Gare d'Orsay enjoyed a chequered history. Used as a German headquarters during the Second World War, in this photo women welcome home French prisoners of war in 1945.

a wooden theatre building erected in the ticket hall and set the stage for a dystopian and dysfunctional society in both Orson Welles's adaptation of Franz Kafka's *The Trial* and Bernardo Bertolucci's film *The Conformist* (both 1962).[9] The station only regained status during the 1970s in reaction to the loss of important examples from the city's late nineteenth-century architectural heritage. Thus the steel structures and classical stone facades of the Gare d'Orsay have been variously lauded, reviled and tolerated, invested with hope and optimism and dismissed as reactionary and regressive. They are objects of culture not simply because of their design but because of the way they have accrued layers of social meanings from the part they play within the varied and dynamic social life of the city.

Mapping and mobilizing: products, journeys and consumers

A pivotal moment in the making of a modern consumer-driven world was the Great Exhibition, held from May to October 1851 in Hyde Park, London. Housed in Joseph Paxton's glass and iron Crystal Palace, the exhibition attracted over six million visitors, equivalent to one-third of the British population. The London & North Western Railway alone carried 775,000 excursionists.[10] Thomas Cook, the travel agent who had initiated the commercially organized excursion by rail in 1841, was responsible for taking 150,000 people to London. The Royal Commission responsible for organizing the exhibition, which included such eminent railway men as Brunel, Cubitt and Robert Stephenson, took early steps to get the agreement of the railway companies to run cheap excursions at a single fare for the return trip, with further reductions for distances over 100 miles. Subscription clubs were organized to enable the working classes to pay the fare by instalments, and in the event the third-class fare from Manchester

Poster advertising excursion trains to the Great Exhibition, 1851. Railways were instrumental in making the Exhibition a national experience while cheap travel to the site in London's Hyde Park helped create the journey as a commodity in itself.

and Leeds, normally over fifteen shillings single, was as low as five shillings return – a day's wages for a craftsman, two days' for an urban labourer and well within the reach of all but the very poor.[11] Thus railways were fundamental to making the Great Exhibition a collective national experience, uniting regions and classes as spectators to marvel at the productive genius of modern industry and the commercial might of Britain. At the same time, the consequences of providing cheap travel to the exhibition helped to create the journey as a commodity in itself as part of a packaged leisure experience in which travel, entertainment and affordability were connected together as a single entity for the consumer/traveller.

Railways certainly exemplify the ways in which commodities and cultures do indeed seem to have become fused together in modernity, a notion aptly captured in the term 'commodity culture'. Considered one way, railway journeys themselves might be thought of as a comparable experience to that of the department store. The bewilderment and sensory overload experienced by visitors to the Great Exhibition and some years later in brightly lit department stores is reflected also in the noise and confusion of the station platform.[12] The sense of gazing without focus at the abundance of goods on sale has some parallel in the habit of panoramic perception adopted by rail travellers to counter the effects of speed on the view from the train. Yet the train journey itself is both a cultural experience for the traveller and an item to be purchased, just as the railway station is both a cultural expression of corporate and civic ideals and a technology for selling travel and delivering that product to waiting passengers. Railways have come to define modern consumers in a wide variety of ways. It is little surprise for example, that Richard Sears, founder of the giant US mail order company Sears, Roebuck & Co., began his career as a railway station agent in Minnesota, where he sold timber, coal and – most importantly for his developing business – watches.[13] Sears, Roebuck pioneered 'scientific salesmanship' which in turn helped to define the modern consumer. At the same time they made the latest and most fashionable consumer goods available to people living in remote rural places, thus helping to build nationally based markets and orientate consumers increasingly towards national and international trends, patterns and styles in the purchase and consumption of goods and services.[14]

The London Underground map illustrates how the marketing of travel goes hand in hand with the making of markets for consumer goods as it facilitates new modes of consumption. It shows how the route network, rendered intelligible through simplification and abstraction, becomes the key to generating new markets for travel. Early underground maps frequently superimposed the railway lines running below ground on a map of the streets lying above. Given the early method of constructing underground railways by 'cut and cover', in which a channel was dug along streets and then covered over to reform the road surface above, it is perhaps not surprising that subsurface railways and the surface street pattern were imagined together.[15] However, producing railway maps that showed the density and complexity of urban commuter railways with topographical accuracy presented a number of problems. Maps became overcrowded towards the centre of cities, while lines that radiated out through suburbia and even deep into the countryside gave rise to maps of unwieldy size incorporating large areas of empty space and irrelevant information.[16]

For London, with the world's oldest and largest metropolitan railway network, the problems were compounded by the size and complexity of the system. In 1901 American railroad magnate Charles Tyson Yerkes (1837–1905), offered to provide financing for the construction of three underground railway lines on the condition that authorization was granted to extend them beyond the city limits into the outlying country. Establishing the Underground Electric Railway Company of London (UERL) in 1902, his decision to invest was underwritten by an expectation that the costs of electrification could be more than offset by profits generated through property development. In 1907 the UERL and the other transit companies agreed to coordinate their schedules and fares, to operate collectively under the trade name Underground and to produce a comprehensive map showing all their routes. Though some aspects of the now familiar London Tube map had been tried before or were already current practice, the revolutionary change in imagining journeys around the city came in 1931 with a diagrammatic sketch of the system drawn by an electrical draftsman,

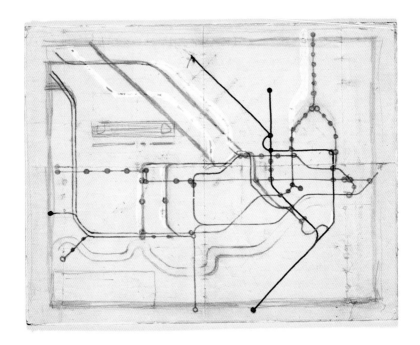

Harry Beck. Using the Central Line as a horizontal midpoint in the composition, Beck's schematic diagram simplified the geography of the system by only using lines which were either horizontal, vertical or at 45 degrees to the horizontal. All curves were either 45 or 90 degrees and stations were represented by either short tags for stops or open circles for connections. Within the city centre stations were spaced to provide clear room for name labels, while in the suburbs and beyond lines were significantly shortened by giving a nominal equidistant spacing to station stops. Each route was colour coded while a schematic representation of the River Thames allowed the traveller to orientate themselves in relation to the city.[17]

Initially sceptical of Beck's uncommissioned proposal, London Underground tentatively introduced it in 1933 and it immediately

An early sketch for the London Underground Map, 1931, by Harry Beck. The origins of his design in the conventions of drawing diagrams for electrical circuits can clearly be seen in this image.

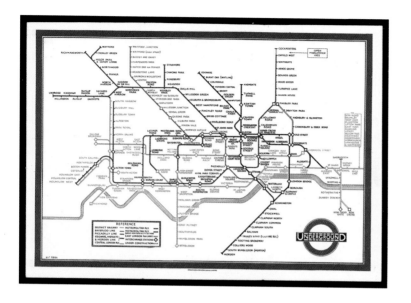

became popular. In January 1933, 750,000 copies were printed and another 100,000 were printed a month later. Though only paid five guineas for full copyright of his design, Beck continued to work on refinements until 1960 and his work is still clearly recognizable. Even more important, Beck's Tube map advanced and consolidated a lexicon of cartographic conventions which have become a world standard for comprehending and negotiating the urban environment. Metro maps from Moscow to Tokyo and Los Angeles to Kuala Lumpur draw on this model. Recently, Beck's map has itself become both an object of art and commerce. There are now numerous versions of the map ranging from advertisements for the Tate Gallery to government illustrations showing school exam results. In 1992 Simon Patterson adapted the official map by replacing the names of stations on specific lines with scientists, saints, philosophers, comedians, explorers, soccer players and other celebrated figures. The title *The Great Bear* refers to the constellation

The first definitive version of the London Underground Map, 1933, by Harry Beck. Its schematic design and legibility advanced a lexicon of cartographic conventions that has become a world standard.

Ursa Major, a punning reference to Patterson's own arrangement of 'stars'. Thus the map draws playfully on the ability of Beck's diagram to make abstract and apparently random connections. At the same time it demonstrates the ways in which the map itself can become a means to create new and novel classifications and modes of order.[18]

The major inspiration for Beck came from the electrical circuit diagrams with which he worked professionally. In such diagrams points of connection, intersection and sequence are most important. Decisions critical to the functioning of the circuit concern the direction and switching of flows rather than estimation of the distance travelled; the transmission of electricity is, after all, relatively insensitive to distance. Beck himself stated the decision to 'ignore geography' in the underground map simply 'seemed common sense. If you're going underground, why do you need bother about geography? It's not so important. Connections', he observed, 'are the thing'.[19]

Like the imposition of 'railway time', Beck's tube map may be seen as a clear manifestation of the process of standardization and abstraction central to the transformation of things into commodities and their subsequent placing within economic circulation. The way in which the map transforms specific geographical locations into equidistant points on a diagram privileging time over space is often thought to be a defining characteristic of modern capitalism. Many theoreticians interpret this as simply a process of abstraction and by implication alienation and estrangement from a 'real world' of familiar things set in a predictable, tangible and familiar geography. As design historian Jan Hadlaw says:

> The places illustrated in Beck's diagram exist purely in the context of their utility within the Underground system, as stations or interchanges. In representation, their function is, as Lefebvre describes, both standardized and specialized. And like the operations in the division of labor,

these spaces are profoundly interdependent, but only in the context of the operations of the Underground itself. Because the places on the various lines were no longer distinguishable from each other, the map's representational priority essentially shifted from the particularity of the places the Underground linked to the idea of the Underground as a conduit for the flow of trains and people, and ultimately, capital itself.[20]

In fact, as Hadlaw further points out, contemporary critics of the diagram insinuated that the real purpose was to deceive the commuting public into believing that the more remote stations were much closer than they really were![21] However, it would be wrong to interpret the London Tube map as simply an exercise in abstraction or indeed obfuscation. Though the map seems to make no distinction between city and suburb, town and country, when considered as part of the broader marketing strategy of London Underground, these distinctions were in fact critical to marketing the network. One only has to contrast the stark abstract graphic image of the Tube map with the richly pictorial advertising posters that UERL and later London Transport used to advertise the life in the suburban estates they developed along, for instance, the route of the Metropolitan Railway. Property development was after all a key objective in Yerkes's initial plan for unification.[22]

Having developed its first housing estate on its northern extension into the countryside of Middlesex and Buckinghamshire north of London at Pinner in 1903, the Metropolitan Railway Company formed the Metropolitan Railway Country Estates Company (MRCE) in 1919. Over a period of thirteen years, the MRCE built a series of new residential estates following the route of the Metropolitan line. Metroland has come to signify a particular form of the English suburban dream, with 'Tudorbethan' cottages with all modern conveniences in a safe and civilized rural idyll located conveniently for the shops. Advertising

images, often featuring cottage gardens and leafy country lanes, were in some respects as much an exercise in idealization as the Tube map itself. First and foremost, such apparently realistic imagery sold a seductive dream of convenient rural living rather than particular pieces of property.[23] An annual guide, *Metro-land*, published by the company from 1915 to 1932, insisted that Metroland existed primarily as an imaginative construction, 'a country with elastic borders that each visitor can draw for himself.'[24]

Though portrayed in a variety of novels, poems and songs, the work of Poet Laureate John Betjeman (1906–1984) is most strongly associated with this landscape of safe comfortable domesticated security. His poem 'The Metropolitan Railway, Baker Street Station Buffet'

This 1933 advertisement for housing in the London commuter suburb of Sudbury Hill sells the prospect of domestic bliss, safe and secure for children and defined by healthy outdoor activities such as gardening.

(published 1954) aptly expresses the interdependence of city and suburb, commerce and domesticity, progress and stability, hope and regret, forged in the imaginative space formed jointly by the idealized realism of Metroland and the universalized abstraction of the Tube map. The poem adopts the journey-biography metaphor familiar from chapter Three to tell a story about living in a fast, clean, efficient, modern, connected world animated by consumer products and material comfort. Given that inspiration for Beck's map came from an electrical circuit diagram it is significant that Betjeman begins with an image in which electric trains, the network of lines and the electric light (this latter a potent symbol of modern consumerism) are drawn together as a symbol of hope for the future.

Early Electric! With what radiant hope
Men formed this many-branched electrolier,
Twisted the flex around the iron rope
And let the dazzling vacuum globes hang clear . . .[25]

Set in the buffet (now long closed) at the Metropolitan Railway's Baker Street terminus, the poet imagines a couple meeting within the confines of its comfortable Arts and Crafts-inspired interior, ready to catch the train back to their home in the new commuter suburb of Ruislip; the husband after spending a day at his office in the financial heart of the city, the wife after shopping in the West End sales. Together, their journey from suburb to city and back represents the symbiosis of work and home that is central to modern consumerism. At work 'The thought of RUISLIP kept him warm inside',

While she, in arc-lit Oxford Street adrift,
Soared through the sales by safe hydraulic lift.[26]

Their forays into the city, he as breadwinner and she as homemaker, service a domestic ideal which provides both justification and antidote for the rush and excitement of city life. The economic transactions of the city both enable home life and act to maintain it as a separate sphere, a pure and uncommodified ideal. Thus, rather than simply creating an alienated no-place disconnected from real geographies, or indeed annihilating space by presenting the world primarily from the perspective of temporal distance, the Tube map seems to work in a rather more duplicitous manner. Suggesting connection on one level (lines and stations) and disguising it on another (actual topography of settlements and suburbs), the map conceals the intimate connection of work and home that enable city and suburb in tandem to become the separate foci for a modern consumerism charged with emotional investment and personal hope.

Locomotives and the aesthetic of the machine age

Under the auspices of Frank Pick (1878–1941) the London Tube map formed an important component of the corporate identity which gave the newly formed London Transport (formed 1933) a clearly identifiable unified modern brand image. For Pick good design meant fitness for purpose and the expression of practical needs but also a harmony signifying moral and spiritual order. Pick was influenced by the German architect Walter Gropius (1883–1969) and the school of modern design he founded, the Bauhaus (1919–33). Under Pick's influence London Transport was influenced by the most advanced design from Europe and North America. Buildings, graphics and fittings of all kinds, as well as vehicles, were redesigned. Historical styles were rejected and an image of modernity was sought in clear unembellished forms that derived their aesthetic value from a logical and efficient adaptation to function.[27] In many respects these design principles were a reaction against the sort of Victorian design encapsulated in the Great Exhibition. Whereas Victorian design often used the power of machinery to create elaborate and highly decorative items which mimicked the dexterity of hand-crafted goods, the new aesthetics which began to emerge from the end of the nineteenth century found its design principles in the machine itself, its efficiency, fitness for purpose and economy of effort. The former adopted the labour power of machines to create more things in existing styles; the latter adopted the labour power of machines as the basis for design itself. In both cases machines not only replaced human labour but transformed the making of things in ways that seemed to transcend human labour. Thus the products of consumer society frequently seem to have made themselves independently of human action. Objects for sale appear to take on a life and value independent of either the complexity of their making or their actual usefulness: historians and social scientists often interpret this as one of the defining characteristics of modernity.[28]

Where railways are concerned, the presence of work has always held a complex place in the marketing of travel. Labour has always been highly visible to the extent that what might be termed 'front of house' – porters, guards, ticket sales and catering staff – work within a highly public domain. In addition public and government interest in railway safety and financial probity has placed aspects of railway operation very firmly in the spotlight at certain times. However it has to be acknowledged that the vast majority of railway work takes place well outside the public gaze in offices, locomotive cabs, along the lineside and in engineering workshops and maintenance depots. Since the late nineteenth century the marketing of travel has balanced service and safety, which require active and visible intervention by workers, with relaxation, comfort and a sense of passenger autonomy, requiring the illusion of minimum staff presence. Thus railway workers have often been figured very carefully as obedient servants. In a parallel move the mechanical effort of the locomotive itself has become increasingly distanced from the experience of travel, through, for instance, technological developments in carriage design. Following the work of Sigfried Giedeon, Wolfgang Schivelbusch argues that the development of sprung coaches and soft, luxuriously upholstered seating were instrumental in the domestication of rail travel. Soft seating not only replicated the interior of the home, but also formed part of a set of technologies whereby travellers became increasingly distanced from the mechanical and human effort of running trains.[29]

During the 1930s steam locomotive design became a key point in articulating the relationship between human labour and machine power. It is certainly true that British steam locomotive design from the late nineteenth century onwards seems to have developed a balance of simplicity and elegance that disguised the physical effort of movement, producing a simplified and in a sense purified concept of locomotion. Such designs initially came to wider public attention in events such as the 'Race to the North' (1888 and again in 1895), staged between London and Scotland, where trains belonging to competing railway companies took the East and West Coast routes. Though apparently exemplifying the machine-age aesthetics of abstraction and simplification, ironically such designs were the result of long-standing craft-based production techniques. However, such British designs seem to encapsulate the essence of 'locomotiveness', resembling at one level the simplified outline of a toy train and at another the understated sophistication of engineering excellence.

Led by events in the US, it was not until the late 1920s that industrial design became an important and consciously articulated commercial issue for railway companies. This resulted in the development of streamlined locomotives and trains during the 1930s across many railway systems in North America, Europe and Japan. The Depression,

heralded by the Wall Street Crash of 1929, hit the railroads harder than many segments of the economy. In addition, by 1930 the automobile had captured three-quarters of the traffic between US cities, while buses enjoyed one-fifth of the remainder. Between 1920 and 1933 the annual number of passenger miles travelled by rail in the USA fell from 47 billion to sixteen billion.[30] Passenger operations had to be made attractive to a public used to increasing levels of comfort, refinement and style in the spheres of domesticity and leisure. Railroad companies strove to offer their customers new standards of luxury and service and, above all, modernity and efficiency. In this context industrial designers became increasingly involved with remaking the form, experience and image of rail travel in line with the aspirations and expectations of the age. Yet it is not without significance that in his pioneering book on the aesthetics of streamlined locomotive design, *Locomotive* (1937), the industrial designer Raymond Loewy (1893–1986) stressed the influence of British locomotive design on his

A photograph taken in the locomotive erecting shops of Vulcan Foundry, Manchester, 1950. The process of assembling locomotives individually by hand remained little changed from the 1850s. A fast-diminishing legacy of empire, these locomotives were under construction for export.

own attempts to simplify, rationalize and modernize the outline of the steam locomotive.[31]

Early experiments with streamlining were pitched at transforming the train using aeronautic and automotive technology. Egmont Arens's 1931 article 'The Train of Tomorrow' outlined plans for a new lightweight aluminium alloy diesel-powered train drawing on automobile and aircraft technology. However it was the publication of *Horizons* by Norman Bel Geddes (1893–1958) in 1932 that attracted serious attention from the railroads. His proposed steam train would bear no resemblance to its predecessors. A smooth aluminium shell enclosed the chimney (US smokestack), pipes, boiler and headlight. Metal shutters covered driving wheels and trucks. A smooth, elastic material would cover openings between coaches. The train would become a single tube with gently rounded sides and roof, a bulging front and a tapered rear. Soon after publication of his design, both the Union Pacific and the Burlington railroad companies, each under new management, began planning lightweight streamliners. Following Arens's model, the companies reached similar solutions, a three-car train with articulated bogie trucks weighing roughly the same as a single Pullman car. Wind-tunnel tests suggested that at maximum speed they would halve the amount of energy required by a steam locomotive with two standard coaches for overcoming wind resistance.[32]

Yet despite innumerable technological innovations, the public responded to the appearance of speed rather than the substance of technological efficiency gains.[33] Thus streamlining as a design strategy was also intimately bound up with both the proliferation of consumer goods and the marketing of leisure and domestic lifestyles and cultures. The career of Raymond Loewy exemplifies this. After emigrating from France in 1919, work as a fashion illustrator for *Vogue* and *Harper's Bazaar* was followed by design and advertising work for Saks and other Fifth Avenue stores. In 1929 he received his first industrial design commission: to modernize the appearance of a duplicating machine by Gestetner.[34] Further commissions followed, including work for Westinghouse and the Hupp Motor Company and styling the Coldspot refrigerator for Sears-Roebuck in 1934. Considered something of a self-publicist, Loewy has developed a subsequent reputation amongst design historians for being market-orientated and consumer conscious. Though Loewy's school education gave him an insight into engineering practice, he never undertook professional training. His style was informed by the sophisticated, elegant domesticity developed in his advertising work. Certainly, his landmark work

Raymond Loewy liked to pose with examples of his designs for streamlined steam locomotives, such as the Pennsylvania S1 class locomotive, pictured here in 1936. They exemplify his aesthetic principles in which form was as important as function in the marketing of distinctive commodities.

for Gestetner and the Coldspot refrigerator succeeded by transforming these objects from machines into desirable items of furniture.[35]

Raymond Loewy's most important commissions for the Pennsylvania Rail Road (PRR) were for the design of steam locomotives. The first of these was a special version of the standard K4 Pacific locomotive redesigned to compete with the streamlined locomotives other railroads were already using. Previous streamlined engines had used a shroud form, enveloping the whole engine. Loewy wanted to use the torpedo shape for K4-S with a pointed cylinder over the boiler and a curved skirt over the front and wheels, resembling a torpedo resting in its cradle. In *Locomotive* he claimed that the wind tunnel tests had shown the shroud form less effective at deflecting smoke from the driving cab, so reducing visibility.[36] However as Wilson shows in his study of Canadian National Railway's CN6400, the wedge-shaped shrouded front could be demonstrably better at dispersing smoke than other forms of streamlining, such as the torpedo. So it is likely that style and visual impact were determining factors. The profile of the locomotive and tender was simply dramatic, and in motion the highlighted strips and rails on the front conveyed an immediate expression of speed. The engine went into service on 3 March 1936. Painted a dark bronze with silver and gold lettering, it pulled the *Broadway Limited* between Chicago and Fort Wayne. Loewy also designed the coach interiors in an Art Deco style reflecting the sophisticated Jazz Age decor drawn from Loewy's experience in designing the interiors for department stores.[37]

Though the early lightweight streamlined diesel multiple units, such as the Burlington Zephyr and indeed Loewy's earlier GG-1 electric locomotive (PRR), produced real design innovation, streamlining steam locomotives was always a matter of style over substance. Adding streamlined cladding to a standard locomotive and tender could add five tons to the weight before any savings in aerodynamic

efficiency were earned.[38] Following the example popularized by Loewy, companies often refurbished older locomotives with tons of sheathing, enclosing boiler, pipes and chimney in a smooth shell. Such redesigned locomotives attracted passengers, but any gain in aerodynamic efficiency was offset by the added weight. In the years of uncertainty which followed the Wall Street Crash of 1929, streamlined trains stimulated public faith in a future fuelled by technological innovation. During 1934 fifteen million people in the United States came out to witness the passing of the Burlington Zephyr and the Union Pacific M-10,000 as they made promotional tours. Streamlined trains played prominent roles at both the Chicago Century of Progress Exposition of 1934–5 and the New York World's Fair of 1939–40, where their

Visitors line up to view the Burlington Zephyr at the Century of Progress International Exposition (Chicago World's Fair), 1934. The diesel-powered, stainless-steel train set a speed record on 26 May 1934, completing the so-called 'Dawn to Dusk Dash' between Denver, Colorado, and Chicago in slightly over 13 hours.

physical presence provided dramatic evidence of American's faith in progress through technology.[39] Simplifying the form of the locomotive, hiding the moving parts and their control mechanisms to emphasise a bold overall outline, translated the effort of locomotion and the work and labour power associated with this into a stylized ideal. This visual language ordered, controlled and domesticated the power of the locomotive and figured this symbolically as both speed in the service of comfort and luxury and as the promise of a readily understandable and widely attainable better tomorrow. The extent to which the streamlining craze penetrated the public imagination is exemplified by its impact on popular culture and cultural ephemera such as movies, toys, novelties and advertising. *The Silver Streak*, a film released by RKO late in 1934, starred the Zephyr itself, racing against time to deliver an iron lung from Chicago to the Boulder Dam. The magazine *Fortune* described streamlining as 'the biggest thing that has happened to the toy-train industry for decades'.[40]

Writing in 1934 as the craze for streamlining was taking hold, Lewis Mumford was a trenchant critic of commercially orientated industrial designers such as Loewy. *Technics and Civilisation* sets out a critical but optimistic tone for technology and examines the relationships between technology, industrialization and society in terms of three historical periods, the eotechnic (1000–1800), the paleotechnic (*c.* 1800–1900) and the neotechnic (*c.* 1900–1930). The paleotechnic phase he describes as a necessary but 'disastrous interlude' marked by 'growth and multiplication of machines' accompanied by exploitation of workers, factory towns that bred disease and alienation, air and water pollution, and – most significant for designers – ugly machine products. The developing neotechnic phase heralds clean electric power, light alloys, synthetics and automation. The contrast between paleotechnic and neotechnic can be characterized as that between labour-intensive and labour-saving technologies, between fussy decoration and clean, simple outlines.[41] Combining elements of both a nineteenth-century industrial aesthetic and a twentieth-century machine aesthetic, it is not difficult to see how the railway as a technology and the steam locomotive in particular fit into Mumford's schema, sitting on the cusp of his paleotechnic and neotechnic phases. In this context the steam locomotive expresses a complex and contradictory relationship with work, energy and effort. It expresses the positive dimensions of labour through its associations with the morally fulfilling social experience of craft design, construction and operation. At the same time, the locomotive also forms part of a machine ensemble that is mass-producing mechanized travel on an unprecedented scale, resulting in an often exploited labour force working very long hours in difficult and dangerous conditions. Yet the marketing of travel and the simplifications and compromises wrought through craft-based practices and customs ironically served to disguise the negative associations of industrial labour behind a simplified facade which translated physical effort into abstract and heroic form. Simultaneously disguising and expressing work, the steam locomotive thus became both an object of nostalgia for the past and hope for the future. It is significant that at the very moment that streamlining propelled the express steam locomotive into the limelight as a symbol of technological optimism, the Electro-Motive Division of General Motors began constructing a $5 million plant to mass-produce complete diesel locomotives (1935). By 1941 GM was producing 48 anonymous and virtually identical box-shaped locomotives a month for railroads across the US and beyond.[42]

Steam locomotives and the nostalgia for progress

Raymond Loewy was often photographed with the K4-S locomotive he designed for the PRR, which fulfilled what he called 'a childhood dream'. In spite of his success elsewhere, this engine was clearly for him a very major design, crowning the second decade of his life in America. Loewy had a lifelong fascination with railways which can be seen in the locomotive sketches he made during his youth. In this respect Loewy was little different from generations of boys who had grown up aspiring to own a miniature steam locomotive of their own and dreaming of eventually being able to drive the real thing. The desire to possess and display images and models of steam locomotives seems to be almost as old as the steam engine itself. There is considerable evidence that professional railway workers, particularly engineers and locomotive crew, were central to establishing the locomotive as an object of pride and possession, personalizing, naming, polishing and decorating the locomotives to which they were assigned. From the beginnings of railway trade unionism in the late nineteenth century, locomotives figured prominently on union banners and insignia, indicating their central place in the formation of work-based identity.[43] However, as the example of streamlining suggests, the locomotive also became a focus for wider public imaginings of the physical presence and transformative potential of railways. The novelty value of early manifestations of steam railway locomotive technology made an early connection between technological innovation and entertainment. Richard Trevithick's 'Catch-me-who-can', for example, ran on a demonstration circular track at a 'steam circus' established in Euston Square, London during the summer of 1808.[44] Toy steam locomotives, known as 'dribblers' ('Birmingham dribblers' in the UK) because of the trail of boiling water and spirit fuel they left in their wake, had been around since the 1840s. By the end of the nineteenth century German and American toy manufacturers were producing quite extensive and relatively sophisticated toy train systems including sidings, signals stations and depots.[45] In Britain images of trains and especially locomotives began to circulate on postcards and in specialist magazines for the amateur enthusiast from the 1890s.[46]

THE HORNBY CLOCKWORK TRAIN

With the introduction of this toy railway system commences a new era in clockwork train construction. Engine, tender and trucks are put together on the Meccano principle. The whole system is built up from standard units, and if one of the parts is lost or damaged, a new part may be purchased and fitted by the user. The engines and trucks are supplied in complete outfits ready built up for instant use, but much pleasure can be derived from taking them all to pieces, and refashioning them. The standardisation is the same as in the Meccano system, and the Hornby train may be looked upon as a Meccano model of an altogether new and delightful type.

The clockwork mechanism is of the finest quality, all the gears being accurately cut, ensuring smooth running. One size only, Gauge 0, in three different colours, to represent the London and North-Western, Midland, and Great Western Railway systems. Each set contains Engine, Tender and one Truck, set of Rails, including a circle and two straights. The engine is fitted with reversing gear, brakes, and regulators.

Complete set in strong attractive box ... ... 27/6 each.

Engines ... ... 17/6 each. | Trucks ... ... 4/6 each.
Tenders ... ... 4/6 ,, | Rails, straight or curved 9/- per doz.

TIN PRINTED CLOCKWORK TRAINS

Strongly built, with reliable clockwork mechanism. One size only, Gauge 0. Each set contains Engine, Tender, and two Passenger Cars, printed in close imitation of the colours of the railway companies' rolling stock, with set of Rails, including a circle and two straights. In London and North-Western, Midland, and Great Northern colours. The engines are fitted with reversing gear, brakes, and regulators.

Complete set, well boxed ... ... 22/6 each.

Engines ... ... 14/- each. Carriages ... ... 2/- each.
Tenders ... ... 2/- ,, Rails, straight or curved 9/- per doz.

VERTICAL STEAM ENGINE

A finely finished steam engine, superior workmanship; each one carefully tested. Oxidised brass boiler; stationary cylinder, and eccentric reversing gear; whistle, spring safety valve, etc., cast base; fittings nickelled and finely finished. Dimensions of boiler, 2¼in. diameter by 3½in. long.

Price, 27/6 each.

This device is printed or stamped on all the toys described here, and it indicates that they have been manufactured by Meccano Ltd. It is a guarantee of quality and workmanship.

Though there is evidence for significant popular interest in railways and locomotives in particular dating back into the late nineteenth century, one has to look to the interwar period, as historian I. Carter suggests, in order to find recognizable foundations for the growth in amateur railway enthusiasm.[47] Founded in Cheltenham Spa in 1927, the organization which became the Railway Travel and Correspondence Society (RCTS) in 1928 specialized in supporting enthusiasts' interest in the contemporary railway scene through rail tours for its members and its journal *The Railway Observer* (established 1929).[48] In the US the National Railway Historical Society (NRHS) was founded

Earliest known Hornby Toy Trains advertisement. Toy trains caricature the locomotive by simplifying its outline.

in 1935 from a merger of local rail-fan clubs in Lancaster, Pennsylvania, Philadelphia, Trenton, New Jersey, and New York City. Both the NRHS and the RCTS combined national organization with a network of regional branches.[49] The interwar years were marked by a series of events across Europe and North America celebrating railway centenaries, starting with that of the Stockton and Darlington Railway in England during 1925. Such events both brought railways to public attention and provoked a period of reflection on a hundred years of achievement. This was rendered more poignant by the economic problems and consequent rationalization plans which beset many railway systems in the aftermath of the First World War.

Throughout this and earlier periods of railway enthusiasm a specific interest in locomotives remains a constant factor. In many respects, for non-professionals the locomotive condenses the meanings of the railway into one highly legible and powerful symbol. As the source of power for railway locomotion, its iconic profile, biomorphic energy (see chapter One), public visibility, physical presence and apparent technological comprehensibility separate it – however unjustifiably – from other pieces of technology as *the* fundamental constituent of railway operation. As such it was in the period following the Second World War that the steam locomotive took on an increasingly particular significance as modernization schemes and railway closures gathered pace around the world. It was during this period, for instance, that the remarkable craze for trainspotting took hold in the UK.[50] In this context the steam locomotive became a highly symbolic marker for the passing of a familiar industrialized world. Its place as an icon of technology on the cusp of Mumford's paleotechnic and neotechnic eras enabled it to carry a multifaceted moral charge. On the one hand its disappearance expressed a sense of loss engendered by the passing of a comfortable, stable social world of heroic industrial labour. On the other its withdrawal undermined the promise of a new modernity delivered via the 'humanized' understandable and acceptable technological means of the railway. Both these aspects of steam locomotives' cultural meaning are evident in the work of photographer O. Winston Link (1914–2001).

Link became a commercial photographer after graduating as a civil engineer from the Polytechnic Institute of Brooklyn in 1937. After the Second World War he became an independent, freelance photographer specializing in industrial subjects.[51] In late January 1955 Link went to Staunton, Virginia, on assignment. With a lifelong passion for steam, and aware that the Norfolk & Western Railway (N&W) passed nearby, he went to check it out. What he found was the last wholly steam-operated mainline (Class 1) network in the US. The N&W was one of the US's most important coal-hauling lines, serving the Appalachian coalfields spanning the Virginias and into Ohio. It had developed steam-locomotive technology to a high point of refinement. Designs with high-capacity boilers, roller bearings on all wheels, mechanized fuel feed and lubrication systems were built at the company's vast workshops at its headquarters in Roanoke, Virginia.[52] Yet in spite of its proud record developing advanced steam locomotive technology, even the N&W could not resist the drive for efficiency and cost-cutting. On 29 May 1955 the N&W announced its first conversion to diesel. Link gained the cooperation of the N&W management and set out to document in photographs the end of the steam era. He made around twenty visits to Virginia, the last in 1960, the year the railroad completed its transition to diesel. By this time he had accumulated 2,400 photographic negatives.[53] In addition to the meticulous documentation of his photographs in notebooks, Link also made sound recordings of the trains, which he issued on a set of six LPs between 1957 and 1977 under the overall title *Sounds of Steam Railroading*.

The major foci of Link's interest were the large modern streamlined passenger and heavy freight locomotives which made the N&W such a distinctive railroad. In one sense this might suggest that his overall approach was little different to many rail enthusiasts taking photographs in the US, the UK and elsewhere. He, like they, were energized to document the last years of the steam railway, to record its highways and byways before they disappeared for ever. Yet even compared with the most highly regarded railway photographers of this period, much of Link's work was highly individual in both style and content. In this regard it drew significantly on his professional work in carefully staged advertising photography. Link was highly critical of what he called 'the wedge shot', an undramatic three-quarter view of a train made by a photographer standing at a 30- to 45-degree angle to the tracks. In these images, so familiar to railway enthusiasts worldwide, the front and side of the locomotive are most prominent, whilst the rest of the train tapers to a distant vanishing point. Deriding these as 'hard ware shots' Link believed that the locomotive and train should be seen in context. Thus he would 'add people, work with the lighting, and position the camera next to signal lights on buildings to avoid the dreaded wedge'.[54]

Many of Link's images were taken during the hours of darkness and demonstrate a sense of theatre rarely paralleled in railway photography or elsewhere. Quoted as saying 'I can't move the sun – and it's always in the wrong place – and I can't even move the tracks, so I had to create my own environment through lighting', Link developed his own system of lighting for large-scale outdoor photography using a power supply which he designed and built himself. This could fire 60 flashbulbs at once while also tripping the shutters of three cameras, all perfectly synchronized together. Together these created what Garver has called a 'theatre of light, controlled and manipulated by the photographer'.[55] Images showing express trains rushing across level crossings, heavy freights paused for a signal check and locomotives under repair in the shops adopt genres long familiar in railway photography. Some of his moody daytime scenes show trains enveloped in misty autumnal atmosphere reminiscent of Alfred Stieglitz's *The Hand of Man* (1902).[56] However, as he and his assistants returned time and again to document the line, staying locally and engaging help and assistance from both rail workers and local people, he increasingly turned his attention towards the workers, buildings and communities along the route. Thus his most distinctive and innovative railroad images place locomotives within uncompromisingly social settings. Perhaps most well known is the image entitled *At the Laeger Drive-In Theater, Willie Allen and Dorothy Christian appear impervious to 'Hot Shot' merchandise on the move* (1956). This picture shows cars lined up at a drive-in movie. Whilst the audience watch a jet plane scream across the screen, a large A-Class locomotive thunders past with a fast freight train. Its massive presence in the background remains completely unnoticed by the filmgoers. Apparently juxtaposing three ages of transport technology – future (jet plane), present (automobile) and past (steam train) – the train is actually one of a new generation of high-speed freight services rather than an antiquated relic of the past. Certainly, the juxtaposition of transport modes is entirely conscious, because the image of the jet plane was collaged onto the photograph in the dark room.[57]

Many images taken in mountainous, remote and 'picturesque' locations accentuate the dominant role of the railway within local economy and society. Link's photographs give locomotives a substantial presence within a range of quotidian and domestic scenes: children play in the river as a train rumbles slowly overhead; old folks sit on the porch totally oblivious to the streamlined express passing just behind the hedge; local residents shop and exchange gossip in the local store while in the background a locomotive can be seen at rest just outside the store window. Most characteristic is an image showing the living room of Hester Fringer's home near Lithia, Virginia. In

an evening scene of apparent domestic tranquility, a woman (Hester Fringer's daughter) reclines in a comfortable chair as the family pets sleep on the mat at her feet. Her young son waves to a train passing close by, illuminated through the open curtains of the picture window. These images and this photograph in particular seem to be both unsettling and reassuring. There are echoes here of the Andrew Melrose's *Star of Empire* (see chapter One), in which the locomotive is a comforting presence in the darkness, protecting homes and communities from the encroaching wilderness. There are also reminders of De Chirico's

At the Laeger Drive-In Theater, Willie Allen and Dorothy Christian appear impervious to 'Hot Shot' merchandise on the move, photograph by Winston Link, 1956. The image combines three generations of travel representing past, present and future.

urban scenes discussed in chapter Three, where the train's marginal presence reminds us of the disturbing and fugitive experience of time as loss or lack. However, it is reassuring to view these pictures in the knowledge that many of the people who feature in Link's domestic scenes are connected to the railroad in one way or another. It is as if these are stills from a movie or perhaps the type of cameo or diorama scene familiar on model railways. In this context, the social relationships carefully organized and staged by Link and frozen in time by the extensive use of flash photography are brought to life by the

Hester Fringer's House near Lithia, Virginia, photograph by Winston Link, 1955. The calm of the domestic interior contrasts uneasily with the massive steam train passing close by outside.

passing presence of the train. Interpreted in this way, the looming presence of the locomotive is a vital life force animating the community. Yet what remains unsettling is the uncanny sense of silence that some of these images suggest irrespective of the visual tumult, the billowing clouds of smoke and steam. In Hester Fringer's living room, the woman sits impassively, the dog continues to lie quietly and the china remains steady in its cabinet, even as the child waves to the passing train. In the photograph of Mr and Mrs Charles W. Lugar, conversation on the porch continues uninterrupted even though the express bears down at full speed. There seems to be a separation between the technological and social subjects as if these two elements exist in different temporalities. Maybe the locomotive is merely a spectral presence, the focus for the collective memory of a past way of life. At the very least, the apparently asynchronous qualities of these photographs suggest a fleeting vulnerability even in the moment of being frozen for posterity.

Link's methods of picture making, designed to freeze the moment and control image content, simplify, abstract and objectify a changing world, trapping, as T. H. Garver puts it, 'man and machine out of time'.[58] Thus Link employs the locomotive to create an idealized past in ways which have much in common with the industrial designers who reshaped the locomotive in streamlined form to create an idealized future. In both instances, reimagining the locomotive as a work of art becomes the starting point for this creative process. It may be fitting therefore that the museum dedicated to the work of O. Winston Link is situated in the former N&W passenger railway station at Roanoke, which was rebuilt in 1949 to designs by Raymond Loewy in a modern streamlined style. Among its claims to fame, Loewy's station pioneered the use of escalators in railroad stations to smooth the flow of passengers through the terminal, nearly fifty years after conveyors had been used to move baggage at the Gare d'Orsay. Opened in 2004 and comprising a 15,000 square foot gallery space, the museum includes much of the archival material related to Link's five-year project on the N&W. More recently the Link Museum has been joined by a gallery devoted to the life and work of Raymond Loewy; 'Raymond Loewy: Designer for a Modern Era'.[59] Thus Roanoke passenger station has become an art gallery dedicated to two men who did much to refigure the railway locomotive as an art form.

The Euston 'Arch', St Pancras Station and the International Style

Popular interest in locomotives during the drive for railway modernization often resulted in neglect of other elements of the railway's technological system. Railway stations are prime illustrations of this. As the examples beginning this chapter suggest, the drive to keep some historic railway architecture came considerably later than that to preserve locomotives. Unlike locomotives, which may only have value as scrap metal, stations are fixed assets with considerable residual value either when adapted to fit the changing needs of the railway or as real estate beyond their useful life as part of the railway system. Locomotives are highly public symbols of the railway's private working environment; their cultural meanings are refined, reinforced and consolidated by our substantially distanced engagement with them across the tracks, beyond the edge of the platform or on the other side of the fence as they race past. In contrast, stations (as we saw in chapter Three) are relatively open semi-public spaces that draw in, juxtapose and refract a multiplicity of individuals, social groups, economic circulations and transactions. Consequently they are quite porous cultural entities. Thus, as we saw with the example of the Gare d'Orsay, stations are inherently contested and many-layered cultural phenomena. Their physical presence, tied to everyday lives and landscapes beyond the railway, ensures that there is much at stake when preserving a building or structure. Thus serious interest in preserving the built environment of railway heritage did not take hold in the UK until the 1960s. It gained momentum through the 1970s, encouraged by a sense of loss generated from the experience of economic crisis, deindustrialization and a widespread feeling that post-Second World War architecture and planning had not produced the social benefits it had promised.[60] In North America the conservation of railway buildings had to await the vogue for culture-led urban renewal based around designated 'historic' and 'cultural' quarters that began to gain momentum during the 1980s. In mainland Europe the legacy of post-Second World War reconstruction in which much railway infrastructure was destroyed often pre-empted debates concerning industrial heritage. In Africa, Asia and South America, station buildings and passenger railways more generally often bore the symbolic legacy of colonialism and were cast aside along with other trappings of the past.[61]

The campaign (1960–61) to save the so-called Euston 'Arch' is often regarded as a turning point in the battle between modernizers and preservationists concerned with Britain's industrial heritage.[62] Though the campaign failed it did galvanize the preservationist movement, particularly in the guise of the Victorian Society (founded in 1958) and its first secretary and vice-president, the poet John (later Sir John) Betjeman. When in 1966 plans were announced to review the future of London's St Pancras station together with that of neighbouring King's Cross, John Betjeman and the Victorian Society were again on hand to marshal the protests. Betjeman had a lifelong affection for both railways and architecture and had been deputy editor of the *Architectural Review* between 1930 and 1935.[63] Though sometimes characterized as merely conservative, reactionary and anti-modern in his architectural tastes, Betjeman had certainly celebrated modernity and modern lifestyles in works such as his poem 'The

Metropolitan Railway, Baker Street Station Buffet'.[64] His fascination with the familiar and everyday no less than the byways of English landscape are reflected in his poetic celebration of the unguarded, unselfconscious moments of English middle-class life. As such his criticisms of modern architecture, particularly that in the international style, are more concerned with building for a human scale and in sympathy with location and history, memory and belonging than with any outright rejection of the new. His portrayal of the new London suburbs of Metroland is testimony to this.

St Pancras Station itself was certainly the most spectacular of London stations and a highly distinctive landmark in the city. Opened in 1868 as the London terminus of the Midland Railway, the station combined what was at the time the largest single-span cast-iron and steel roof in the world measuring 74 m (243 ft) span, by 213 m (700 ft) long and about 30 m (100 ft) high, with a grand hotel and offices in an ornate Gothic Revival style (completed 1873) by George Gilbert Scott (1811–1878).

Interim reports on the modernization of St Pancras suggested that King's Cross would be levelled in favour of a combined new station. In this case William Barlow's (1812–1902) train shed might be allowed to remain as an exhibition hall or sports centre. Alternately the St Pancras train shed might be capable of accommodating the trains from King's Cross in conjunction with a new concourse building to be erected on the site of the Midland Grand Hotel. It is ironic that the fortunes of St Pancras and its neighbour King's Cross were linked so closely in these proposals. As Bradbury shows, the architectural qualities of both stations were contrasted in debates between champions of modernism and preservation.[65] The architecture of King's Cross suggested an unadorned practicality attributed to rational engineering practice and providing historical lineage for modernist functionalism. However, opinion was divided regarding St Pancras.

Barlow's train shed had a clear design pedigree dating back to the Crystal Palace and the Great Exhibition of 1851 and was given status as an example of engineering excellence. However, Scott's hotel was roundly dismissed as an example of gross and grotesque Victorian bad taste. Even the way in which Scott's design sat slightly apart on the site from Barlow's train shed was criticized because it suggested that engineering science (represented by the iron canopy) and decorative art (represented by the Gothic hotel) were seen by Victorians as mutually distinct and incompatible. Support for St Pancras station from architectural critics was at best half-hearted. Robert Furneaux Jordan wrote in 1969 that Scott's hotel was 'the culminating masterpiece of its epoch' only in that '[it] combines all the qualities of the [eighteen-] sixties: stylistic display and solid philistinism'.[66]

St Pancras station, London, 1927, showing the Gothic extravagance of the luxury Midland Grand Hotel, Euston Road, designed by Sir George Gilbert Scott and completed in 1876.

It was evident that arguments based on architectural merit alone were not going to sway either an architectural establishment firmly dedicated to the aesthetics of international style modernism or a government committed to economic, social and technological modernization. These arguments were played out in the letters pages of *The Times* newspaper in the weeks subsequent to the publication of the redevelopment proposals. As Bradle shows, one alternative approach was voiced by the photographer, architectural historian and friend of John Betjeman, Eric de Maré. He argued that St Pancras was itself now part of history, a precious embodiment of communal memory. Another correspondent recollected sheltering in the station from air raids in the company of an elderly London County Council clerk of works, who declared the hotel the finest example of the bricklayer's craft in existence.[67] Both writers drew on the moral virtue of the building, not as an exemplar for logical planning and rational behaviour or aesthetic merit, but as a product of human labour, craftwork and skill, a repository of human values and memories. Knowingly or

King's Cross Station, London, built to the designs of Lewis Cubitt in 1852 as the terminus of the Great Northern Railway. The relatively unadorned functional design of its facade contrasts strongly with neighbouring St Pancras.

not, this formulation was reminiscent of that Victorian champion of Gothic architecture, John Ruskin. Gathering these sentiments together at a time when Britain's place in the world was becoming increasingly uncertain, the Victorian Society built its argument in favour of preservation around issues of heritage and national identity, placing the building within a deeper historical context. St Pancras should be preserved in its entirety, epitomizing 'the greatest period of British history', when the nation was at its zenith of influence and power.[68] Represented in these terms, St Pancras was no longer an eclectic Victorian architectural confection, or an aesthetic monstrosity demonstrating nouveau riche bad taste. Rather it was a poignant reminder of former glories, of times full of confidence and optimism. On the second of November 1967 St Pancras was added to the national list of protected buildings at Grade I, the highest level, placing it in the same category as Westminster Abbey, St Paul's Cathedral or Windsor Castle.[69]

In November 2007 St Pancras became the London terminal for high-speed Eurostar services to Paris, Brussels and continental Europe via the new high-speed rail link to Dover and the Channel tunnel. The historic hotel and train shed, repaired, restored and adapted to their new use, formed the focal point for a major national investment in rail travel and for the redevelopment of the run-down urban areas around St Pancras and King's Cross. Today train services to those areas of the East and North Midlands traditionally served from St Pancras are displaced to a new part of the station while sleek, streamlined, silver, electric high-speed multiple units belonging to Eurostar glide away from under the cavernous roof of Barlow's vast arched train shed. Running diagonally under the station are newly constructed interchange platforms for the upgraded Thameslink line, giving direct rail access across London and between the Midlands and the south coast. Scott's Gothic Revival building will once again serve its original function as a luxury hotel while the top-most rooms will be converted for high-status loft living. The undercroft, supporting the railway's elevated approach to the city over the Regent's Canal and originally designed to store ales and beers brought to London from the Midlands, now hosts an airport-like customs, security and departure lounge. Alongside these facilities, where the platform level has been cut through, creating an impressive atrium open to spectacular views of the pale blue train shed, a mall of shops, cafes and restaurants provide an upmarket ambience for consumers and travellers alike.[70]

St Pancras is testimony to the resurgence in rail travel in Britain, Europe and many other parts of the world which has taken place over the past fifteen years. It is also evidence of the success of aircraft-style streamlined intercity travel originally envisioned in the depression of the 1930s and brought to fruition with innovations in high-speed travel developed from the 1960s, such as the Japanese Shinkansen and the French TGV. The redevelopment demonstrates the current vogue for a fusion of travel, leisure and shopping typified by the modern airport and arguably presaged in attempts by Raymond Loewy and others to bring high-street fashion and domestic design to transport engineering. What Loewy and others may not have foreseen was that such a culture of consumption would be carried not by a smooth, rational, convenient modern construction but in a compromised, adapted, eclectic, rambling, Gothic folly. In this respect St Pancras gives justification to the vision and determination of preservationists such as John Betjeman and the Victorian Society. Yet many who argued for the 'preservation' of St Pancras may never have imagined such an active and interventionist transformation of the building and its site. In many respects it can be argued that the redevelopment is wholly true to the history and ethos of the original buildings. The historical conjunction of rational engineering and conspicuous display is reflected in the station's new status as a fitting departure point between England's capital city and mainland Europe. Yet for all the sympathy in design the building has not been preserved like a cathedral or palace but has been radically transformed and adapted for the twenty-first century.

In this respect St Pancras – like so many contemporary station developments, whether new build or refurbishment – is more than the gateway to the city described by Wolfgang Schivelbusch. Perhaps St Pancras exemplifies something new in the way railway stations have become 'significant urban locations' in themselves.[71] There is evidence for this in the resurgence of railway station architecture as a distinctive art form freed from the constraints of functionalism and able to work with the symbolism of styles and engineering structures suggested by the multiplicity of historical examples. One key to this is of course renewed investment in railway infrastructure commensurate with the resurgence in traffic. However, one might also argue that as locomotives morph into power cars for multiple units increasingly indistinguishable from other less heroic forms of rolling stock, so the station itself comes to carry the symbolic weight of the railway as a humanized technology. Certainly the contrast between the engineering rationality of Barlow's train shed and the luxury exuberance of Scott's Midland Hotel echoes something of the tension between the labour-intensive and labour-saving technologies that situated the steam locomotive between Mumford's paleotechnic and neotechnic eras. These ideas are certainly present in the arguments between modernizers and preservationists during the 1960s that invoked concepts of craftwork, engineering rationality, decoration and functionalism to both damn and defend the station. Perhaps the evident popularity of the statue to John Betjeman, hand on hat, staring in wonder at the newly painted roof, suggests our continued need to connect the railway as a technology with progress on a human scale. Perhaps also relevant is the conception of 'terminal' present in the work of architectural critic Martin Pawley (1939–2008) and deriving both from the transport hub

Shoppers browse the new stores and cafes of the St Pancras undercroft, while beneath the vast single-span train shed drinkers wait at the bar and Eurostar trains leave for the Continent.

and the computer. In this conception a terminal is a nodal point for the access and exchange of a heterogeneous mix of information, flows and services.[72] Thus for Ferrarini the contemporary conception of the railway station based on the maximization of its income-generating capacity is envisaged as a junction for different kinds of traffic, a 'fulcrum for the reorganization of the surrounding area itself'. This marks a 'transformation in the very conception of the railway station'.[73] Like the computer terminal the station has become a junction point within a territorial system of mixed traffic flow; a place in which movement

The statue of John Betjeman, hat on head, marvels at the splendours of the redeveloped St Pancras station: a fitting tribute to one of the station's most articulate and vociferous defenders.

is translated into millions of individual lifestyle choices, acquisitions and purchases; a site in which desires, wants, needs and expectations suggested by Schivelbusch's 'gateway' are both generated and fulfilled. Perhaps this recognizes a key factor in the cultural role of railways set out at the beginning of this chapter. Stations exemplify the points where objects or actions are translated from one mode or register of circulation to another. The act of translation or transhipment marks their cultural location, their value as tradable commodities and their significance within socially meaningful interactions. Such a conception has a clear resonance with Harry Beck's London Tube map, derived from the form of a circuit diagram in which stations are nodal points within switchable electric circuits. One can only speculate how John Betjeman would have imagined his comfortable middle-class couple from Ruislip meeting at the St Pancras champagne bar, ready to depart for a city break to browse the museums and boutiques of Paris.

5 Entrainment: Tracks to a Railway Ecology

Politics, Environment and the Rail Revival

On 17 January 2008 Barack Obama, president-elect of the United States, undertook a 137-mile ceremonial train journey from Philadelphia south to Washington, DC. For Obama, the USA's first president of African-American descent, the journey consciously retraced that taken by his hero Abraham Lincoln in 1861. Along the route crowds gathered and cheered as the train slowed to allow the President-elect to wave back. The train made several stops en route, notably at Wilmington, Delaware, and latterly at Baltimore, where Obama addressed an enthusiastic crowd of around 40,000 people, echoing the whistle-stop tours typical of elections from a previous age.[1] During his speech he recalled the troops at Maryland's Fort McHenry who had defeated the British during the War of 1812: 'Only a handful of times in our history has a generation been confronted with challenges so vast.' He concluded with a phrase from Lincoln's inaugural address:

> What is required is a new declaration of independence, not just in our nation but in our own lives – from ideology and small thinking, prejudice and bigotry – an appeal not to our easy instincts but to our 'better angels'.[2]

Barack Obama and wife Michelle arrive at Wilmington, Delaware, on the trip from Philadelphia to Obama's presidential inauguration in Washington, DC, 17 January 2008.

It is significant that Obama should choose a railway journey to set the tone for a presidency styled as more egalitarian, more caring, more reflective and more inclusive. Most would agree Obama was right to say that America will face real challenges during the years of his presidency and beyond. As his train rolled down to Washington the world was in the grip of the worst economic recession since the 1930s while simultaneously involved with armed conflict in Iraq and Afghanistan. Potentially even more catastrophic are the impending impacts of human-induced climate change, given greater public awareness in the US through the impact of extreme weather events such as Hurricane Katrina in 2005.

On 17 February 2009 President Obama signed the Recovery and Reinvestment Act. This Act of Congress was intended to provide a stimulus to the US economy in the wake of the economic downturn. The measures, nominally worth $787 billion, included federal tax cuts, expansion of unemployment benefits and other social welfare provisions, and domestic spending in education, health care and infrastructure, including the energy sector. Remarkably, after generations of neglect by governments of all persuasions, these measures contained a set of proposals to revive rail travel in the USA.[3] Set out by President Obama in a speech made on 16 April 2009, the plan allows for an investment of $8 billion and a further $1 billion per year for five years. The money was to be used for two purposes: to improve existing rail lines so that trains could go 100 mph or faster; and to construct new high-speed rail corridors between various major cities within specific metropolitan regions. The report identified ten high-speed rail corridors as potential recipients of Federal funding; these included corridors in California, the Pacific North West, along the Gulf Coast, in the north-east and a Midwest hub around Chicago.[4]

What we're talking about is a vision for high-speed rail in America. Imagine boarding a train in the centre of a city. No racing to an airport and across a terminal, no delays, no sitting on the tarmac, no lost luggage, no taking off your shoes. (Laughter.) Imagine whisking through towns at speeds over 100 miles an hour, walking only a few steps to public transportation, and ending up just blocks from your destination. Imagine what a great project that would be to rebuild America.[5]

In his Wilmington speech Obama drew on the historic figure of President Lincoln to lend authority and moral trajectory to his presidency.[6] In addition to his other triumphs in binding the nation together, Lincoln also presided over the construction of much of the First Transcontinental Railroad. In his speech Obama carefully tied unification by railroad to social and political inclusiveness: 'President Lincoln was committed to a nation connected from East to West, even at the same time he was trying to hold North and South together.' The proposals have also been likened to President Eisenhower's national network of interstate highways; these were developed as an instrument of strategic defence and economic regeneration during the period after 1955. However it might be better to find the core of Obama's inspiration in the hand-drawn map of the US marked with eight superhighway corridors which President Franklin D. Roosevelt gave Thomas MacDonald, his chief of the Bureau of Public Roads, for study in 1938. Obama acknowledges his admiration of Roosevelt, and the 2009 rail proposals are certainly in the spirit of the Keynesian welfare economics which helped bring the US and the UK out of the Depression in the 1930s. As part of an economic stimulus package designed to create employment, the proposals simultaneously tick other important boxes of national concern, including those relating to energy security and climate change. Improving inter-urban public transport should help to decrease dependence on the private automobile, thus helping to curb emissions of greenhouse gases, while at the same time helping to reduce dependence on fossil fuel reserves from the Middle East. Thus Obama characterized the proposals as 'a giant environmental down payment'.[7]

It is appropriate that the USA should rediscover the value of railways during the presidency of a senator from Chicago, America's archetypal railway city. Yet through the last decades of the twentieth century and into the new millennium railways seem not only to have gained increasing importance as a means of transport, as evidenced by increasing usage and investment for both passenger and freight services, but to have also become charged with a distinctive moral authority in the context of environmental concerns over urban gridlock and 'global warming'.

> Now all of you know this is not some fanciful, pie-in-the-sky vision of the future. It is now. It is happening right now. It's been happening for decades. The problem is it's been happening elsewhere, not here.[8]

In Europe it is certainly true that some countries witnessed a dramatic increase in railway usage during the ten years around the new millennium. Between 1995 and 2006 Germany experienced a 23 per cent increase in rail passenger traffic while Spain, Belgium and France also enjoyed strong growth: 32, 42 and 42 per cent respectively. In the UK the figure was a staggering 56 per cent (calculated in terms of passenger-kilometres travelled). In terms of freight the figures for some countries are also impressive: Germany showed a 30 per cent increase, Belgium 35 per cent and the UK 77 per cent. Elsewhere in Europe, outside its established, modernized, urbanized and industrialized Western extremities, rail travel has showed a disturbing decline over the same period. Passenger traffic is down 48 per cent in Bulgaria, 57 per cent in Romania and 62 per cent in Lithuania. There are similar statistics for freight traffic, which was 28 per cent down in the Czech Republic, 39 per cent down in Bulgaria, 37 per cent down in Poland and 52 per cent down in Romania.[9] These countries constitute those parts of the new Europe recently experiencing rapid capitalist economic development. Such statistics have disturbing environmental implications given that the transport sector is a significant and growing contributor to greenhouse gas emissions. Transport is responsible for 34 per cent of all anthropogenic emissions of greenhouse gases and 23 per cent of world CO_2 emissions from fossil fuel combustion. Among the various means of mechanized transport, rail is by far the most environmentally friendly. Rail is three times more efficient than taking a car and four times better than taking a plane. In the EU figures suggest that rail accounts for between 7 and 10 per cent of journeys but produces only 1.6 per cent of total greenhouse gases.[10]

The disparities between 'old' and 'new' Europe are indicative of the processes that have been ongoing since relatively cheap individual motorized transport first became available in the US in the 1920s. Ownership of a private vehicle remains one of the most sought after, enduring and emotionally charged aspirations for the modern consumer-citizen. It symbolizes affluence, status, individual freedom, self-expression and lifestyle choice. Yet since the 1990s transport planners have begun to talk of a 'new realism', a conscious attempt to move beyond the long-accepted practices of predicting growth in automobile and air travel and using this as the basis for developing future provision.[11] Experience has shown that traffic levels expand to fill available road space; as road speeds increase commutes get longer; and business strengthens its reliance on just-in-time provisioning. Environmentalists watch with concern as India, China and the former Soviet Bloc Eastern European countries move rapidly towards a society based on a Western model of industrialized mobile consumerism. Yet, as evidenced in President Obama's pronouncements, the cultural status of railways has begun to change. No longer so widely perceived as an inflexible, dirty, mass mover representing an outmoded industrial age, railways have begun to take on some of the character of an enlightened lifestyle choice – for those wealthy enough to choose. Obama's carefully calculated contrast between rail and air travel casts the railway as the fast, comfortable, efficient, time-saving alternative. As working practices become more flexible in Western economies that are increasingly focused on service and tertiary sector employment, so railway travel in the digital age provides extended office space for white-collar workers connected into mobile networked media technology. As issues of quality of life and lifestyle choice become increasingly important within the affluent developed world, the cultural status of the automobile is challenged by its very ubiquity, the incivilities, stresses and inconveniences of overcrowded roads and the increased costs of car ownership. In this respect the evidence stacks up well in favour of railways. Its infrastructure occupies between two and three times less land per passenger or freight unit than other modes of transport and its overall external costs – including government subsidies and the indirect costs of pollution, accidents and congestion – may be less than 1 per cent of those of road transport, according to figures relating to Europe prepared by the Community of European Railway and Infrastructure Companies (CER) and the International Union of Railways (UIC).[12] Railways, tramways and urban light rail (Light Rapid Transit LRT) have thus come to occupy an important position within the debate concerning environmental sustainability. They offer what might prove to be the best opportunity for developed countries to retain high levels of mobility while providing a clean and efficient means of transport which will help mitigate the environmental effects of industrialization in developing countries. Thus Kjell Larsson, then the Swedish Minister for the Environment, speaking at an international conference on railways and sustainable transport, *Is Rail on Track?* (2001), felt able to call for 'the need to prioritise expansion of the railway in planning and decision making in all countries'.[13]

Sustainable development was defined in the Bruntland Report commissioned by the World Commission on Environment and Development (1987) as development that meets the needs of the present without compromising the ability of future generations to meet their own needs.[14] Some argue that the very idea of sustainable 'development' is an oxymoron: that sustainability and development are antithetical because development inevitably leads to greater resource use, depletion and degradation, whatever measures are taken to minimize and ameliorate impacts. Radical environmentalists would probably argue that universally available mechanized transport, including rail, is a luxury we simply cannot afford. To counter this, theorists tell us that sustainable development should: (a) not allow the use of renewable resources to exceed their rates of regeneration; (b) not draw on non-renewable resources at rates which exceed that at which alternative renewable resources are developed; and (c) restrict pollution emissions to levels which do not exceed the assimilative capacity of the environment.[15] Others argue that a society cannot be called sustainable if it does not provide its members with minimum levels of subsistence, wellbeing, civil rights and justice. Thus sustainability is more than simply a matter of environmental protection. It involves three pillars: social justice, prudent and balanced economies and environmental conservation. As a result, any one of the three pillars of sustainable development (economic, social, environmental) can be emphasized in the interests of publics or environments defined in a multiplicity of ways.[16] When President Obama wrapped his plans for rail within a broader set of economic, social and environmental measures they received immediate and vehement criticism from both political allies and opponents alike and much of this was only tangentially related to the specificities of railway development. Thus what constitutes sustainability, sustainable transport and railway development in particular remain susceptible to claim and counter-claim, to the vagaries of political expedient and economic opportunity. In the UK, for example, representatives of the rail industry have called for the doubling in size of the railway system within 30 years.[17] As is the case in the US, Europe and elsewhere this has been championed both as a solution to growing environmental demands and a way to pump-prime the economy and provide a range of broader-based social benefits in the wake of the worldwide depression in 2009–10. At the same time 'environmentally sustainable' railway technology is viewed by government and industry as providing emerging market opportunities that combine elements of a knowledge economy, project-management expertise and manufacturing. In China, for instance, the substantial rail-building plan has resulted in the construction of 17,000 km (10,655 miles) of new passenger and freight rail lines costing an estimated $190 million in the five years 2005–2010.[18] It has included high-tech, high-profile schemes such as the Shanghai airport Maglev (2004), which reaches speeds of 430 km/h (267 m/ph), the high-altitude Qinghai–Tibet line and a number of high-speed intercity routes. The Asian Development Bank, has provided fourteen loans for rail construction projects between 1989 and 2008 amounting to $3 billion. It lists 'protecting the environment' alongside increasing personal incomes, industrializing rural areas, developing tourism and supporting economic growth corridors and agricultural development among the objectives of these new rail schemes.[19] Both the Dubai Metro, with its cutting-edge technology, computerized driverless trains running in a heavily engineered, energy-intensive, air-conditioned environment – and the proposed Kielder Forest Railway, a short steam-hauled narrow-gauge heritage tourist line projected to use timber biomass energy

from renewable managed woodland sources – describe their respective missions in terms of 'sustainability'.[20]

Environmental change and the permanent way

Cast as the saviour of modern lifestyles in a post- or at least low-carbon future, the rehabilitation of railways in the early twenty-first century seems to have conveniently forgotten the central place railways have played in making the carbon-centred economy. Many climate scientists now recognize a new period in the earth's history termed the Anthropocene. This environmental age is characterized

Opened in 2004, the Shanghai airport Maglev uses a magnetic levitation monorail system rather than conventional rails and has an operational top speed of 431 km/h. This flagship technology sends a clear message to the world regarding China's economic ambition.

by the impact of human action.[21] Though scientists argue about the starting-date for this period, with some dating it back to the origins of settled agriculture 8,000 years ago, one influential formulation proposes the latter part of the eighteenth century. This is the period when data retrieved from glacial ice cores show the beginning of a growth in the atmospheric concentrations of several 'greenhouse gases', in particular CO_2 and CH_4.[22] Significantly, such a starting-date also coincides with James Watt's invention of the steam engine in 1784, forming a highly symbolic marker for an age in which human actions have had global effects.

It cannot be denied that railways have made possible dramatic environmental change. Railway development encouraged both rural depopulation in rapidly industrializing countries such as the UK, and long-distance migration and colonization in for instance the American West and Siberia. In the case of North America this resulted in

Albert Bierstadt, *The Last of the Buffalo*, 1888. Though the picture implies that Native Americans were responsible for the demise of the buffalo, this is at best a romantic fiction and at worst pure railroad propaganda: the railroads encouraged professional hunters and sportsmen to kill for profit and amusement.

the large-scale harassment and displacement of indigenous populations. Railway development also resulted in wholesale ecological change, deforestation in India and the demise of the buffalo in North America, resulting in profound and destructive change for indigenous ways of life in many places. In India the rapid expansion of the railway system after the rebellion of 1857–8 was spurred on by commercial opportunity as well as strategic considerations. By 1910, India had the fourth largest railway network in the world, with more than 32,000 miles of track playing a significant part in what David Arnold calls India's 'environmental revolution'.[23] Elsewhere railways were central to colonial economies of sugar, rubber, sisal and other agricultural raw materials in countries such as Angola, Argentina, Australia, Cuba, Fiji, India, Indonesia, Japan, the Philippines and Zimbabwe. Thus railways have played an important part in the ecological transformation of the earth, providing the infrastructure that enabled the profitable introduction of alien species and the simplification of

A narrow-gauge sugar-cane railway in Fiji. Railways have been instrumental in the sort of ecological imperialism that has allowed alien species to be grown as monocultures in the developing world.

ecosystems, allowing cash crops to be grown in areas which were economically marginal but full of ecological potential.

Environmental changes facilitated by railway development have been relatively subtle as well as profound. Railway tracks, like roads and highways, have often been the means of enabling non-native invasive species to colonize particular ecosystems. Stray seeds hidden in packing materials or carried in the folds and crevices of packages, cargoes and vehicles may be distributed along the lineside, allowing species to invade new territories and even entire continents. They are carried into new habitats where they may thrive either because they are more vigorous or have fewer natural predators. Railways themselves create a distinctive set of habitats, leading to new human-made natures only made possible by culturally infused actions and activities. Railway beds are usually built on a bed of compacted earth and aggregate, with drainage channels designed to carry water away from the tracks. At the same time, this run-off often accumulates in

After escaping from the Oxford Botanic Garden around 1719, Oxford Ragwort spread across Britain via the railway system. Trackbeds rich in cinders and clinker replicated the lava-soils of its native Sicily.

areas fairly near the tracks where drainage is poor, forming small artificial wetlands. Embankments, cuttings and small areas of ground cut off from other uses at junctions and sidings create untamed areas with sometimes distinctive and localized geological and environmental conditions in which plants and wildlife may thrive. Thus railway tracks provide corridors along which particular species can spread and thrive, even when the surrounding areas might be less hospitable to them. In Britain a classic example is Oxford Ragwort. A native of Sicily, where it grows in volcanic ash, the plant was brought to the Oxford Botanic Garden some time around 1719. The plant grew for many years in and around the old stone walls of Oxford and its colleges. When Oxford became connected to the railway system, the plant gained a new habitat in railway trackbeds rich in cinders and clinker from steam locomotives which replicated characteristics of the lava-soils of its native home in Sicily. In such a conducive environment the plant gradually spread via the railway to other parts of the country, carried on board trains and migrating along the track bed.[24] In North America railways have been responsible for colonization by non-native invasive species such as *Ailanthus altissima*, *Paulownia tomentosa*, the Siberian elm and the Norway maple, and notoriously invasive non-woody plants such as Japanese knotweed. The expansion of China's rail system westward may result in similar environmental changes. The recently completed 1,100 km Qinghai–Tibet railway links the high Tibetan plateau (4,000 metres in elevation) to the rest of the country. Goldenrod and common ragweed (*Ambrosia aertemisiifolia L.*), both of which are invasive in eastern China, and other alien species are expected to spread readily to remote and environmentally sensitive western China along the rail line.[25]

Kelly Reichardt's film *Wendy and Lucy* (2008, based on the short story 'Train Choir' by Jon Raymond) tells of a young woman

Taylor had told me that this was one of the few places in the West where you can see the entire mile-long length of a coal train as it curves around the side of the mountain. I looked back, watching the cars obediently trailing along – seventeen thousand tons of coal and iron rolling up the hill. It was a glorious, awe-inspiring feat of industrial might, even if there was something absurd about deploying so much horsepower on such a grand adventure just to haul a few thousand tons of coal to the other side of the country. But this is how America keeps the lights on.[31]

It was not surprising therefore when on 13 June 2008 protestors halted a coal train carrying fuel for Drax power station in Yorkshire, UK. Dressed in white overalls and canary outfits, the protestors used a red flag to stop the train on a bridge overlooking the power station. They climbed on board and dumped coal off onto the tracks while unveiling a banner carrying the message 'Leave it in the Ground!' Protestors used a network of climbing ropes to suspend themselves under the bridge from the train to prevent the train from moving. The choice of both train and Drax power station is highly symbolic.[32] As the largest coal-fired power station in western Europe, supplying 3,960 megawatts or about 7 per cent of the UK's electricity needs, Drax is also the UK's largest emitter of CO_2. Since deep-mined coal production has been wound down in the UK, an increasing proportion of coal is brought from Australia, Colombia, Poland, Russia and South Africa. The coal, brought to the power station exclusively by unit train, amounts to some 36,000 tons every week, on 35 trains each day six days per week. Given its high profile, much has been done to ensure that this plant meets and exceeds contemporary environmental standards. However it remains a focus for debate concerning the politics of coal, climate change and environmental damage. The protesters form part of a growing international coalition of individuals and groups protesting against the increasing use of coal.

Activities have included a series of climate camps and protests at Drax and other power stations in the UK.[33] Direct action has come to be a prominent force in environmental politics since the 1990s and the actions taken in the coal train protest are familiar from the repertoire of tactics previously deployed elsewhere. Using ropes, wires and chains to suspend themselves from the train under the bridge, the Drax protest uses techniques of passive resistance familiar from road protests and airport development campaigns in the UK. The symbolic shovelling of coal off the train on to the track is itself reminiscent of the spoiling of crops in the presence of mass media by activists protesting against genetically modified (GM) crops. In the light of legal and physical security measures designed to inhibit protests at the power station site itself, focus on the train may indeed have been a pragmatic decision for the protestors. However, giving the train visible presence in the debate concerning coal, climate change and CO_2 production certainly challenges claims that railway development is a purely benign force in creating a sustainable low-carbon future.

Climate-change protestors halt a coal train heading for Drax power station in Yorkshire, June 2008.

229

Compared with other means of mechanized transport, railways project an aura of solidity and durability. The very term 'permanent way', given to rail tracks and their related earthworks, is instructive. It is certainly true that in the past much railway infrastructure has been significantly over-engineered, either through an uncritical adoption of over-cautious standards, active boosterism and self-promotion in design, or simply through profligate and inefficient management. Yet the idea remains an enduring one. The permanent way signifies an ongoing commitment to public service, a set of tacit contractual relationships given voice in steel, concrete, brick and earth. In the UK the battle to save the former Midland Railway mainline through the rugged limestone fells of the northern Pennines between Settle and Carlisle illustrates both the impermanence of the permanent way and our cultural and emotional investment in the solidity of its structures. Born out of concerns regarding spatial monopoly, the Settle–Carlisle line was constructed during the 1870s to enable the Midland Railway Company independent access to Scotland when a rival deliberately obstructed the transit of the trains sharing their tracks. Designed primarily for long-distance express running rather than local traffic, the line was heavily engineered and thus proved both extremely expensive to construct and ultimately expensive and difficult to maintain. Most notable is the 24-arch Ribblehead Viaduct, which is 104 ft (32 m) high and 440 yards (402 m) long. The viaduct piers are sunk 25 ft (8 m) into the soft bog peat.[34] In 1983 British Rail announced its intention to close the line. BR claimed that a replacement was required for Ribblehead Viaduct at a cost of £4.5m, and that government and local authority refusal to fund the project would put the future of the line in jeopardy.[35] Engineering reports argued that the waterproof membrane placed under the track bed at the time of construction had decayed and had been allowing water to seep through the bridge and down the inside of the stone piers,

damaging the bridge from the inside out. Evidence suggested that water running down inside the bridge was washing mortar out from the joints, loosening the stone blocks and damaging the structure of the brick arch sections. The extreme weather conditions at Ribblehead – wind, frost, snow and up to 90 inches (228 cm) of rainfall per annum – have clearly taken their toll on the structure, particularly given the relatively poor weathering qualities of alkaline limestone, which is susceptible to becoming soluble in contact with the mild acidity of rain water.

Ribblehead Viaduct, itself a favourite haunt of railway photographers, featured centrally in the story of saving the Settle–Carlisle line, both during the fierce battle against closure and subsequently. Emblematic in logos, headings and photographs representing the line, Ribblehead features in much promotional and descriptive material. Used by BR to illustrate the high infrastructure costs of maintaining

The grand structure of Ribblehead Viaduct became a key symbol in the battle to keep open the railway line between Settle and Carlisle through the scenic Yorkshire Dales. Today it is a major tourist attraction.

the line and the burden of responsibility carried by BR, for protest groups the bridge has become a symbol of neglect demonstrating BR's long-term failure of duty to uphold maintenance of the line. A report into the line made in 1983–4 and sponsored jointly by the local authorities and BR concluded that the line could indeed become economically viable, though it uncovered a backlog of maintenance which it described as 'wanton neglect'.[36] To make matters worse, when the viaduct was eventually given thorough maintenance and repair immediately after the line's reprieve in 1989, it was found that the damage was not as extensive as had been feared and the cost considerably less that some of BR's more pessimistic estimates made as part of the case for closure.[37] Thus for pro-rail groups Ribblehead is also a constant reminder of corporate duplicity and deceit in the face of what they argue is an overwhelming and contrary greater public interest.

In 1987 the status of the Viaduct as a structure of national significance was recognized when English Heritage granted £1 million as a contribution towards its repair. This award established the historic status of the structure and acknowledged its place as an object of particular significance within the natural landscape. At the time this award for the conservation of a Grade II listed structure was the largest single grant ever made by England's commission for historic buildings and monuments. In the controversy generated by plans to transform the line into what the press dubbed a '70 mile Disneyland in the Dales',[38] Ribblehead came to symbolize the authenticity and inviolability of these 'wild places'. It was argued that Ribblehead, like other highly valued locations, should be left to their solitude, unpolluted by the 'make-believe' of mass tourism. A cartoon published in the June 1989 edition of *Railnews*, a monthly publication aimed at rail industry employees, shows a Ribblehead Viaduct with its arches converted into bijou holiday homes. In the foreground stand a sheep farmer, a rail worker and a man with a clipboard, while two figures dressed in hiking clothes stand on the formerly wild expanse of peat-bog, now paved over as a car park, trying to find a way past 'Viaduct Villas' – 'a public-private partnership'.[39] It is not insignificant that farmer, rail worker and walker are depicted together as victims. It is also apt that a row of holiday lets situated beneath track level now provide dubious and inappropriate physical and by implication financial support for the train rumbling overhead.

Today the line is open 24 hours a day, seven days a week. The generous standards adopted in construction of the line coupled with congestion on other routes have provided renewed scope for freight traffic. In the ten years from 2008 Network Rail projects growth on the Settle–Carlisle line of approximately 37 per cent, equivalent to 2.7 per cent per annum.[40] In 2008–9 Network Rail invested £18 million in new, enhanced signalling for the route; these improvements are designed to enable the line to cope with greatly increased freight traffic rather than to upgrade the still relatively modest passenger services. The heaviest freight flows in the whole north-west region are concentrated on the Settle and Carlisle line and comprise imported coal from as far away as Asia and South America, bound for power stations in Yorkshire, the Trent Valley and the East Midlands.[41] According to the Lancashire and Cumbria Rail Utilisation Strategy 2008, with 'the continuing uncertainty in gas and oil prices and the time lag to build nuclear power stations, coal looks set to remain in demand for the foreseeable future'. Thus coal traffic along the Settle and Carlisle route is expected to rise from the current level of approximately twelve to sixteen trains per day each way, with a projected additional extra six trains by 2014/15.[42] It is perhaps an irony characteristic of contemporary debates concerning sustainability that the rail traffic which ensures the viability of the Settle–Carlisle line as an environmentally friendly means of bringing economic and social development to the sensitive and precious Dales landscapes is also part of

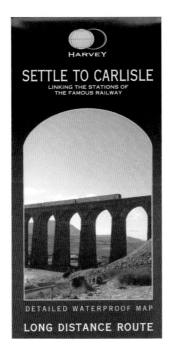

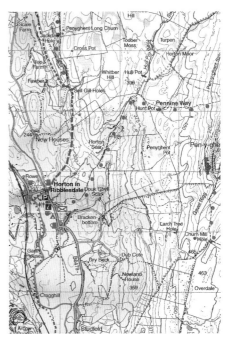

a global flow in 'dirty' and potentially environmentally damaging fossil fuel, which is a major source of greenhouse gases and the particulates that create acid rain. The Drax coal train protestors would probably be the first to point out that this acidulated rainwater attacks historic limestone structures such as Ribblehead Viaduct, while at the same time threatening fragile alkaline ecosystems like those of the Dales themselves.

Community, competition and the railway corridor

Railways and environmental histories are entwined in ways that both exceed and inform debates around sustainable development. Railway locomotives have often been imagined as an 'endangered species'. This is certainly one implication of the biomorphic analogy which figures steam railway locomotives as living, breathing 'iron horses'

The Settle–Carlisle railway has become a focus for tourism strategy in the region. Today a wide range of leisure, recreation and heritage activities cluster around the route.

(see chapter One). David Shepherd (1931–), the popular British painter of locomotives and railway scenes, is also known for his depictions of romanticized heroic portraits of African elephants, lions and tigers. His work is found in prints and books, on pottery and other memorabilia, and its combination of almost photographic realism and passionate impressionism demonstrates a heartfelt intensity. Shepherd turned to painting after visiting Kenya, where he had hoped to become a game warden.[43] He is equally well known for his work in railway preservation and wildlife conservation, receiving a CBE for his services to charity and wildlife conservation in 2008. In books such as *Steam Safari* (1974) and *Iron Dinosaurs* (1976), the photographer Colin Garrett describes himself as cataloguing 'ecological diversity' and tracing an 'evolutionary history' for unusual designs of steam locomotive.

Symbolic of an old declining industrial order, railways are central to an ecological aesthetic of decline, decay and renewal by which

Giants at Rest by David Shepherd, 2003, freight locomotives between duties.

Britain in particular but also Europe and North America have endeavoured to come to terms with the consequences of post-industrialism. The sculpture *The Iron Road* (1986) by Keir Smith is situated on the trackbed of an old mineral railway, and is carved from twenty equally spaced old railway sleepers. Part of the Forest of Dean Sculpture Trail in Gloucestershire, it is set in a young beech wood at the side of the family cycle path on a curved track running through the historic former coal mining region.[44] Designed to 'bring the spirit of the Forest's industrial past to life', the individual sleepers are carved with 'poetic images of natural or industrial life – a feather, a leaf, a wheel, a factory or a cloud'. In this context ecological metaphors act as a means of explaining the effect of industrial cycles on the landscape. The Forest is a landscape which shows the traces of human activity like layers of organic material which provide a culture out of which grows the next generation of productive activity. According to the organizers of the Sculpture Trail:

> Nothing is permanent in the forest, and these artistic interventions are no more than the latest marks left by man on the land. From the first excavations, the forest has been inscribed with lines of passage – paths, railways and watercourses; dug into and sculpted by mines; or cut down and replanted along avenues and in well-defined plots.[45]

Rather more than the picturesque conception of decline as a means of coming to terms with industry as already worn out (see chapter One), this formulation interprets decay as a positive and inevitable stage in the process of renewal and reinvigoration.[46]

Yet as we can see from the Obama plan and elsewhere, railways currently play a more complex cultural role in negotiating the consequences of industrialization than simply forming a focus for the loss of a recent past, though this remains an important locus for their

cultural positioning within contemporary society. These ideas have a history situated in mid-twentieth-century thinking around technology and culture in which railways played an important part. The engineer, writer on industrial archaeology and pioneer of railway preservation L.T.C. (Tom) Rolt (1910–1974) set down his reflections on the relationship between humans, technology and environment in the book *High Horse Riderless* (written in 1943 and published in 1949), now recognized as a classic of green philosophy. He argued that a mechanical, materialistic and substantially urban world produced impoverished lives, human exploitation and degradation of natural resources. Mass production, he concluded, could never truly satisfy individual needs, merely subdue individuality by imposing conformity.

> For the effect of concentrating productive capacity and knowledge always toward that which can be produced with the greatest facility is to create, not only monopolies, but a widening gulf between producer and

Tom Rolt, chatting to passengers at Abergynolwyn during his time as general manager of the Talyllyn Railway, Mid-Wales, the world's first preserved railway, in 1951.

consumer. The wider this gap the more complex and unwieldy becomes the problem of distribution and of relating production with consumption and consequently the greater the waste. Swifter and swifter methods of transport become necessary . . . [47]

His vision for society posited a new balance between machines, science, arts and spirituality based on organic principles of self-sufficiency; it envisaged a form of society based in local democracy and local production. This philosophy is reflected in his pioneering efforts in railway preservation and particularly his role co-ordinating the campaign to save the Talyllyn Railway in Mid-Wales during 1949. This was one of a number of distinctive narrow-gauge railways in Wales

Tom Rolt standing beside the Giesl ejector chimney fitted to Talyllyn locomotive No. 4 Edward Thomas in Pendre Yard, 1958.

that were primarily constructed to serve the local slate-quarrying industries and their working communities. After a successful campaign Rolt spent the summer of 1951 as the operating manager of the world's first preserved railway. In the third volume of his autobiography, *Landscape with Figures* (1992), he described how he became fascinated with the Talyllyn Railway after a cottage holiday in Wales in 1943. Waiting in vain for one of its thrice-weekly trains, he walked the line and explored its antique and thoroughly worn-out track and stock. In his capacity with the Inland Waterways Association, which he had helped form in 1946, Rolt was familiar with the new Labour government's proposals to nationalize transport. He viewed these proposals with dismay:

> Instead of 'our railways' it seemed to be that they were far more likely to become nobody's railways under nationalisation. They would fall into neglect and decay just because they had become political pawns about which nobody felt responsible and nobody cared.[48]

In a letter in the *Birmingham Post* bemoaning the demise of the Talyllyn Railway he stressed the importance of grass roots initiative in the face of passive dependence on the state:

> Surely it is a sorry symptom of the decline of individual initiative at the present time that we often grumble and say: 'Why don't they do something about it?' and so seldom pause to consider whether we might not be doing something about it ourselves.[49]

Rolt was highly sceptical of what he called 'the machine state' because he believed that it stifled the full realization of the creative individual. For him this term encompassed both industrial capitalism and state-socialism. As an antidote, he championed a bottom-up, self-reliant, collaborative life based on a politics of village and region. In this view he was among a number of environmental thinkers critical of a modern technological progressivism perceived to be out of control and insensitive to human needs and the human scale in the aftermath of the Second World War. This is characterized as the 'High Horse Riderless' of his book's title. Thus for Tom Rolt, the campaign to save the Talyllyn was a means of celebrating what he perceived to be more fulfilling craft-based jobs in which employees took a pride in their work, while at the same time providing an opportunity to exercise his brand of collaborative self-help. Writing long before E. F. Schumacker had coined the term 'appropriate technology', from this perspective the railway itself represents a fitting scale for human-machine relationships. Such narrow-gauge railways pragmatically winding their way through valleys, round headlands and up mountainsides suggest individualistic and idiosyncratic responses to specific needs, economic circumstances and the challenges posed by landscape and environment.[50]

Tom Rolt's perspective on technology, society and environment is itself tense and contradictory. Setting himself in favour of a realistic history of 'the common people' and against the idealizations of the Arts and Crafts movement, his perspective on the railway worker as a self-fulfilled and unalienated artisan is clearly itself a romanticization. A vehement champion of radical bottom-up democracy, he certainly found his personal brand of collectivism difficult to unite with both his own management style and the practical requirements of everyday business at the Talyllyn Railway. The British Ealing comedy film *The Titfield Thunderbolt* (dir. Charles Crichton, 1953) presents an idealized version of a locally run train service taken over from the nationalized British Railways and was directly inspired by the restoration of the Talyllyn Railway. Yet rather than being grounded in local initiative and local need, it is arguable that the Talyllyn preservation movement was substantially an externally generated enterprise. Support for the project was after all substantially gathered at meetings of English enthusiasts in Birmingham. Rolt alludes to the tensions generated by this when reporting the antagonistic attitudes of some long-standing local Welsh railway workers during his period as manager.

In many respects, however, Tom Rolt's environmental views were quite prescient. Where mass-transport systems are concerned, his identification of transport as a symptom of the current consumerist malaise is certainly echoed by many current thinkers. His recognition of a new role for mechanized mass-transport systems within a global society based on local and regional self-sufficiency is also in tune with aspects of present-day green thought. In this context transport plays an ethical and social rather than a purely economic role: it becomes the medium for ameliorating inequalities in available resources, thereby creating equality of opportunity. However, it was Rolt's recognition of ecology as the means to reconcile progressive science and moral philosophy, individual and collective needs, human culture and raw nature that constitutes arguably his single most original thought. For Rolt, ecology was a means to transform the modern world from 'an eternal ferment of conflicting forces', into a 'harmonious association of opposites in perfect balance'.

> the scientist of the future may join hands with the artist and the vision-ary by gathering together the broken threads of knowledge from a past when the words 'science' and 'philosophy' were synonyms. It is the field of ecology, in the study, that is, of the relationship of living things, including man himself, to each other and to their environment, that the most hopeful advances in this direction are being made.[51]

Rolt was not alone amongst mid-twentieth-century historians of technology concerned with the broader environmental consequences of technologically driven modernization. Like Tom Rolt, Lewis Mumford (see chapter Four) looked forward to a future which would be 'organic' and characterized by common ownership. Though Rolt would not have used Mumford's term 'communist' to describe such a future, he would certainly have endorsed Mumford's assertion that technology should not be rejected, but that the mechanical should be made more 'organic' and therefore more effective when rendered harmonious with our living environment.[52] Significantly, Mumford's writings were an important influence on the thinking of Barry Commoner (1917–), the American pioneer of modern environmentalism. Commoner's four laws of ecology, outlined in his book *The Closing Circle: Nature, Man and Technology* (1971), set out an approach to environmental action grounded in principles of sustainability. Commoner drew on both the laws of energy conservation and cybernetic theories of systems control in order to develop an organic conception of interconnection and interdependency between human and natural worlds. This in turn was grounded in American nature writing such as that by Henry David Thoreau (see Preface). Commoner's formulation of ecology for the 'new environmentalism' certainly resonates with that of Tom Rolt, who characterized the place of humanity within the global environment as

> a delicately ordered system of mutual dependencies so finely poised, so intricate, and so infinite in its scope that it is doubtful whether the human mind can ever hope to encompass a tithe of it.[53]

Key terms linking ecological processes to social organization are encapsulated in the morally charged metaphors of community and competition. The term community implies interdependency and the grounds for organic growth, while competition is both a contrasting and complimentary term that hints at Darwinian processes of natural selection and survival of the fittest. Together they suggest processes leading to the exploitation of specific ecological/economic competencies and the domination of particular niches within a system of interdependencies. The metaphor of a railway line as a tree with trunk, roots and branches is one such means of identifying and describing properties of organic interdependency which link with notions of community and competition. In the case of the Settle–Carlisle line, for example, this was used by protestors to invoke a wide understanding of the railway within the service of a broadly drawn understanding of community. When in 1984 BR produced figures to suggest that the line was unviable, these appeared to be based on the lack of any substantial local traffic. Protestors claimed that BR reasoning wrongly judged the line in isolation without recourse to its role of functioning as part of the wider BR network or the income drawn from this. A lesson to be learned from the BR modernization plan of the 1960s, they suggested, was that withdrawal of feeder services had a disproportionate affect on the number of passengers travelling long distance and adversely disadvantaged poorer social groups, thereby affecting the viability of the system as a whole. As Abbott and Whitehouse wrote in their book on the Settle–Carlisle campaign, *The Line that Refused to Die* (1990), one needs to appreciate that 'if you cut the roots and branches from a tree the trunk will wither'.[54] Perhaps not surprisingly, the BR rationalization plans of the 1960s have become widely known as the Beeching 'Axe'.

The metaphor of the corridor is another important means by which railways are imagined as an ecological community. Though the idea of a corridor might suggest something that is designed and fabricated rather than organic and spontaneous, it is frequently used in an ecological sense to denote a pathway or ribbon of valued and vital habitat. In this context the idea of the corridor or 'growth corridor' as it is termed by planners links lives and landscapes to geologies and economies, long-distance flows and local social networks, national histories and local knowledges. For John R. Stilgoe in *Metropolitan Corridor: Railways and the American Scene* (1983), a book about the impact of railways on North American culture during the period 1880–1930, the railway corridor is a place of activity and transformation, connecting technology to society and environment by moulding spaces, structures and ways of thinking in new and different ways. Trains and rights-of-way 'transformed adjacent built environments', 'nurtured factory complexes, electricity generating stations and commuter suburbs while enfeebling Main Streets and other traditional places'.[55] Thus 'trains, right-of-way, and adjacent built form had become part environment, part experience, a combination perhaps best called metropolitan'. Stilgoe concludes: 'the metropolitan corridor objectified in its unprecedented arrangement of space and structure a wholly new lifestyle'. Along the tracks and through the corridor 'flowed the forces of modernisation, announcing the character of the twentieth century'.[56] 'For one half-century moment, the nation created a new sort of environment characterized by technically controlled order.'[57]

For Peter Bishop, like Stilgoe, railway corridors 'gather' the elements of landscape and culture, thereby creating new places, perspectives, meanings and experiences both around and within them. For Bishop railway corridors have a characteristic 'poetics of space', one which is built around contrasting elements of the impersonal and the intimate, the public and the private, flow, eddy and stillness. In his study of the Alice Springs to Darwin railway (opened 2004), Bishop is particularly concerned with the idea of the 'corridor' as a tool of practical planning and a means of marshalling the hopes and aspirations of national identity. Construction of the north–south transcontinental railway from Adelaide via Alice Springs to Darwin, is a physical manifestation of Australia's new position in the world as part of an Asian-Pacific economy growing towards global dominance. Yet at the same time the line passes through territories and towns, it also negotiates a range of histories, lifestyles and aspirations. In this context the rail corridor has to manage issues of national integration within a nation divided by European fears of Asian dominance, memories of colonial rule, discrimination against Aboriginal peoples and regional antagonisms between coast and interior. The corridor is therefore a site of difference, struggle and reconciliation, between European, Aboriginal and Asian conceptions of being Australian. Central to notions of reconciliation are the trains themselves. Promotional literature shows the highly colourful trains often decorated with Aboriginal-style art crossing vast open expanses of desert, sometimes with a frilled-necked lizard or kangaroo in the immediate foreground. Thus the train becomes inserted into the outback on par with native fauna and Aboriginal culture. In this way the railway connects the historical baselines of Australian identity, Aboriginal culture and outback landscape to a progressive conception of national future (see chapter Two) at once both progressive and redemptive.[58]

Some locomotives used on the Adelaide–Darwin railway are painted in a style imitating Aboriginal painting, connecting the origins of Australian identity to a national future powered by technology.

In the case of the Settle–Carlisle line, as both private companies and anti-closure groups formulated proposals for the economic rehabilitation of the line during the mid-1980s they increasingly fixed on formulae which stressed the broader environmental role of the corridor. The proposal from Sian Johnson & Associates, a London-based marketing consultancy, was to develop 'major high intensity tourist magnets' using the railway as a 'theme corridor' with the aim of ultimately attracting a million passengers a year on ten or twelve trains a day.[59] Major tourist attractions would be complemented by 'lineside development and tourist services such as shops, pubs, amusements, indoor and evening entertainments, sporting activities, holiday accommodation in nearby towns and villages'.[60] Yet to this day, plans for a themed heritage corridor remain largely unrealized. Ironically, as protestors are quick to point out, a series of relatively minor changes in business practice coupled with efforts to raise support for the line locally and nationally were sufficient to effect a transformation. Though never formally implemented, over the years certain aspects of the heritage corridor have certainly come to pass as tourism and leisure activities have congregated around and along the line, taking advantage of the opportunities it affords. With guided walks and outdoor activities, tourist accommodation, special ticket rates for local residents, themed trains and steam-hauled specials, clothing and merchandising, websites and promotional literature, the line is now thoroughly embedded within the tourism and rural development strategies for Cumbria and the Yorkshire Dales. Today the Settle–Carlisle Railway Development Company (formed 1992), a not-for-profit partnership of local authorities and public sector bodies in the region surrounding the railway, promotes the line in the interests of those businesses and communities, towns and villages along the route. Anti-closure protestors are justifiably proud of this apparently bottom-up form of development. As Abbott and Whitehouse conclude:

It may be that quite simply, the future of the Settle–Carlisle lies, not as part of a sanitised 'heritage project' but as a working – and workaday – railway carrying a healthy mixture of people who actually want to get from A to B, with those who want a pleasant and relaxing day out taking up the next seat.[61]

By contrasting the lifeless sterility of imposed heritage with the liveliness of 'authentic' indigenous development, Abbot and Whitehouse draw on a conception of community which is steeped in notions of vitalist heterogeneity as the life force behind progress and improvement. This is a response Tom Rolt may well have endorsed.

Entrainment

In his book *We Have Never Been Modern* (1991, English trans. 1993) the sociologist of science Bruno Latour addresses the hubris of modernity substantially captured by Rolt's figure of the 'high horse'. In many respects Latour adds to environmentalist criticism of widely held assumptions concerning human dominion over nature which have developed since the time of Thoreau and Emerson. Latour adopts the metaphor of a railway network in part to express the intricate and infinite connections between physical and social worlds, material objects and human actions, that which is close by and that which is distant.

Is a railroad local or global? Neither, it is local at all points, since you always find sleepers and railroad workers, and you have stations and automatic ticket machines scattered along the way. Yet it is global, since it takes you from Madrid to Berlin or from Brest to Vladivostok. However, it is not universal enough to be able to take you just anywhere. It is impossible to reach the little Auvergnat village of Malpy by train, or the little Staffordshire village [sic] of Market Drayton. There are continuous paths that lead from the local to the global, from the circumstantial to the universal, from the contingent to the necessary, only so long as the branch lines are paid for.[62]

According to Latour, these hidden and unrecognized connections are key to maintaining the fiction of separation between human and natural worlds. At the same time, these bifurcating pathways represented by train tracks form a conduit for the concealed and distanced implications of human action. For Latour, the processes which connect decaying limestone to the threat of line closure are salutary. These processes link calls for a socially responsive railway to the production of acid rain and a reinforced threat of change to the very bedrock on which everyday life is built. They are a constant reminder that things are not necessarily under control, that the human-made structures we rely on are not as permanent as we might like to believe and that ultimately social responsibility means that we have to embrace even the most humble parts of nature. Thus the railway as a technological network demonstrates the interconnection of local actions and distanced consequences, expressed in the environmentalist slogan 'think global – act local'.

As we have seen from the Obama plan and elsewhere, transport has become a major issue in contemporary debates concerning environmental sustainability. Within these debates, railways have been figured as part of the problem, part of the solution and as a metaphor for the forgotten connections between physical and social, human and natural worlds that arguably helped create the problem in the first place. Yet in spite of the environmental contradictions indicated for example by their role as major coal haulers, railways and high-speed rail in particular still seem to hold out a particular hope for the continuation of modern life into the future. Yet this ignores the fact that high-speed rail is itself ultimately highly controversial from an environmental perspective. Electrification of the conventional rail network plus other investments in energy and resource-efficient technology can have a greater effect on overall energy use and bring benefits to a wider travelling public even though high-speed lines may have a greater ability to compete for traffic with air travel. Further, though the localized impact of high-speed lines can be significant, specific local benefits are often limited. High-speed lines require very substantial earthworks in order to maintain a straight level track bed; they need to be newly cut rather than following existing sinuous routes; levels of visual, auditory and landscape intrusion may be substantial. Yet few towns and villages along the route will have direct access to services aimed squarely at regional and national intercity passengers.

Like the unit train, the promise of high-speed rail depends on the prospect of technologically mediated seamless interconnection. When President Obama asks citizens to imagine a transport system where there is 'no racing to an airport and across a terminal, no delays, no sitting on the tarmac, no lost luggage, no taking off your shoes'; where one is whisked 'through towns at speeds over 100 miles an hour, walking only a few steps to public transportation, and ending up just blocks from your destination'; his vision for future high-speed rail corridors in America draws on this conception. This is a pervasive concept in the realization of contemporary technology. It is present in the smoothness, simplicity, flow, efficiency and ergonomics of modern design. It is also evident in 'just-in-time' logistics which maximize availability on demand and the design and use of digital, mobile computer and communications systems where real-time co-presence and the portability of information from application to application are important considerations. In this sense high-speed rail is a logical extension of a modernist ethic of technological mastery which distances nature behind a protecting envelope of complex environmental engineering.

It gives expression to the idea of untrammelled personal freedom that is fundamental to conceptions of mobile individualism (see chapter Three). From this perspective high-speed rail is merely another flagship high-tech national project.

However, there are clearly other expectations generated by high-speed rail. Evidence for this might be found in the symbolic status of the Japanese Shinkansen (bullet train) as a potent and aspirational symbol for a socially and environmentally engaged rapprochement between nature and culture, modernity and tradition, technology and environment, entrepreneurial energy and social responsibility. It is certainly the case that the East Japan Railway Company (JR East), operator of the most iconic of Shinkansen services, is itself a model for socially and environmentally responsible capitalism. With 71,000 employees JR East is the largest railway company in the world. Since 2000 JR East's glossy and substantial environmental report has charted a range of environmental initiatives from recycling and in-house design for commuter bicycles to sustainably managed forestry, carbon offsetting and innovative uses of renewable energy.[63] Photographs of the Japanese Shinkansen set against the towering presence of Mount Fuji have become a very powerful and internationally recognized symbol of modern Japan.[64] Typically such images juxtapose the sleek metallic horizontal trajectory of the train against the rugged pyramidal peak of the mountain. Clearly a contrast is being made between a future that is fast, fleeting, mobile and high-tech and the solid transcendent natural beauty of Mount Fuji, whose dramatic outline is vested in deep layers of history, myth and national identity. Yet these visual images also set up a series of correspondences, between the angled slope of the mountain and the nose of the train, glistening white paintwork and snow-capped peak. As the latter reaches up to the heavens piercing the sky, so the former cuts the air and reaches forward into the future. As examples of perfection in form, train and mountain together suggest an order and harmony paying homage equally to Japan's natural and cultural heritage. Such images constantly remind us of the rich wealth of philosophical and religious thinking concerning nature that informs Japanese approaches to industrial design and business practice.

In this way images of the Shinkansen reflect the railway's place as a carrier for those senses of connection and community present in the thinking of Tom Rolt and the suggestion of society–nature network-building present in Latour's railway metaphor. Railways seem to have a fortunate knack of embodying the apparent separation of humans and nature while providing a route to their psychic and cultural resolution. Such a sense is developed through the resilient technological complexity discussed in chapter Two and in the aesthetic union of objects and social values described in chapter Four. It is present in the juxtaposition of disturbance and quiet discussed as part of the technological sublime in chapter One and in the fusion of cyclical and linear trajectories which encourage us to think of individual biographies in terms of personal and collective journeys described in chapter Three. In this context, and given its metaphorical capacity to link technology, culture, society and environment, it may be significant that contemporary ways of imagining railways as part of a more environmentally sustainable transport system often invoke the idea of the corridor. In one respect this is a very practical matter. Fixed-route public transport systems such as railways and inter-urban tramways cannot provide individual mobility in the dispersed, on-demand way that automobiles can. Rather, they adopt routes that cut through population centres in order to maximize points of accessibility. In addition, the corridor provides a convenient means of imagining and drawing some sort of a boundary around the broader external costs and benefits which are often unrecognized when investment in rail is compared to that of road. In another

Images of Japanese Shinkansen (bullet trains) set against Mount Fuji are a powerful and internationally recognized symbol of modern Japan. Train and mountain together suggest an order and harmony that pays homage equally to Japan's natural and cultural heritage.

respect, the railway corridor is both a way of understanding the physical interaction between railways and their environments and something which shapes thought. Stilgoe's conception of the railway corridor 'molding spaces, structures and ways of thinking' resonates strongly with Michel Foucault's characterization of the 'extraordinary' nature of railways as a cultural product and producer of modern life. For Foucault (see chapter Three) the train is 'something through which one goes, it is also something by means of which one can go from one point to another, and then it is also something that goes by'.[65] The apparent permanence of the tracks and the routine, rhythmic dependability of the train schedule engages and enrols us in ways which are both conscious and unconscious. Such activity might be described by recent theorists working on the communal experience of dance and music as a form of resonant sympathetic behaviour as a process of 'entrainment'. In the quote that opens the introduction to this book Henry David Thoreau recognized the sound of the train whistle as the rallying cry organizing farmers and traders, country people and townsfolk. He was describing the role of this culture in a broader ecology of connection. Though the railway corridor is built out of a multiplicity of social, economic, geological and biotic processes, sound seems to have particular qualities which mark its spaces. In Stilgoe's 'metropolitan corridor', for instance, the train whistle 'sounds the space of modernity', permeates and colours the environment, resonates through sensate and insensate bodies alike, questions conventional notions of distance, touching directly, resonating, resounding and decaying over a broad field, providing points of focus and infinite traces of faint echo. It is hardly surprising then that the sounds of the train features so prominently in popular culture and personal memory, songs, stories and reminiscences. Such sounds evoke physical power, environmental transformation, collective hope and personal sadness. When President-elect Barack Obama addressed the United States from the train on his journey from Philadelphia to Washington, DC, his words and vision for the future were amplified, shaped and given deep historical meaning by this distinctive cultural ecology.

References

Preface

1 H. D. Thoreau, *Walden* (London, 1995), p. 80.
2 W. Schivelbusch, *The Railway Journey: The Industrialization of Time and Space in the 19th Century* (Leamington Spa, 1986).

1 Nature, Culture and the Train Landscape

1 Colin Garrett, *Steam: An Evocative Tribute to the Last Days of Steam Trains* (London, 2006), p. 37.
2 W. Wordsworth, 'On the Projected Kendal and Windermere Railway' [1844], in *The Poetry of Railways*, ed. K. Hopkins (London, 1966), p. 72; J. Simmons, *The Victorian Railway* (London, 1991), pp. 163–4; J. Mulvihill, 'Consuming Nature: Wordsworth and the Kendal and Windermere Railway Controversy', *Modern Language Quarterly*, LVI/3 (1995), pp. 305–26.
3 J. Urry, *Consuming Places* (London, 1995), pp. 203–4; J. Buzard, *The Beaten Track: European Tourism, Literature and the Ways to 'Culture' 1800–1914* (Oxford, 1992), p. 25.
4 M.J.T. Lewis, 'Railways in the Greek and Roman World', in *Early Railways: A Selection of Papers from the First International Railway Conference*, ed. A. Guy and J. Rees (London, 2001), pp. 8–19.
5 B. Trinder, *The Making of the Industrial Landscape* (London, 1982), pp. 32–3, 144–5.
6 D. Cardwell, *The Fontana History of Technology* (London, 1994), p. 89.
7 Fanny Kemble, 'Mr Stephenson', from a letter of Fanny Kemble to a friend, printed in her *Records of a Girlhood* [1878], reprinted in *Pandemonium*, ed. H. Jennings (London, 1985), p. 174.
8 M. Freeman, *Railways and the Victorian Imagination* (New Haven, CT, and London, 1999), pp. 38–44.

9 Ibid., p. 38.

10 T. Clayton and A. McConnell, 'Alken Family (per. 1745–1894)', *Oxford Dictionary of National Biography* (*ODNB*, Oxford, 2004); online edn, January 2008, at www.oxforddnb.com/view/article/65029, accessed 5 July 2010.

11 S. J. Daniels, *Train Spotting: Images of the Railway in Art*, exh. cat., Nottingham Castle Museum (Nottingham, 1985), pp. 5–6.

12 R. M. Ballantyne, *The Iron Horse or Life on the Line: A Tale of the Grand National Trunk Railway* (London, 1871), p. 1.

13 L. Kirby, *Parallel Tracks: The Railroad and Silent Cinema* (Exeter, 1997), pp. 198–219.

14 D. Nye, *America as Second Creation: Technology and Narratives of New Beginnings* (Cambridge, MA, 2003), p. 154.

15 Ibid., pp. 154–5.

16 Freeman, *Railways and the Victorian Imagination*, p. 44.

17 S. Danly and L. Marx, *The Railroad in American Art: Representations of Technological Change* (Cambridge, MA, 1988), p. 5.

18 D. Nye, *American Technological Sublime* (Cambridge, MA, 1994), p. 76.

19 R. W. Emerson, '"The Young American": A Lecture Read Before the Mercantile Library Association', 7 February 1844, at www.munseys.com/diskone/youngam.pdf, accessed 5 July 2010, p. 1; also J. R. Stilgoe, *Metropolitan Corridor: Railroads and the American Scene* (New Haven, CT, and London, 1983), p. ix.

20 W. Schivelbusch, *The Railway Journey: The Industrialization of Time and Space in the 19th Century* (Leamington Spa, 1986), pp. 129–33; Simmons, *Victorian Railway*, pp. 146–7; Freeman, *Railways and the Victorian Imagination*, pp. 84–6.

21 Nye, *American Technological Sublime*, p. 55.

22 Daniels, *Train Spotting*, pp. 6–7; I. Carter, *Railways and Culture in Britain: The Epitome of Modernity* (Manchester, 2001), pp. 76–8.

23 K. Marx, 'The Future Results of the British Rule in India' [22 July 1853], *New-York Daily Tribune*, 8 August 1853; reprinted in *Railways in Modern India*, ed. I. J. Kerr (Oxford, 2001), pp. 62–7.

24 S. J. Daniels, *Fields of Vision: Landscape Imagery and National Identity in England and the United States* (Cambridge, 1993), pp. 126–9.

25 J. Gage, *J.M.W. Turner: 'A Wonderful Range of Mind'* (New Haven, CT, and London, 1987), p. 234.

26 Daniels, *Fields of Vision*, p. 136.

27 Simmons, *Victorian Railway*, pp. 163–4.

28 G. Biddle, 'Railways, their Builders and the Environment', in *The Impact of the Railway on Society in Britain: Essays in Honour of Jack Simmons*, ed. A.K.B. Evans and J. V. Gough (Aldershot, 2003), pp. 117–28.

29 Simmons, *Victorian Railway*, pp. 156–7.

30 Ibid., p. 273.

31 Daniels, *Train Spotting*, p. 12.
32 J. T. Ward, and G. R. Wilson, eds, *Land and Industry: The Landed Estate and the Industrial Revolution* (Newton Abbot, 1971).
33 Daniels, *Train Spotting*, p. 12.
34 G. Rees, *Early Railway Prints: A Social History of the Railways from 1825 to 1850* (Oxford, 1980), pp. 20–21.
35 C. Dickens, *Dombey and Son* (Harmondsworth, 1970), p. 65.
36 F. Klingender, *Art and the Industrial Revolution* (London, 1972), pp. 31, 36, 43.
37 J. Richards and J. M. MacKenzie, *The Railway Station: A Social History* (Oxford, 1988), p. 23; J. Simmons, *The Railways of Britain* (London, 1961), pp. 101–2; G. Biddle, *The British Railway Station* (Newton Abbot, 1977).
38 Richards and MacKenzie, *Railway Station*, pp. 25–30.
39 M. Rosenthal, *British Landscape Painting* (Oxford, 1982), p. 48; M. Andrews, *Landscape in Western Art* (Oxford, 1999), pp. 116–20.
40 Daniels, *Train Spotting*, p. 13.
41 Daniels, *Fields of Vision*, pp. 162–7.
42 I. Kennedy, 'Crossing Continents: America and Beyond', in *The Railway: Art in the Age of Steam*, ed. I. Kennedy and J. Treuherz (New Haven, CT, and London, 2008), p. 124.
43 Stilgoe, *Metropolitan Corridor*, pp. 139.
44 Nye, *American Technological Sublime*, pp. xi–xiii.
45 Danly and Marx, *Railroad in American Art*, pp. 21–31; Michael Freeman, 'The Railway Age: An Introduction' in *The Railway: Art in the Age of Steam*, ed. Kennedy and Treuherz, pp. 131–9.
46 Simmons, *Victorian Railway*, p. 299.
47 G. Norden, *Landscapes under the Luggage Rack: Great Paintings of Britain* (Bugbrooke, Northants, 2001), p. 10.
48 R. Williams, *The Country and City* (London, 1985), pp. 253–62; D. Matless, *Landscape and Englishness* (London, 1998) pp. 87–90.
49 Schivelbusch, *The Railroad Journey*, pp. 63–64.
50 R. L. Stevenson, 'From a Railway Carriage' [1885], reprinted in *The Poetry of Railways: An Anthology*, ed. K. Hopkins (London, 1966), p. 233.
51 Schivelbusch, *The Railroad Journey*, p. 53; Simmons, *Victorian Railway*, p. 212.
52 Carter, *Railways and Culture*, pp. 119–21; Ian Kennedy, 'Impressionism and Post-Impressionism', in *The Railway: Art in the Age of Steam*, ed. Kennedy and Treuherz, pp. 155–71.
53 M. Proust, *Remembrance of Things Past*, Part II: *Within a Budding Grove*, trans. C. K. Scott Moncrieff (London, 1924); also L. Kennedy, ed., *A Book of Railway Journeys* (London, 1980), p. 300.
54 Kennedy, 'Impressionism and Post-Impressionism', pp. 171–81.
55 Danly and Marx, *Railroad in American Art*, p. 41.
56 E. Longley, 'Thomas, (Philip) Edward 1878–1917', *ODNB*, at www.oxforddnb.com/view/article/36480, accessed 6 July 2010; J. Lucas,

'Discovering England: The View from the Train', *Literature and History*, VI/2 (1997), pp. 43–7.

57 E. Thomas, *Collected Works* (London, 1920), p. 52, also W. Cooke, *Edward Thomas: A Critical Biography: 1898–1917* (London, 1970), pp. 253–7.

58 Carter, *Railways and Culture*, pp. 261–3; I. Jeffrey, *The British Landscape, 1920–1950* (London, 1984), pp. 14–15.

59 'Train Tracks', *BBC Radio 4*, 10 April 2009.

60 W. Whitman, 'To a Locomotive in Winter', in *Leaves of Grass*, ed. J. Loving (Oxford, 1990), p. 359; R. Christ, 'Walt Whitman: Image and Credo', *American Quarterly*, XVII/1 (1965), pp. 92–103; G. Ferris Cronkite, 'Walt Whitman and the Locomotive', *American Quarterly*, VI/2 (1954), pp. 164–72.

2 The Machine Ensemble and the Nation-state

1 A. C. Mierzejewski, *Hitler's Trains: The German National Railway and the Third Reich* (Stroud, 2005), pp. 32–43; also A. C. Meizejewski, *The Most Valuable Asset of the Reich: A History of the German National Railway*, vol. II, *1933–1945* (Chapel Hill, NC, 2000).

2 Mierzejewski, *Hitler's Trains*, pp. 30–32, 38.

3 A.J.P. Taylor, *War by Timetable: How the First World War Began* (London, 1969).

4 J. Joll and G. Martel, *The Origins of the First World War* (London 2007), p. 125; J. Black, *Why Wars Happen* (London, 1998), p. 178.

5 A.J.P. Taylor, *From the Boer War to the Cold War*, ed. C. Wrigley (London, 1995); A. F. Thompson, 'Alan John Percivale Taylor (1906–1990)', in *Oxford Dictionary of National Biography* (*ODNB*, Oxford, 2004), online edn, October 2008, at www.oxforddnb.com/view/article/39823, accessed 7 July 2010.

6 J. Simmons, *The Victorian Railway* (London, 1991), p. 364.

7 W. Schivelbusch, *The Railway Journey: The Industrialization of Time and Space in the 19th Century* (Leamington Spa, 1986), pp. 70–71.

8 Ibid., p. 34.

9 A. Mattelart, *Networking the World, 1794–2000* (Minneapolis, MN, 2000), p. 160; N. Faith, *The World the Railways Made* (London, 1990), pp. 83–5.

10 K. Starr, 'Introduction', in F. Norris, *The Octopus* (New York, 1986).

11 Norris, *Octopus*, p. 51.

12 Ibid., p. 289; S. Kern, *The Culture of Time and Space* (London, 1983), pp. 213–14.

13 Faith, *World the Railways Made*, pp. 81–2; G. Kolko, *Railroads and Regulation, 1877–1916* (New York, 1965), pp. 20–29; D. Sven Nordin, *Rich Harvest: A History of the Grange: 1867–1900* (Baton Rouge, LA, 1974).

14 Schivelbusch, *Railroad Journey*, p. 25.

15 Ibid., pp. 26–7.

16   D. Lardner, *Railway Economy: A Treatise on the New Art of Transport* (London, 1860), pp. 421–2, italics original.

17   Schivelbusch, *Railroad Journey*, p. 16–32.

18   M. Bonavia, *The Organisation of British Railways* (London, 1971), p. 12.

19   P. Lecount, Letter to *The Times* in 1840; Simmons, *Victorian Railway*, p. 214.

20   J. A. Ward, 'Image and Reality: The Railway Corporate-State Metaphor', *Business History Review*, LV/4 (1981), p. 494; J. A. Ward, *Railroads and the Character of America, 1820–1887* (Knoxville, TN, 1986), pp. 145–50.

21   T. Gourvish, *Mark Huish and the London and North Western Railway: A Study in Management* (Leicester, 1972), pp. 20–28.

22   W. W. Tomlinson, *The North Eastern Railway* (London, 1880), p. 240; also F. McKenna, *The Railway Workers* (London, 1980), p. 31.

23   Ward, *Railroads*, p. 153.

24   Ward, 'Image and Reality', p. 498.

25   Gourvish, *Mark Huish*, p. 27; also Bonavia, *Organisation*, pp. 11–15; H. Pollins, 'Aspects of Railway Accounting before 1868', in *Studies in the History of Accounting*, ed. A. C. Littleton and B. S. Yamey (London, 1957).

26   Bonavia, *Organisation*, pp. 11–12.

27   P. W. Kingsford, *Victorian Railwaymen: The Emergence and Growth of Railway Labour, 1830–1870* (London, 1970).

28   Bonavia, *Organisation*, p. 15.

29   L. Jenks, 'Multiple-Level Organization of a Great Railroad', *Business History Review*, XXXV/3 (1961), p. 181.

30   G. Revill, 'Working the System: Journeys Through Corporate Culture in the "Railway Age"', *Environment and Planning D: Society and Space*, 12 (1994), pp. 714–17.

31   F. McKenna, *The Railway Workers, 1840–1970* (London, 1980), p. 40.

32   J. D. Orton and K. E. Weick, 'Loosely Coupled Systems: A Reconceptualization', *The Academy of Management Review*, XV/2 (1990), pp. 203–23.

33   D. Puffert, 'The Economics of Spatial Network Externalities and the Dynamics of Railway Gauge Standardization', *Journal of Economic History*, 52 (1992), pp. 449–52.

34   T. Fischer, *Transcontinental Train Odyssey: The Ghan, The Khyber, The Globe* (Crows Nest, NSW, 2004), pp. 22–3.

35   J. Simmons and G. Biddle, eds, *The Oxford Companion to British Railway History* (Oxford, 1997), pp. 523–4.

36   H. J. Dyos and D. H. Aldcroft, *British Transport: An Economic Survey from the Seventeenth Century to the Twentieth* (Harmondsworth, 1974), pp. 128–32.

37   J. Simmons, *The Railways of Britain* (London, 1968), pp. 19–21.

38   D. Puffert, 'The Standardization of Track Gauge on North American Railways, 1830–1890', *Journal of Economic History*, 60 (2000), pp. 933–60.

39   D. J. Puffert, 'Path Dependence in Spatial Networks: The Standardization of Railway Track Gauge', *Explorations in Economic History*, 39 (2007), pp. 282–314.

40 L. Tissot, 'The Internationality of Railways: An Impossible Achievement?', *Die Internationaliität der Eisenbahn*, ed. M. Burri, K. T. Elsasser and D. Gugerli (Zurich, 2003), pp. 263–71; G. Hafter, 'Berne and All That', *Modern Railways* (April 1992), at www.crowsnest.co.uk/gauge.htm, accessed 10 August 2009.

41 B. Stone, 'Interoperability: How Railways became European. Or, One Step Forwards and Two Steps Back', in *Internationalität der Eisenbahn*, pp. 237–43; 'Towards the Rail Transport European Integration', Europa press release, at http://ec.europa.eu/transport/rail/index_en.html.

42 National Audit Office, *Progress on the Channel Tunnel Rail Link* (London, 2005).

43 V. Guigueno, 'Building a High-Speed Society: France and the Aérotrain, 1962–1974', *Technology and Culture*, XLIX/1 (2008), pp. 21–40.

44 Ibid., p. 40.

45 Mattelart, *Networking*, pp. 15–17; A. Picon, *French Architects and Engineers in the Age of Enlightenment* (Cambridge, 1988).

46 A. L. Dunham. 'How the First French Railways Were Planned', *Journal of Economic History*, I/1 (1941), pp. 12–13.

47 A. Mitchell, *The Great Train Race: Railways and the Franco-German Rivalry* (New York, 2000), p. 5.

48 Ibid., p. 6.

49 Ibid., p. 7.

50 Faith, *World the Railways Made*, pp. 60–61.

51 S. J. Ericson, *The Sound of the Whistle: Railroads and the State in Meiji Japan* (Cambridge, MA, 1996).

52 H. J. Hobsbawm, *The Age of Capital Revolutions* (London, 1975); Simmons, *Victorian Railway*, pp. 365–7.

53 N. Faith, *Locomotion: The Railway Revolution* (London, 1993), pp. 78–84.

54 D. Headrick, *Tools of Empire: Technology and European Imperialism in the Nineteenth Century* (Oxford, 1981), pp. 182–3.

55 C. Divall, 'Railway Imperialisms, Railway Nationalisms', in *Internationalität der Eisenbahn*, pp. 195–211; D. Arnold, 'Europe, Technology, and Colonialism in the 20th Century', *History and Technology*, XXI/1 (2005), p. 94.

56 Faith, *World the Railways Made,* p. 317.

57 Mitchell, *Train Race*, p. 60–66.

58 B. Anderson, *Imagined Communities: Reflections on the Origin and Spread of Nationalism* (London, 1983).

59 Faith, *World the Railways Made*, pp. 86–8.

60 L. Mitchell, *Language, Emotion and Politics in South India* (Bloomington, IN, 2009), pp. 2, 27–8.

61 M. K. Gandhi, *An Autobiography: The Story of My Experiments with Truth*, Chapter 35 [Ahemadabad, India, 1927], at www.mkgandhi.org/autobio/chap33.htm, accessed 20 May 2010.

62 M. Aguiar, 'Making Modernity: Inside the Technological Space of the Railway', *Cultural Critique*, 68 (2008), p. 73.

63 Guardian.co.uk, 'Buenos Aires Hit by Rush Hour Rail Riot', 6 May 2008, at www.guardian.co.uk/world/2007/may/16/argentina/print, accessed 7 November 2009; *Daily Telegraph*, 'Argentinians Torch Train Over Delays', 5 September 2008, at www.telegraph.co.uk/news/worldnews/southamerica/argentina/ 2686366/Argentina, accessed 7 November 2009.

64 S. Parissien, *Station to Station* (London, 1997), pp. 111–35.

65 Faith, *Locomotion*, pp. 87, 90.

66 *BBC News Online*, 'Rail Link Reconnects Two Koreas', 11 December 2007, at http://news.bbc.co.uk/1/hi/world/asia-pacific/7137739.stm., accessed 12 November 2009.

67 *BBC News Online*, 'Kenya's Crumbling Railways', 21 August 2000, retrieved from http://news.bbc.co.uk/1/hi/world/Africa/889966.stm, accessed 13 November 2009; Joe Bavier, 'Congo Hopes to Get Ageing Railways Back on Track', *Reuters.uk*, retrieved from http://uk.reuters.com/article.idUKL0786539120070807?, accessed 13 November 2009.

68 S. G. Marks, *Road to Power: Trans-Siberian Railroad and the Colonization of Asian Russia, 1850–1917* (London, 1991).

69 M. Strage, *Cape to Cairo* (London, 1977); G. Tabor, *The Cape to Cairo Railway* (London, 2003).

70 H.S.W. Corrigan, 'German-Turkish Relations and the Outbreak of War in 1914: A Re-Assessment', *Past and Present*, 36 (1967), pp. 144–52; A. P. Maloney, 'The Berlin-Bagdad Railway as a Cause of World War I', *Centre for Naval Analysis: Professional Paper 401* 1984, at www.cna.org/documents/5500040100.pdf, accessed 15 February 2010.

71 Mitchell, *Train Race*, p. 141.

72 I. J. Kerr, ed., *Railways in Modern India* (New Delhi, 2001), p. 13.

73 *BBC News Online*, 'China Torch Relay: Lhasa', 20 June 2008, at http://news.bbc.co.uk/1/hi/world/asia-pacific/7373290.stm, accessed 13 November 2009.

74 A. A. den Otter, *The Philosophy of Railways: The Transcontinental Railway Idea in British North America* (Toronto, 1997).

75 B. Hrabal, trans. Edith Pargeter, *Closely Observed Trains* (London, 1968); D. Malcolm, 'Jiri Menzel: Closely Observed Trains', Guardian.co.uk, 7 October 1999, at www.guardian.co.uk/film/1999/oct/07/derekmalcolmscenturyoffilm, accessed 13 November 2009; R. Hillman, 'Closely Observed Trains', *Senses of Cinema* (2002), at http://archive.sensesofcinema.com/contents/cteq/02/23/ closely_observed.html.

3 Journeys, Stories and Everyday Lives

1   J. Simmons, *The Victorian Railway* (London, 1991), pp. 205–6; D. Kramer, *Cambridge Companion to Thomas Hardy* (Cambridge, 1999), pp. 28–9.
2   T. Hardy, *A Pair of Blue Eyes* (Oxford, 2005), pp. 104–5.
3   D. Spooner, 'Reflections on the Place of Larkin', *Area*, XXXII/2 (2005), pp. 209–16; A. Thwaite, 'Philip Arthur Larkin (1922–1985)', *Oxford Dictionary of National Biography* (*ODNB*, Oxford, 2004), online edn, May 2009, at www.oxforddnb.com/view/article/31333, accessed 10 July 2010.
4   P. Larkin, *The Whitsun Weddings* (London, 1964).
5   T. A. Whalen, *Philip Larkin and English Poetry* (Basingstoke, 1986), pp. 84–91; J. Keibetanz, 'Philip Larkin: The Particular Vision of the Whitsun Weddings', *Modern Language Quarterly*, XLIII/2 (1982), pp. 156–73.
6   L. Flint, 'Marcel Duchamp, Nude (Study), Sad Young Man on a Train', in *Peggy Guggenheim Collection* (New York, 1983), plate 13.
7   L. Marcus, 'Psychoanalytic Training: Freud and the Railways', *The Railway and Modernity: Time, Space and the Machine Ensemble*, ed. M. Beaumont and M. Freeman (Oxford, 2007), pp. 155–76.
8   W. Schivelbusch, *The Railway Journey: The Industrialization of Time and Space in the 19th Century* (Leamington Spa, 1986), pp. 134–58.
9   S. Freud, *Standard Edition of the Compete Psychological Works of Sigmund Freud*, ed. A. Strachey and A. Tyson (London, 2001), p. 202.
10 I. Carter, *Railways and Culture in Britain: The Epitome of Modernity* (Manchester, 2001), p. 137.
11 J. Treuherz, 'States of Mind', in *The Railway: Art in the Age of Steam*, ed. I. Kennedy and J. Treuherz (New Haven, CT, and London, 2008), pp. 202–6; J. Thrall Soby, *Giorgio de Chirico* (New York, 1955), pp. 13–14; M. Holzhey, *De Chirico* (Köln, 2005), pp. 23–4; W. Schmeid, *Giorgio De Chirico: The Endless Journey* (Munich, 2002).
12 M. De Certeau, *The Practice of Everyday Life* (Berkeley, CA, 1984), p. 115.
13 Z. Bauman, *Liquid Modernity* (Cambridge, 2000); M. Castels and G. Cardoso, eds, *The Network Society: From Knowledge to Policy* (Washington, DC, 2006).
14 M. Serres and B. Latour, *Conversations on Science, Culture and Time* (Ann Arbor, MI, 1995), p. 66.
15 M. Foucault, 'Of Other Spaces', *Diacritics*, 1 (1986), pp. 23–4.
16 E. McLuhan and F. Zingrone, eds, *Essential McLuhan* (London, 1997).
17 B. Massumi, *Parables for the Virtual: Movement, Affect, Sensation* (Durham, NC, 2002).
18 A. Sargeant, *British Cinema: A Critical History* (London, 2005), p. 155.
19 J. Richards and J. M. MacKenzie, *The Railway Station: A Social History* (Oxford, 1988), p. 137.
20 S. J. Daniels, *Train Spotting: Images of the Railway in Art*, exh. cat., Nottingham Castle Museum (Nottingham, 1985), p. 18; M. Freeman, *Railways*

and the Victorian Imagination (New Haven, CT, and London 1999), p. 237; Treuherz, 'States of Mind', pp. 96–8.

21 M. Cooper and H. Chalfont, *Subway Art* (London, 1984), pp. 32–4, 50.

22 D. Ehrlich and G. Ehrlich, 'Graffiti in Its Own Words: Old-timers Remember the Golden Age of the Art Movement that Actually Moved', *New York Magazine*, 25 June 2006, at http://nymag.com/guides/summer/17406/index4.html, accessed 28 July 2010.

23 C. Williams [Oats], *One More Train To Ride: The Underground World of Modern American Hoboes* (Bloomington, IN, 2003), p. xiii.

24 T. Cresswell, *The Tramp in America* (London, 2001), pp. 35–6.

25 Williams [Oats], *One More Train To Ride*, p. xiv.

26 W. C. Handy, *Father of the Blues* (New York, 1941), p. 78.

27 T. Fleming, 'Railroad Blues', at http://phlegm.mnsi.net/railroad_blues.html; W. Barlow, *Looking Up At Down: The Emergence of Blues Culture* (Philadelphia, PA, 1989).

28 G. H. Douglas, *All Aboard! The Railroad in American Life* (New York, 1992), p. 64.

29 D. A. Zabel, *The (Underground) Railroad in African American Literature* (New York, 2004).

30 N. Cohen, *Long Steel Rail: The Railroad in American Folksong* (Urbana, IL, 2000), p. 480.

31 P. W. Kingsford, *Victorian Railwaymen: The Emergence and Growth of Railway Labour 1830–1870* (London, 1970); G. Revill, '"Railway Derby": Occupational Community, Paternalism and Corporate Culture 1850–1890', *Urban History*, XXVIII/3 (2001), pp. 378–404.

32 D.E.C. Eversley, 'The Great Western Railway and Swindon Works in the Great Depression', in *Railways in the Victorian Economy*, ed. M. Reed (Newton Abbot, 1969), pp. 111–37.

33 E. J. Hobsbawm, *Labouring Men* (London, 1964); R. Gray, *The Aristocracy of Labour in Nineteenth-Century Britain, c. 1850–1914* (London, 1976).

34 H. Wojtczak, *Railway Women: Exploitation, Betrayal and Triumph in the Workplace* (Hastings, 2005).

35 F. McKenna, *The Railway Workers 1840–1970* (London, 1980).

36 G. Revill, 'Working the System: Journeys through Corporate Culture in the "Railway Age"', *Environment and Planning D. Society and Space*, 12 (1994), pp. 705–25.

37 Simmons, *Victorian Railway*, pp. 316–17.

38 Ibid., pp. 320–21.

39 Richards and MacKenzie, *Railway Station*, p. 138.

40 A. Richter, *Home on the Rails: Women, the Railroad, and the Rise of Public Domesticity* (Chapel Hill, NC, 2005), p. 81.

41 Ibid., p. 83–4.

42 Richards and MacKenzie, *Railway Station*, p. 145.

43 Schivelbusch, *Railroad Journey*, pp. 80–81.

44 Ibid., p. 83.

45 J. Treuherz, 'The Human Drama of the Railway', in *The Railway: Art in the Age of Steam*, ed. Kennedy and Treuherz, p. 84.

46 L. Mulvey, *Visual and Other Pleasures* (Basingstoke, 1989); S. Žižek, *Looking Awry: An Introduction to Jacques Lacan through Popular Culture* (Cambridge, MA, 1991); N. K. Denzin, *The Cinematic Society: The Voyeur's Gaze* (London, 1995).

47 Schivelbusch, *Railroad Journey*, p. 83.

48 Richter, *Home on the Rails*, p. 38.

49 Ibid., p. 50.

50 G. Letherby and G. Reynolds, *Train Tracks: Work, Play and Politics on the Railways* (Oxford, 2005), pp. 164–7.

51 J. Yardly, 'Indian Women Find New Peace in Rail Commute', *New York Times*, 15 September 2009, at www.nytimes.com/2009/09/16/world/asioa/16ladies.html, accessed 28 September 2009; *ABC NEWS Internet Ventures*, 'Japan tried Women-Only Train Cars to Stop Groping', at www.abcnews.go.com/GMA?International/Story?id+803965&CMP+OTC-RSSFeeds0312, accessed 28 September 2009.

52 F. Bonnet, 'Managing Marginality in Railway Stations: Beyond the Welfare and Social Control Debate', *International Journal of Urban and Regional Research*, XXXIII/4 (2009), p. 1037; G. Verstraete, *Tracking Europe: Mobilty, Diaspora and the Politics of Location* (Durham, NC, 2010), pp. 95–109.

53 K. Maher, 'Sin Nombre', Times Online, 14 August 2009, at http://entertainment.Timesonline.co.uk/tot/arts_and_entertainment/film/film_reviews, accessed 6 August 2010; C. Chataigne, 'A Journey on the Railroad: An Interview with Cary Fukunga', *Socialist Review*, July 2009, at http://socialistreview.org.uk/article.php?articlenumber=10896, accessed 06 August 2010.

54 T. Chronopoulos, 'Neo-liberal Reform and Urban Space: The Cartoneros of Buenos Aires 2001–2005', *City*, X/2 (2006), pp. 171–4.

55 J. M. Garcia, 'The White Train', *Virginia Quarterly Review* (Fall 2007), at www.vrqonline.org/articles/2007/fall/garica-white-train/, accessed 8 February 2008.

56 R. Lehan, *The City in Literature: An Intellectual and Cultural History* (Berkeley, CA, 1998), p. 197.

57 Ibid., pp. 198–9.

58 R. C. Bannister, *Social Darwinism: Science and Myth in Anglo-American Social Thought* (Philadelphia, PA, 1979).

59 G. Revill, 'Liberalism, Paternalism and Corporate Culture: Local Politics in "Railway Derby", 1865–75', *Social History*, XXIV/2 (1999), pp. 196–214.

60 Lehan, *City in Literature*, p. 200.

61 A. D. Keating, *Chicagoland: City and Suburbs in the Railroad Age* (Chicago, IL, 2005), pp. 3–21.

62 R. A. Holland, *Chicago in Maps: 1612 to 2002* (New York, 2005), pp. 186–9.

63 Keating, *Chicagoland*, pp. 93–7.

64 R. E. Park and E. Burgess, *The City* (Chicago, IL, 1925); T. Cresswell, *On the Move: Mobility in the Modern Western World* (London, 2006), pp. 36–7.

65 Lehan, *City in Literature*, p. 200.

66 R. Lindner, *The Reportage of Urban Culture: Robert Park and the Chicago School* (Cambridge, 1996); D. Frisby, *George Simmel* (London, 2002), p. viii.

67 D. N. Levine, *On Individuality and Social Forms* (Chicago, IL, 1971), p. 21: Z. Bauman, *Freedom* (Minneapolis, MN, 1988), p. 9.

68 G. Simmel, 'The Metropolis and Mental Life', in *The Sociology of Georg Simmel*, ed. D. Weinstein (New York, 1950), pp. 409–24.

69 S. Kern, *The Culture of Time and Space* (London, 1983), pp. 217–18.

70 Z. Bauman, *Hermeneutics and Social Science: Approaches to Understanding* (London, 1992), p. 226.

4 Moving Objects: Stations, Locomotives and the Arts of Commerce

1 S. Rose, 'What goes around . . .', *The Guardian*, 29 May 2006, at www.guardian.co.uk/artanddesign/2006/may/29/architecture, accessed 12 June 2009; B.W.C. Cooke, 'Notes and News: Camden's Round-house', *Railway Magazine* (October 1964), pp. 800–1.

2 A. Ferrarini, *Railway Stations: From the Gare de L'Est to Penn Station* (Milan, 2005), pp. 5–12.

3 C.L.V. Meeks, *The Railroad Station: An Architectural History* (New Haven, CT, 1956), pp. 27–8.

4 S.P.A. Montesi and R. Deposki, *St Louis Union Station* (Charleston, SC, 2002); 'St Louis Union Station: The Last Place for Commonplace', at www.stlouisunionstation.com, accessed 15 June 2009.

5 S. Parissien, *Station to Station* (London, 1997), pp. 111–14.

6 Ibid., pp. 190–96; 'Cincinnati Museum Center: At Union Terminal', at www.cincymuseum.org, accessed 15 June 2009.

7 G. Plum, *La Gare D'Orsay* (Paris, 2007), pp. 24–7.

8 Ibid., p. 42.

9 Ibid., pp. 43–6.

10 H. Perkin, *The Age of the Railway* (Newton Abbot, 1970), p. 228.

11 Ibid., p. 101; P. Brendon, *Thomas Cook: 150 Years of Popular Tourism* (London, 1991), pp. 57–63.

12 K. Hetherington, *Capitalism's Eye: Cultural Spaces of the Commodity* (New York, 2007), pp. 16–17.

13 'Narrative History of Sears', *Sears Archives* internet resource, at www.searsarchives.com/index.htm, accessed 13 November 2009.

14 W. Cronin, *Nature's Metropolis: Chicago and the Great West* (New York, 1991),

pp. 136–40; A. Chandler, *The Visible Hand: The Managerial Revolution in American Business* (Cambridge, MA, 1977), pp. 230, 235.

15 S. Taylor, *The Moving Metropolis: A History of London's Transport since 1800* (London, 2001), pp. 54–5.

16 M. Ovenden, *Metro Maps of the World* (Harrow Weald, Middlesex, 2003), pp. 6–9, 20–23.

17 J. Hadlaw, 'The London Underground Map: Imagining Modern Time and Space', *Design Issues*, XIX/1 (2006), pp. 29–30.

18 Ibid., pp. 34–5.

19 Ibid., pp. 32.

20 Ibid., pp. 34.

21 Ibid., pp. 34–5.

22 Taylor, *The Moving Metropolis*, pp. 178–81; D. Edwards and R. Pilgrim, *London's Underground Suburbs* (London, 1986), pp. 10–11; C. Wolmar, *The Subterranean Railway* (London, 2004), pp. 172–3.

23 Ibid., pp. 236–53; S. Halliday, *Underground to Everywhere: London's Underground Railway in the Life of the Capital* (Stroud, Gloucestershire, 2001), pp. 102–21.

24 Wolmar, *The Subterranean Railway*, pp. 236–8.

25 J. Betjeman, 'The Metropolitan Railway, Baker Streed Station Buffet', *John Betjeman's Collected Poems* (London, 1958), p. 212.

26 Ibid., p. 213.

27 J. Heskett, *Industrial Design* (London, 1980), p. 134.

28 G. Debord, *The Society of the Spectacle* (London, 2005); R. Bocock, *Consumption* (London, 1993); M. Douglas, *The World of Goods* (New York, 1979).

29 W. Schivelbusch, *The Railway Journey: The Industrialization of Time and Space in the 19th Century* (Leamington Spa, 1986), pp. 121–3.

30 J. L. Meikle, *Twentieth Century Limited: Industrial Design in America, 1925–1939* (Philadelphia, PA, 2001), p. 155.

31 R. Lowey, *Locomotive* (London, 1987).

32 Meikle, *Twentieth Century Limited*, p. 157.

33 Ibid., p. 158.

34 P. Jodard, *Design Heroes: Raymond Loewy* (London, 1994), pp. 19–27.

35 Ibid., pp. 33–47; Meikle, *Twentieth Century Limited*, p. 104.

36 Jodard, *Design Heroes*, pp. 53–4; Meikle, *Twentieth Century Limited*, p. 184.

37 Jodard, *Design Heroes*, pp. 55.

38 G. Wilson, 'Designing Meaning: Streamlining, National Identity and the Case of Locomotive CN6400', *Journal of Design History*, XXI/3 (2008), pp. 243; Jodard, *Design Heroes*, pp. 58–9.

39 Meikle, *Twentieth Century Limited*, p. 160.

40 Ibid., p. 162.

41 L. Mumford, *Technics and Civilization* (London, 1934), Meikle, *Twentieth*

Century Limited, p. 135; R. Williams, 'Classics Revisited: Lewis Mumford's *Technics and Civilization*', *Technology and Culture*, LXI/1 (2002), pp. 2002.

42 Meikle, *Twentieth Century Limited*, p. 162.

43 N. Mansfield, 'The Contribution of the National Banner Survey to Debates on Nineteenth-Century Popular Politics', *Visual Resources*, XXIV/2 (2008), pp. 133–43; D. Weinbren, 'Beneath the All-Seeing Eye; Fraternal Order and Friendly Societies' Banners in Nineteenth- and Twentieth-Century Britain', *Cultural and Social History*, III/2 (2006), pp. 167–91.

44 P. Payton, 'Richard Trevithick (1771–1833)', *Oxford Dictionary of National Biography* (*odnb*, Oxford, 2004), online edn, October 2007, at www.oxforddnb.com/view/article/27723, accessed 15 July 2010.

45 M. Freeman, *Railways and the Victorian Imagination* (New Haven, CT, and London 1999), pp. 212–13; P. Carlson, *Toy Trains: A History* (London, 1986).

46 M. I. Bray, *Railway Picture Postcards* (Ashbourne, Derbyshire, 1986), pp. 96–7.

47 I. Carter, *British Railway Enthusiasm* (London, 2008), pp. 55–64.

48 J. Simmons and G. Biddle, eds, *The Oxford Companion to British Railway History* (Oxford, 1997), p. 414.

49 F. G. Tatnall, 'NRHS: A Story of Growth', reprinted from the *National Railway Bulletin No 5 of 1985, The 50th Anniversary Issue*', *NRHS: A Story of Growth (The Origins of the NRHS)* at www.nrhs.com/about.htm#origins, accessed 14 July 2010.

50 Carter, *British Railway Enthusiasm*, pp. 97–101.

51 T. H. Garver, *The Last Steam Railroad in America* (New York, 1995), p. 6.

52 B. Solomon and P. Yough, *Coal Trains: The History of Railroading and Coal in the United States* (Minneapolis, MN, 2009), pp. 49–57; T. Hensley, *America's Last Steam Railroad: Steam, Steel and Stars* (New York, 1998), pp. 8–9.

53 Garver, *The Last Steam Railroad*, p. 15.

54 Ibid., p. 38.

55 Ibid., pp. 20, 38–9.

56 I. Kennedy and J. Treuherz, 'The Machine Age', in *The Railway: Art in the Age of Steam*, ed. I. Kennedy and J. Treuherz (New Haven, CT, and London, 2008), pp. 224–5.

57 Ibid., p. 253.

58 Garver, *The Last Steam Railroad*, p. 15.

59 'Raymond Loewy: Designer for a Modern Era', at www.linkmuseum.org/loewy.html, accessed 15 July 2010.

60 R. Hewison, *The Heritage Industry: Britain in a Climate of Decline* (London, 1987).

61 J. Dethier, *All Stations: A Journey through 150 Years of Railway History* (London, 1981), p. 113.

62 P. Thompson, 'The Victorian Society', *Victorian Studies*, VII/4 (1964), pp. 388, 390.

63 K. Amis, revd M. Clare Loughlin-Chow, 'Betjeman, Sir John (1906–1984)',

ODNB (Oxford, 2004); online edn May 2009, at www.oxforddnb.com/view/ article/30815, accessed 15 July 2010; J. Delafons, *Politics and Preservation: A Policy History of the Built Heritage, 1882–1996* (London, 1997), pp. 84–5; M. Tewdwr-Jones, '"Óh, the Planners Did their Best": The Planning Films of John Betjeman', *Planning Perspectives*, XL/20 (2005), pp. 389–411.

64 T. Mowl, *Stylistic Cold Wars: Betjeman versus Pevsner* (London, 2000).
65 S. Bradley, *St Pancras Station* (London, 2007).
66 Ibid., pp. 86–7.
67 Ibid., p. 158.
68 Ibid., p. 159.
69 Ibid., p. 160.
70 A. Lansley, S. Durant, A. Dyke, B. Gambrill and R. Shelton, *The Transformation of St Pancras Station* (London, 2008).
71 Ferrarini, *Railway Stations*, p. 12.
72 M. Pawley, *Terminal Architecture* (London, 1998).
73 Ferrarini, *Railway Stations*, p. 11.

5 Entrainment: Tracks to a Railway Ecology

1 *BBC News*, 'Diary: Railroad to the White House', at http://news.bbc.co.uk/1/hi/world/americas/7828467.stm, accessed 18 September 2009; *BBC News*, 'Obama Train Arrives in Washington', at http://news.bbc.co.uk/hi/world/americas.obama_inauguration/7835253.stm, accessed 18 September 2009; *CNN Politics.com*, 'Obama to Crowds: 'I Love You Back', at http://edition.cnn.com/2009/POLITICS/01/17/obama.train/index.html, accessed 18 September 2009.
2 *CBS News.com*, 'Transcript: Obama's Baltimore Speech. Inauguration 09', at www.cbsnews.com/8301-503544_162-4730806-503544.html, accessed 18 September 2009.
3 United States of America Department of Transportation, News, 'President Obama, Vice President Biden to Announce $8 Billion for High-Speed Rail Projects across the Country. Projects Will Help Create Construction Jobs, Revitalize US Manufacturing Sector' (28 January 2010), at www.dot.gov/affairs/briefing.htm, accessed 28 January 2010; United States of America Department of Transportation, 'Chronology of High-Speed Rail Corridors' (19 October 2005) , at http://fra.dot.gov/downloads/Research/hsr_corridors_2009_LV.pdf, accessed 12 April 2010.
4 M. D. Sheer, 'Obama Pushes Vision for High-Speed Rail', *Washington Post.com*, 16 April 2009, at http://voices.washingtonpost.com/44/2009/04/16/by_micheal-d_shear_declaring.html accessed 18 September 2009; S. Goldenberg, 'Barack Obama Announces High-speed Rail Plan for 10 Busiest US Routes', *Guardian.co.uk*, 16 April 2009, at

http://guardian.co.uk/environment/2009/apr/16/barack-obama-high-speed-rail/pr, accessed 10 September 2009.

5 The White House Press Office, 'Remarks by the President and Vice President on a Vision for High-Speed Rail in America', 16 April 2009, at www.whitehouse.gov/the_press_office/Remarks-by-the-President-and the-Vice, accessed 18 September 2009.

6 *BBC News*, 'Obama Train Arrives in Washington'.

7 White House, 'Remarks by the President'.

8 Ibid.

9 OECD, *Trends in the Transport Sector 2008* (Paris, 2008).

10 European Rail Research Advisory Council, 'Rail 21: Sustainable Rail Systems for a Connected Europe' (www.errac.org, 2006); OECD/ITF, *Transport and Energy. The Challenge of Climate Change: Research Findings* (Leipzig, 2008).

11 G. Vigor, *The Politics of Mobility: Transport, the Environment and Public Policy* (London 2002), pp. 86–92, 97–205; R. Haywood, *Railways, Urban Development and Town Planning in Britian: 1948–2008* (Farnham, Surrey, 2009), pp. 3, 185, 193.

12 CER/UIC, *Rail Transport and Environment: Facts and Figures* (Paris, 2008); Community of European Railway and Infrastructure Companies, *CER Fact Sheet: External Costs of Transport and the Eurovignette Revision* (Brussels, 2008).

13 Banverket – Swedish National Rail Administration, 'A Sustainable Transport System Requires that Expansion of the Railways is Prioritised' (2001), at http://feed.ne.cision.com/wpyfs/00/00/00/00/00/02/3A/16/bit0003.pdf, accessed 15 January 2010.

14 World Commission on Environment and Development, *Energy 2000: A Global Strategy for Sustainable Development* (London, 1987).

15 D. L. Greene and M. Wegener, 'Sustainable Transport', *Journal of Transport Geography*, V/3, p. 178.

16 P. Johnston, M. Everad, D. Santillo and K.-H. Robèrt, 'Reclaiming the Definition of Sustainability', *Environmental Science Pollution Research*, XIV/1 (2007), pp. 60–66; J. Hayat and S. Atkins, *Sustainable Development and the Railway in Great Britain* (2007), at www.etcproceedings.org/paper/download/2913, accessed 15 January 2010; W. R. Blackburn, *The Sustainability Handbook* (London, 2007).

17 S. Griffiths, 'Railways "Must Double in Size" Within 30 Years', 28 May 2009, at www.building.co.uk/story.asp?storycode=3141426, accessed 12 January 2010; UK Trade & Investment, *The UK Railway Sector: Business Excellence in Sustainable Development* (London, 2008), atwww.uktradeinvest.gov.uk, accessed 15 January 2010.

18 B. Bremner, 'China's Great Rail Spree Continues', *Business Week*, 20 March 2007, at www.businessweek.com/globalbiz/content/mar2007/gb20070320_138627.htm, accessed 30 January 2010.

19 M. Parkash, *Building Railways in the People's Republic of China: Changing Lives* (Manila, 2008), at www.adb.org, accessed 30 January 2010, p. viii.

20 E. Arpi, 'Dubai Launches New Metro, But Will it Work?' *The City Fix.com*, 17 September 2009, at http://thecityfix.com/dubia-launches-new-metro-but-will-it-work/, accessed 18 September 2009; Andy K., 'Kielder Forest Railway', *Narrow Gauge Heaven*, at www.narrow_gauge.co.uk/forums/read.php?1,1052, accessed 30 January 2010.

21 P. J. Crutzen and E. F. Stoermer, 'The Anthropocene', *International Geosphere-Biosphere Programme Newletter*, 41, pp. 17–18; P. Crutzen, 'The "Anthropocene"', in *Earth System Science in the Anthroposcene*, ed. E. Ehlers and T. Kraft (Berlin, 2006), pp. 13–18.

22 P. J. Crutzen and W. Steffen, 'How Long Have We Been in the Anthropocene Era?' *Climate Change*, LXI/3 (2003), pp. 251–7; J. Zalasiewicz et al., 'Are We Now Living in the Anthropocene?', *GSA Today*, XVIII/2 (2008), pp. 4–8; E. Kolbert, 'The Anthropocene Debate: Marking Humanity's Impact', *Yale Environment 360* (17 May 2010), at http://e360.yale.edu/feature/the_anthropocene_debate_marking_humanitys_impact_/2274, accessed 17 May 2010; C. Brahic, 'Have Humans Created a New Geological Age?' *New Scientist Environment Blog*, 24 January 2008, at www.newscientist.com/blog/environment/2008/01/have-humans-created-new-geological.html, accessed 20 January 2010.

23 D. Arnold, *The Problem of Nature: Environment, Culture and European Expansion* (Oxford, 1996), p. 178.

24 S. A. Harris, 'Introduction of Oxford Ragwort, *Senecio squalidus L.* (Asteraceae), to the United Kingdom', *Watsonia* (Botanical Society of the British Isles), 24 (2002), pp. 31–43; C. Sargent, 'The British Rail Land Survey', in *Ecological Mapping from Ground, Air and Space*, ed. R, M. Fuller (1983), pp. 47–56.

25 J. Ding, R. N. Mack, P. Lu, M. Ren and H. Huang, 'China's Booming Economy is Sparking and Accelerating Biological Invasions', *BioScience*, LVIII/4 (2008), pp. 317–24.

26 M. De Landa, *A Thousand Years of Non Linear History* (New York, 1997); M De Landa, 'Deleuze and the Genesis of Form: on the Philosophy of Gilles Deleuze', *Art Orbit*, 1 (1998), at www.artnode.se/artorbit/issue1/index.html, accessed 10 October 2008.

27 J. T. Starr Jr, *The Evolution of the Unit Train 1960–1969* (Chicago, IL, 1976); B. Solomon and P. Yough, *Coal Trains: The History of Railroading and Coal in the United States* (Minneapolis, MN, 2009), pp. 65–95.

28 N. Pierce, 'Obama Puts Nation on a Path to Serious Train Service', *The Seattle Times*, 6 May 2009, at http://seattletimes.nwsource.com/html/opinion/2009198365_opinc10pierce.html, accessed 18 September 2009; 'Drunk Engineer', 'FRA Sabotages Passenger Rail Again', *Systemic Failure Blog*, 9 January 2010, at http://systemicfailure.wordpress.com/2010/01/09/fra-sabotages-passenger-rail-again/, accessed 18 July 2010.

29 Center for Global Development, 'Carbon Dioxide Emissions From Power Plants

Rated Worldwide', *ScienceDaily* (15 November 2007), atwww.sciencedaily.com_/
releases/2007/11/071114163448.htm, accessed 19 July 2010.

30 J. Goodell, *Big Coal: The Dirty Secret Behind America's Energy Future*
    (New York, 2006), pp. 92–3.

31 M. Wainwright, 'Climate Change Protestors Hijack Coal Train', *Guardian.co.uk*,
    13 June 2008, at http://guardian.co.uk/environment/2008/jun/13/
    activists.climatechange/print, accessed 22 December 2010.

32 Wikipedia, 'Drax Power Station', at
    http://en.wikipedia.org/wiki/Drax_Power_Station, accessed 23 January 2010.

33 *BBC News Online*, 'Police Hold 29 Train Protestors', 14 June 2008, at
    http://news.bbc.co.uk/go/pr/fr/-/1/hi/england/north_yorkshire/7453846.stm,
    accessed 22 January 2010; *UK Indymedia*, 'Leave it in the Ground: Drax Coal
    Train Halted', 13 June 2008, atwww.indymedia.org.uk/en/2008/06/401022.html,
    accessed 22 December 2010.

34 S. Abbott and A. Whitehouse, *The Line that Refused to Die: The Story of the
    Successful Campaign to Save the Settle and Carlisle Railway* (Hawes, North
    Yorkshire, 1990), p. 25.

35 Abbott and Whitehouse, *The Line that Refused to Die*, pp. 55–6.

36 S. Abbott, *To Kill a Railway* (Hawes, North Yorkshire, 1986), pp. 95–105;
    J. Towler, *The Battle for the Settle and Carlisle* (Sheffield, 1990), pp. 122–35.

37 Abbott and Whitehouse, *The Line that Refused to Die*, pp. 164–5.

38 Ibid., p. 141.

39 Ibid., pp. 143–4.

40 Network Rail, *Lancashire and Cumbria Route Utilisation Strategy: August 2008*
    (London, 2008), p. 66.

41 Ibid., p. 37.

42 Ibid., pp. 38, 67.

43 The Guild of Railway Artists, 'David Shepherd CBE OBE' (2003), at
    www.railart.co.uk/gallery/shepherd.html, accessed 3 February 2010.

44 R. Martin, *The Sculpted Forest: Sculptures in the Forest of Dean* (Bristol, 1990),
    p. 63.

45 Ibid., p. 61.

46 G. Revill, 'The Forest of Dean: Art, Ecology and the Industrial Landscape', in
    *Place Promotion: The Use of Publicity and Public Relations to Sell Towns and
    Regions*, ed. J. Gold and S. Ward (London, 1993), pp. 233–45.

47 L.T.C. Rolt, *High Horse Riderless* (Bideford, Devon, 1988), p. 139.

48 L.T.C. Rolt, *Landscape with Figures* (Stroud, Gloucs, 1992), p. 7.

49 Ibid., p. 11.

50 Ibid., p. 6.

51 Rolt, *High Horse Riderless*, p. 166.

52 D. M. Pepper, *Modern Environmentalism: An Introduction* (London, 1996),
    p.244.

53 Rolt, *High Horse Riderless*, p. 166.

54 Abbott and Whitehouse, *The Line that Refused to Die*, p. 47.
55 J. R. Stilgoe, *Metropolitan Corridor: Railroads and the American Scene* (New Haven, CT, and London, 1983), p. ix.
56 Ibid., p. ix.
57 Ibid., p. 339.
58 P. Bishop, 'Gathering the Land: The Alice Springs to Darwin Rail Corridor', *Environment and Planning D; Society and Space*, 20 (2002), pp. 295–317.
59 Abbott and Whitehouse, *The Line that Refused to Die*, p. 141.
60 Ibid., p. 142.
61 Ibid., pp. 151–2.
62 B. Latour, *We Have Never Been Modern* (Cambridge, MA, 1993), p. 117.
63 S. Kamata, 'JR East Takes up the Challenge of Searching for a Railway that is Kinder to the Earth', *Proceedings of the Institute of Mechanical Engineers*, 214, Part F: *Journal of Rail and Rapid Transit* (2000), pp. 117–22; JR East Group, *Sustainability Report 2009*, at www.jreast.co.jp/e/environment/pdf_2009/all.pdf, accessed 24 November 2009.
64 C. P. Hood, *From Bullet Train to Symbol of Modern Japan* (London, 2006).
65 M. Foucault, 'Of Other Spaces', *Diacritics*, 1 (1986), pp. 23–4.

Select Bibliography

Bradley, S., *St. Pancras Station* (London, 2007)

Carter, I., *Railways and Culture in Britain: The Epitome of Modernity* (Manchester, 2001)

Cronin, W., *Nature's Metropolis: Chicago and the Great West* (New York, 1991)

Daniels, S. J., *Fields of Vision: Landscape Imagery and National Identity in England and the United States* (Cambridge, 1993)

—, *Train Spotting: Images of the Railway in Art,* exh. cat., Nottingham Castle Museum, (Nottingham, 1985)

Danley, S., and L. Marx, *Railroad in American Art: Representations of Technological Change* (Cambridge, MA, 1988)

Ferrarini, A., *Railway Stations: From the Gare de L'Est to Penn Station* (Milan, 2005)

Freeman, M., *Railways and the Victorian Imagination* (New Haven, CT, and London, 1999)

Goodell, J., *Big Coal: The Dirty Secret Behind America's Energy Future* (New York, 2006)

Kennedy, I., and J. Treuherz, eds, *The Railway: Art in the Age of Steam* (New Haven, CT, and London, 2008)

Kern, S., *The Culture of Time and Space* (London, 1983)

Kirby, L., *Parallel Tracks: The Railroad and Silent Cinema* (Exeter, 1997)

McKenna, F., *The Railway Workers, 1840–1970* (London, 1980)

Meeks, C.L.V., *The Railroad Station: An Architectural History* (New Haven, CT, 1956)

Meikle, J. L., *Twentieth Century Limited: Industrial Design in America, 1925–1939* (Philadelphia, PA, 2001)

Nye, D., *America as Second Creation: Technology and Narratives of New Beginnings* (Cambridge, MA, 2003)

Parissien, S., *Station to Station* (London, 1997)

Rees, G., *Early Railway Prints: A Social History of the Railways from 1825 to 1850* (Oxford, 1980)

Richards, J., and J. M. MacKenzie, *The Railway Station: A Social History* (Oxford, 1988)

Richter, A., *Home on the Rails: Women, the Railroad, and the Rise of Public Domesticity* (Chapel Hill, NC, 2005)

Rolt, L.T.C., *Landscape with Figures* (Stroud, Gloucs, 1992)

Schivelbusch, W., *The Railway Journey: The Industrialization of Time and Space in the 19th Century* (Leamington Spa, 1986)

Simmons, J., *The Victorian Railway* (London, 1991)

Stilgoe, J. R., *Metropolitan Corridor: Railroads and the American Scene* (New Haven, CT, and London, 1983)

Vigor, G., *The Politics of Mobility: Transport, the Environment and Public Policy* (London, 2002)

Acknowledgements

I would like to thank Colin Divall for his unfailing help and advice and sharing with me his invaluable knowledge of railway history and culture. Particularly I would like to thank him for reading earlier draft chapters and for his encouraging and constructive comments. The many errors and omissions are of course entirely my fault. Thanks to Eleanor for her patience and understanding during the writing process and for agreeing to proofread yet another manuscript chapter about railways; I am greatly in your debt. Thanks also to Tim Strangleman, David Matless, John Gold, Nigel Clark and Dan Weinbren for providing continual intellectual stimulation and for allowing me to discuss railways at any available opportunity.

I would like to thank the Open University's Openspace Reseach Centre for financial help towards the production of images, and John Hunt for producing the cartography for chapter Two.

Lastly, I must say a big thank you to Michael Leaman, Vivian Constantinopoulos and everyone else at Reaktion for their patience and understanding during the research and writing of this book.

Photo Acknowledgements

Bigstock: pp. 102 top left (Hadrian), 222 (Paha_L); Bridgeman Art Library: p. 174 (Victoria & Albert Museum, London / The Stapleton Collection); Nick Cobbing: p. 229; www. CartoonStock.com: p. 33; Cincinnati Museum Center, Ohio: p. 168; Corbis: pp. 97 (Bettmann), 108 (Hou Deqinang / Xinhua Press), 185 (Bettmann); © Eurotunnel: pp. 19, 85; Harvey Maps: p. 234; Stuart Herbert: p. 231; John Hunt: pp. 79, 90; A. M. Hurrel: p. 88; GeoWombats: p. 245; Getty Images: pp. 99, 133, 169, 187; Istockphoto: pp. 102 bottom right (Harryfn), 103 top (SF photo), 166 top (Steve Geer), 219 (Holger Mette), 221 (John Kirk); © Japan National Tourism Organization: p. 74 (©Japan Convention Services, Inc.); Library of Congress, Washington, DC: pp. 140, 141; Musée d'Orsay, Paris: p. 162; London Transport Museum: pp. 175, 176; © O. Winston Link / Image Courtesy of the O. Winston Link Museum: pp. 196, 197; George Revill: pp. 103 bottom, 156, 207; Oxyman: p. 209; Estate of Eric Ravilous, all rights reserved, DACS 2011: p. 55; Rex Features: pp. 100 (Marbella Photos), 104 (CSU Archives / Everett Collection), 132 (Sipa Press), 210; Roundhouse, London: pp. 165 top, 165 bottom (Sophie Laslett); Science and Society Picture Library: pp. 20 (© National Rail Museum Pictorial Collection), 202 (National Railway Museum); By Kind Permission of David Shepherd: p. 235; Shutterstock: pp. 84 (Stefan Ataman), 251 (Hiroshi Ichikawa); Swiss-image.ch: p. 87 (Jungfrau Railways); reproduced with kind permission of the Thomas Cook Archives: p. 171; William Wessen: p. 166 bottom.

Index

dribblers 190
Hornby Toy Trains advertisement *191*
track gauges 78–82, *79–80*
trackbeds
  and plant growth 222–3, *222*
  as wildlife corridors 224
  'wrong side of the tracks', origins of
  156
trade unionism 78, 189
'Train Choir' (Raymond) 223–4
Train Landscape (Ravilious) 53–5, *55*
Train in the Snow at Argenteuil (Monet)
  49–50, *51*
*The Trainspotter as Twentieth-Century
  Hero* (Whittaker) 127–8
trainspotting 13, 127–8, 192–4
  see also amateur enthusiasts
tramroads 23–4
Trans-Siberian railway 105–6, *105*
travel as commodity 170–82, 184–6,
  189–90
travel writing 159–60
travelling salesmen 147
Trevithick, Richard, 'Catch-me-who-can'
  locomotive 24–5, *24*, 190
Turner, J.M.W., *Rain, Steam and Speed*
  34–6, *35*, 50, 58–9

Uganda Railway poster *106*
UK
  Beeching Axe 129, 243
  Birmingham, Curzon Street Station
  41
  Birmingham dribblers 190
  Channel Tunnel *see* Eurotunnel
  competition between railway
  companies 47–8
  Drax power station protest 228–9,
  229, 234
  Eurotunnel *see* Eurotunnel
  Flying Scotsman 101
  Forest of Dean Sculpture Trail 236
  Gladstone's Act (1844) 140–42

GPO, *Night Mail* (film) 59–61, *60*
Great Eastern Railway 46
Great Western Railway 34–6, *35*,
  80–81
Highland Railway guidebook 46
History of the English Railway
  (Francis) 38
Kendal & Windermere Railway 22
Kielder Forest Railway 218–19
landowners' hypocrisy over railways
  37–8
Leeds, Middleton Colliery *25*, 26
Liverpool & Manchester Railway 25,
  26, 32, 38–9, 75–6, *79–80*
Manchester, Vulcan Foundry *183*
merry-go-round trains 225–7, *228*
Midland Railway Company 40–41, *47*,
  77, 230
nationalization of railways 92,
  239–40
Newcastle upon Tyne, coal wagonway
  225
nostalgic ruralism 46–7, 53–6
Railway Travel and Correspondence
  Society (RCTS) 191, 192
Ribblehead Viaduct 230–34, *231*, *234*
Settle–Carlisle line 230–34, *231*, *234*,
  243, 246–7
Shrewsbury & Chester Railway 42–3,
  43
Somerset, Prior Park *20*
Stockton & Darlington Railway 80,
  192
Surrey Iron Railway 70
Talyllyn Railway, Mid-Wales *237–8*,
  238–40
Victorian Society 200–201, 204
West Coast Mainline, steam traction,
  end of 21–2
UK, London
  Euston 'Arch' preservation campaign
  200–201
  Euston Road School 52

286